GW00771227

PRODUCING FOR
FILM AND TELEVISION

'The filmmaker requires money, camera and film.'

PRODUCING FOR
FILM AND TELEVISION

SUE AUSTEN

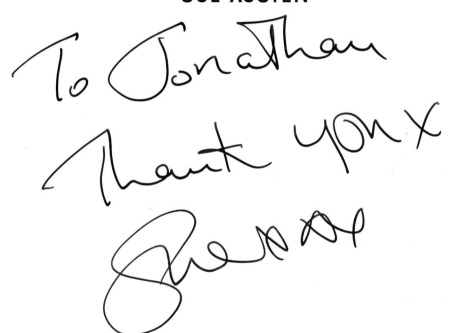

To Jonathan
Thank you x
Sue xx

THE CROWOOD PRESS

ACKNOWLEDGEMENTS

I would like to thank everyone whose advice and expertise has helped me to write this book. Particular thanks are due to Steve Coombes, Tracy Bass, Richard Kwietniowski, Rose Cussen, Nigel Bristow, Gemma Dempsey, Andrew Woodyatt, Matthew Button and the students of the London Film School and MA Filmmaking at Goldsmiths University of London.

PHOTOGRAPH CREDITS

My grateful thanks to Matthew Button, Frederic Kau, Robert Smith and Dheeraj Malhan for permission to use their work and photographs in this book.

First published in 2019 by
The Crowood Press Ltd
Ramsbury, Marlborough
Wiltshire SN8 2HR

www.crowood.com

© Sue Austen 2019

All rights reserved. No part of this publication may be reproduced or transmitted in any form or by any means, electronic or mechanical, including photocopy, recording, or any information storage and retrieval system, without permission in writing from the publishers.

British Library Cataloguing-in-Publication Data
A catalogue record for this book is available from the British Library.

ISBN 978 1 78500 531 2

Typeset by D & N Publishing, Baydon, Wiltshire

Printed and bound in India by Replika Press Pvt Ltd

CONTENTS

INTRODUCTION

HOW I BECAME A PRODUCER

I have been lucky enough to have worked in the film and television industry for thirty-five years. I am continuing this work now at film schools, sharing my knowledge and experience with another generation of filmmakers.

The industry has changed a lot over these years. There have been huge technological advances, and the way we physically make and view films continues to evolve. When you read this book more changes will have happened, though some fundamentals will remain. Films are still created, financed and produced in broadly the same way as they always have been. We still need writers to provide us with inspiring stories, and directors to interpret them for the screen. We will always need directors of photography, production designers, editors, sound designers, composers, actors and skilled technicians to deliver this vision. And, more than anything, we still need creative producers to bring all these different and diverse talents together to give their best work.

I left university in 1980 with a degree in English and European Literature, and no very clear idea what I wanted to do with the rest of my life. After a brief spell in publishing, I secured a temporary secretarial job at a now legendary company, Goldcrest Films and Television Limited. I spent four years there in different departments, working my way to the position of script editor in the television production division and learning a lot along the way. The story of Goldcrest's rise and fall is meticulously told by the company's founder Jake Eberts in his co-authored book *My Indecision is Final*. Anyone interested in the business of film should read this book.

For me personally, Goldcrest was a wonderful place to understand film and television at a time when the industry was changing significantly in the UK and in Europe. Whilst I was there, the UK's fourth television channel went on air, sourcing its programmes for the first time from independent production companies such as Goldcrest, rather than making them solely 'in house' as the BBC and ITV had done until then. There was the first of many revivals of the British film industry, and Goldcrest won multiple Academy Awards for *Gandhi* and *The Killing Fields*. It was an exciting time to be starting out in what became my chosen profession.

After Goldcrest closed its television division I moved to become Head of Development at Granada Films. From working in the television part of a film company, I was now in the film part of a major television company. At Granada we developed and produced only a handful of films before being shut down in a company reshuffle. But it was great experience, and for me the highlights included meeting a real Hollywood legend, Lauren Bacall, and making the enormous leap from development into becoming a producer.

One of the projects I had developed for Granada Films was a medical thriller, *Paper Mask*, based on a novel by former doctor, John Collee. I optioned the novel before publication and developed the screenplay with John, who had no previous screenwriting experience at the time. Christopher Morahan came on board as director and producer, and with his support, I left Granada to be the co-producer of the film. I was thirty years old and doing something I had never dreamed possible. A year later *Paper Mask* was selected as the closing film of Director's Fortnight at the 1990 Cannes Film Festival.

Since then I have continued to earn a living in the precarious world of film and television. I never had another permanent job after Granada and remained a self-employed freelancer. I have produced many kinds of films and television dramas over the years in many different places. These have included single films, drama serials, continuing drama series (soaps) and children's dramas, as well as features. On some productions I have worked as a 'producer for hire', and on some I have devoted years of my life to bring them to the screen. Some of my favourite projects are still waiting to be funded. Like every producer I haven't given up hope that they will be made one day.

HOW TO USE THIS BOOK

In this book I have tried to explain some of the fundamentals of producing for film and television. All these basics can be equally applied to the production of documentaries and short films. The book will mainly refer to 'film', but most of the information applies equally to the production of dramas for television or streaming services. Where there are specific variations they will be discussed. But overall the process of filmmaking is more or less the same, whether you are making *The Queen* for theatrical release or *The Crown* for Netflix.

The book uses gender-neutral titles throughout. So for example, the term 'actor' will be used whether the individual is male or female. One of the biggest changes since I first entered the industry is the opening of all roles to a more diverse workforce, and I celebrate this development.

I apologize for any errors or mistakes in what follows. I hope you will both enjoy this book and find it a helpful guide as you begin your own journey to becoming a creative producer.

Sue Austen

Handwritten notes:
- Set build in Studio? or location?
- Will need at least 2 identical dogs
- 2nd Unit / Footage? greenscreen?
- No ... 24.

Script text:

NS FLAT] DAY.

...VOICE

...nd a muzzle three inches from his
...e features and long silky ears, is
...Lead in her mouth. Charlie snatches
...de. He grumpily crosses to his
...irt from his enormous collection of

CHARLIE
...I have plans for the...l,
...I plan to go to...
...get drunk and I...
...oo.

...ack th...
...kitch...

...nowing her the bowls and

...(continued)
...perallergenic sleeping rug.
...g and goodbye.

...away the lead again and walks out, shutting the

...inness' sad brown eyes.
...him.

...snarls and takes the

T. KINGS ROAD. DAY.

...e joins Sam and hundreds of other Chelsea fans strolling
...the Kings Road to Stamford Bridge.

CHARLIE
Any luck last night?

SAM
...just went home for a Dogger.

CHARLIE
...you're shipping
...try out a new

1
WHAT IS A PRODUCER?

A producer is a man with a dream. I say 'I don't write, I don't direct, I don't act, I don't compose music, I don't design costumes'. What do I do? I make things happen.

David Wolper, Producer
(*Willy Wonka and The Chocolate Factory, LA Confidential, Roots*)

Most people interested in film and television, whether they are a consumer or a practitioner, know broadly speaking what a director does. He or she directs the cast towards their Academy or Emmy award-winning performance, designs the set-ups and shots, supervises the edit and much more. Many people also have an understanding of the job of the production designer, cinematographer, editor, sound recordist, screenwriter and other key roles in filmmaking. But many of these same people have only a very sketchy idea of what the producer of a film actually does.

The traditional image of the Hollywood producer is typically of a large rich man (and yes, it was then always a man!) smoking a huge cigar. Nowadays this is a long way from the truth. This book will mainly focus on the modern independent producer, the person I describe as a 'creative producer'. This individual does not have major studio backing, and is probably earning their living on a project-by-project basis. They may very well be working across film and television, drama and documentary. They will be someone who develops film and series ideas, works closely with the writer or writers, finds the right director and talent with whom to collaborate, raises the finance to make the project happen, hires the team to work

OPPOSITE: Many people have no idea what the producer of a film actually does.

with, produces the film or series, supervises the post-production, delivers the finished work, and is still involved when it comes to distribution, festival screenings, marketing and transmission.

I think of production as a drama in five acts. As will become apparent through the next chapters, the producer will have a crucial and evolving job to do throughout these different stages, which are:

Act One: Development
Act Two: Pre-production
Act Three: Production
Act Four: Post-production
Act Five: Distribution

DEFINING THE PRODUCER'S ROLE

One of the difficulties of precisely defining the producer's role is that it is ever changing. There are as many different types of producer and as many titles as there are formats and genres. At the start or end of most feature films and more and more drama series and documentaries, there will be a number of people – sometimes as many as ten – who have some kind of producer credit. In addition to the term 'producer', we often see credits for the following:

Executive producer
Line producer
Development producer
Associate producer
Co-producer

The rest of this book will focus on the creative producer, but who are all these other people, and what do they actually do?

EXECUTIVE PRODUCERS

The credit of 'Executive Producer' is in reality a courtesy title. This doesn't mean that this person is not very important: they most definitely are, and without them the film or series would probably never get made. But they don't necessarily have a tangible role on the production. The executive producer may have invested money into the film or series. They may work on the permanent staff of one of the major funders of the film – for example a film fund or broadcaster. They may represent the production company. They might be the writer. They might be a piece of key talent, such as an actor, whose commitment to the project has been instrumental in getting it funded.

They may work for the distribution company, the studio, or even the bank who is cash flowing the shoot. They have definitely earned their credit. But if you are working as a member of the crew on the film you may never see them, except at the film's premiere or on Oscar night.

LINE PRODUCERS

By contrast the 'Line Producer' has a vital and very tangible role in making dramas and documentaries happen. All productions need a line producer and their team. One way of understanding the line producer's role is to think of the top sheet of the standard film budget. It is divided into two main sections: 'above the line' and 'below the line'. 'Above the line' sit the fees and payments to the writer, director, producer, executive producers and main cast. 'Below the line' is everything else.

The line producer is essentially responsible for the 'everything else' part of the budget. He or she runs the production office, manages the budget, negotiates deals with facilities houses, personnel, suppliers, studios and key locations. The line producer also shares responsibility for certain health and safety requirements, including risk assessments and insurance. They must also ensure that all departments are accurately reporting their spending on a weekly basis. Ultimately it is their job to make sure the shoot is completed on time and within budget.

This is a complex and critical job. On some very low-budget films, shorts and dramas, the producer may do some of the line producer's work, and there might be a production manager instead. But this is more or less the same job, just less well paid. On very large productions with multiple units there might be both a line producer and a production manager.

DEVELOPMENT PRODUCERS

It is becoming increasingly common to see the credit of 'Development Producer' on films and series. Usually this means the person who has developed the project up to the point when it has been 'green lit' for production. In some cases this may be someone who works on staff at a production company or studio or broadcaster, and whose job it is to find, develop and sell ideas.

Development producers have important key relationships with agents, publishers and writers. They know when a 'hot' book is coming out and how to get advance copies. They know which writers sell, and they nurture these relationships to make sure they get a first look at their new project. They will work on the scripts, may attach directors and other key talent, and may be involved in pitching and fundraising – but they will then step aside when the film or series goes into production. Normally they will be working on multiple projects at once.

ASSOCIATE PRODUCERS

An associate producer is often a more junior job, and the title may be offered to a promising young producer with limited experience. In documentary and factual programming, the 'Associate

Producer' credit may be given to a person stepping up from being a researcher but not quite ready to be made a producer. The role may involve development, research, packaging or supervising other departments. In fiction and drama the 'Associate Producer' credit might be given to someone from a small production company who initially developed the project but is not considered experienced enough to be the sole producer or to be offered a 'Co-Producer' credit.

Co-Producers

The term 'Co-Producer' is another catch-all title. Almost all film and television drama now involves some kind of co-production. Aside from studio pictures, which may still be fully funded from a single source, the majority of films have multiple investors. Some of these may be described as co-producers, but as we have seen earlier, they are as likely to be given the title of producer or executive producer on the credit roll. A co-producer may also be a junior producer, or an individual who is not quite important enough to have a full 'Producer' credit, but has still made a valuable contribution to the production.

There is more about co-production in Chapter 5, 'Raising Production Finance'.

The Writer as Producer in US Television

The US television system for creating drama series is somewhat different from that which has traditionally operated in the UK and Europe. On this side of the Atlantic we tend to commission individual writers to create new dramas, and to credit them with the authorship of the work. If other writers are brought in to write further episodes in the series, this is normally in consultation with the original writer. Writers take ownership of their episode, and receive a credit as the writer or screenwriter on it. The original writer may receive an additional credit, such as 'based on an idea by', or 'series created by'.

In the USA, however, a system is operated known as 'the writers' room'. A number of writers, usually between eight and twelve, gather together every day to conceive, create, plot and write the series. The lead writer and originator of the series is known as the 'showrunner', while the other members of the room will range in experience from those with a lot of network credits, to those who have just graduated from film school. Vince Gilligan (*Breaking Bad*, *Better Call Saul*), David Simon (*The Wire*, *Treme*, *The Deuce*), Matthew Weiner (*Mad Men*) and Alan Ball (*Six Feet Under*, *True Blood*) are examples of American showrunners.

On US drama series everyone who belongs to the writers' room and has contributed to the final script of an episode of the series receives an on-screen credit as a producer. This may be as executive producer, producer, or co-producer. This situation has come about because of restrictions placed on the credit system by the all-powerful Writers Guild of America. All writing credits have to be approved by the Guild, so to get around this restriction, the writers customarily take a producer credit instead. This is despite the fact they may have had nothing at all to do with the production processes other than as a writer. The actual producer of the show is listed under the credit 'produced by'.

WHO IS THE PRODUCER?

At the 2017 Academy Awards ceremony in Los Angeles there was an unprecedented and embarrassing mistake when Faye Dunaway announced the winner of Best Picture as *La La Land* when in fact *Moonlight* had won. The person who stepped forward to correct the error was not *La La Land*'s director Damien Chazelle, but its producer, Jordan Horowitz. This is because the Academy awards its highest honour, the prize for Best Picture, to the film's producers. In Hollywood's profit-driven world they understand very well that it is producers, and not directors, who make films.

In the early days of the cinema industry the studios controlled all aspects of production. They owned the studios, the back lots, the directors, the writers, the actors, the technicians, the laboratories and processing plants, and the cinemas. They paid their staff to write scripts, employed their staff to direct and film them, they cast the actors they had under contract, and finally they showed the films in their own cinemas. This was known as 'vertical integration', and the early movie moguls (the producers) made a lot of money this way.

But in 1938 the US Department of Justice brought an anti-trust case against the studios, accusing them of creating a monopoly. The main defendant was Paramount Pictures, which at the time was the largest of the Hollywood studios. But in reality, the case was brought against them all – namely MGM, Warner Bros, RKO, 20th Century Fox, Universal Studios, Columbia Pictures and United Artists. The studios resisted change, entered into a bitter battle, and appealed for almost ten years. Finally, in 1948, the case reached the US Supreme Court, which ruled against the studios, insisting that they give up some of their control over the industry. They were forced to sell their cinemas and give up the exhibition side of their businesses.

Although initially the move caused a slump in audience figures, it opened the way for independent distributors and allowed independent producers to get access to audiences for the first time. Now it was possible for talented individuals to create films and put them before a paying public without having to go to a studio and have the studio interfere in how the film was made. This was the birth of the independent producer.

At the same time as the Hollywood studios were losing some of their grip on the industry, a new medium was emerging: television. In the USA there were three main networks or broadcasters: NBC, CBS and ABC. There was also a much smaller public broadcasting system known as PBS. Television production soon moved from the east to the west coast, and live broadcasting made way for filmed dramas and documentaries as well as sporting events, news and entertainment shows.

In the UK there was just one channel to begin with: the British Broadcasting Corporation, known as the BBC. Then in 1956 an alternative channel known as ITV was launched. The critical difference between the two networks was that the BBC was publicly funded via a compulsory tax known as 'the licence fee', and ITV was a commercial station whose income derived from selling advertising slots. But both networks operated a production system not dissimilar to that of the US film studios. They made programmes 'in house', and then showed them on their own network. There were producers on staff, directors on staff, cameramen (no camerawomen then!), editors, designers and sound recordists, all on staff. Only the actors and writers were hired on a project-by-project basis. This is how all UK television programming was created until the early 1980s.

In 1982, the UK's first new channel for more than a decade was launched as Channel Four. The important difference between C4 and its predecessors was that it did not intend to make any of its own programmes, but rather would source them from independent production companies. C4 operated like a publishing house, in that its commissioning editors chose the projects they liked, and then handed over control to the producers, who were expected to deliver back completed programmes on time and on budget. If there was a shortfall between the sum that C4 paid for the series and its cost of production, it was up to the producer to fill that gap. But the producer also benefited from the opportunity to exploit the programmes in other territories or markets by selling them to other networks and stations.

This new model created a whole new breed of independent producer and production companies, and a new industry was born. But C4 was a small broadcaster with limited funds. The independent sector lobbied for more access, and in 1990 the UK Government passed legislation that forced all the channels, including BBC and ITV, to take 25 per cent of their programming from independent producers.

As new markets and channels have continued to emerge from the 1980s onwards, there have been more and more places to sell and pre-sell ideas and projects. Cable channels such as HBO,

Showtime and Canal+ have commissioned some of the most ambitious and bold stories. Netflix, Amazon and Hulu's entry into the market has recently had a major impact. All have deep pockets and are investing heavily in new drama series, documentaries and feature films, and this has created even more opportunities for ambitious creative producers.

To be a successful producer you will need a range of skills and talents, and by far the most important of these is a love of film and television, and a determination to produce the best new work. Nobody can survive in this industry without the passion to keep going. The next quality you will need is the ability to spot an excellent idea or script. It will be you, the producer, who will turn a story idea into a finished film, and it will be you who must raise the money to enable a brilliant script to be shot.

Throughout this book we will see how the producer steers the project from start to finish. To do this, he or she must have infinite patience and enthusiasm, and be ready to play the long game. In one way or another, the producer is always selling the project, so they must also be persuasive, articulate and charming. The producer's main job is to convince others to share their vision and to join them on the journey into production – whether these others are investors, contributors, distributors or audiences.

Producers must be trustworthy and reliable. If they are not, nobody will work with them a second time. They must be part entrepreneur and part nanny. They must nurture talent and promote it with confidence and authority. They should be clever about how to raise money, and keep themselves continually informed of new streams of funding. They will have to work under pressure, but must remain smiling throughout. They need to know when to intervene, and when to hold back. Above all, the producer must always be looking for creative solutions to any problem.

2
DEVELOPMENT

A producer is a marathon runner who plods along, believing against all reasonable hope that at some point he or she is going to go through the tape and actually win.

David Puttnam, Producer (*Chariots of Fire*, *The Killing Fields*)

The time it takes to nurture a project from the seed of an idea to the start of production may be many years. In the film industry this period is known as 'development', and it is frequently described as hell. The development period is frustrating and unpredictable. Things can – and definitely will – go wrong for all kinds of reasons. During this time it is the producer's job to keep the ship on course and to keep the goal – making the film – in everyone's mind. Along the way there will be many icebergs, and it will be his or her job to navigate a course through these.

FINDING YOUR PROJECT

Every great drama or documentary starts with a good story. As a producer, stories will come to you from many different sources, and part of your job is to sift through them and make decisions about which ones to pursue and develop, and which ones to pass on or let go. All the best producers have passed on a project that went on to become a brilliant film. This is not necessarily because they failed to spot the potential, it may be that their slate was already too full, or they didn't like or trust the talent associated with the project, or the agent was asking too much money, or something else.

The first and most obvious place to start looking for a project is to meet and talk to writers. As a creative producer, your most important asset is a good relationship with talented writers, and the

trust and respect of their agents. Writers' agents are powerful people and can strongly influence their clients' choices. Over time, producers develop relationships with writers and their agents. Sometimes these may be formalized into what is known as a 'first look deal', when the writer is obliged to offer all their new ideas and projects to the producer first, before shopping them around on the open market. But in most instances there is a more informal arrangement between friends and colleagues. A writer whose last film or series was successfully and happily delivered by a particular producer may very well choose to take his or her next project to the same company. Equally, a writer who is disappointed by the final product may choose never to work with that producer or production company again.

Many producers start their career path in the industry working as script readers, script editors and development producers. This gives them a head start in knowing writers with whom they want or like to work. If you have been to film school or studied with writers, you may know those you would like to work with again. Maybe you produced a short film and can talk to the writer about the feature film idea they have been burning to write for years. Or there may be a writer whose work you greatly admire whom you may approach via his or her agent and ask for a meeting.

In many of these cases you will be talking to them about an original idea, which belongs to the writer. At the time it first comes to your attention, the idea

Every great drama or documentary starts with a good story.

may already be written down as a script, or it may be in the form of a treatment. Or it may be something that exists only in the writer's imagination, and which is pitched to you verbally. Whatever the form, if you decide to pursue the project you need to draw up a contract with the writer, clearly setting out the terms of your arrangement with them. The process for doing this is described later in this chapter.

But original ideas are not the only, or even the most likely, source material for films, drama series or documentaries. The majority of films produced in the UK and in North America are based on a previously published work or on a real story. This means they were based on something that already existed in another form. In most cases that form is written material – a novel, published work of non-fiction, biography, short story, comic book, graphic novel or similar. In some cases the form may be a play written for the theatre or for radio. It may also have been originally a television series or a film. For example the television series *Fargo* is derived from the 1996 film by the Coen Brothers, and the Netflix original series *House Of Cards* began life as an adaptation of an old BBC television series of the same name, which was itself based on a novel by Michael Dobbs.

So, let's start by assuming that you (the producer) have read something in print, which you think could form the basis of a drama. The first thing you have to do is find out if the material is still in copyright or not, and if it is, who owns that copyright.

UNDERSTANDING COPYRIGHT

Copyright law originated in the UK from a concept known as 'common law'. In 1911 the British Government passed the Copyright Act. The current act is the Copyright, Designs and Patents Act 1988. The Copyright (Computer Programs) Regulations 1992 extended the rules covering literary works to include computer programs.

The law gives the creators and authors of certain types of work the right to control the ways in which their original material may be used, and to object to unauthorized reproductions, misuse or distortions of their work. The works covered include literary, dramatic, musical and artistic works, sound recordings, broadcasts, films and magazines. The rights cover broadcast and public performance, copying, adaptation, renting and lending copies to members of the public.

Music copyright is an important area for producers to understand, and is covered in greater detail in Chapter 8, 'Post-Production'. The use of other copyright works, such as photographs, artistic works and logos, is discussed in Chapter 6, 'Pre-Production'. The Berne Convention of 1886 is an international agreement that established some of the ground rules of copyright, maintained today. Amongst these are the concept of non-registration and fixed copyright, and a requirement that members of the convention recognize the copyright of citizens of other countries.

What this means in practice is that when an author creates an original work it is 'fixed' and therefore automatically in copyright. There is no need for the work to be formally registered for the copyright to be theirs. However, to qualify, the work must be regarded as original and 'exhibit a degree of labour, skill or judgement', which is unique to the author (or authors). This is generally interpreted to mean the independent creation or treatment of the subject, rather than the idea itself. So, as an example, you may be inspired by the story of *Romeo and Juliet*. Shakespeare died in 1616, so his play is out of copyright and you can reinterpret his story. But if you choose to do so by setting it on New York's West Side, making the Capulets and Montagues into rival street gangs, and turning it into a musical, you are infringing copyright. Updating *Romeo and Juliet* may be an original idea but your interpretation is not, because the copyright in *West Side Story* doesn't belong to Shakespeare but instead belongs to Arthur Laurents, Leonard Bernstein, Stephen Sondheim and Jerome Robbins.

The same may apply to characters. When Walt Disney named the seven dwarfs, he created the copyright to their story, even though the fairytale of *Snow White* had existed for centuries before. If you write a book on a subject, the content is yours. This won't prevent someone else writing another book on the same subject, but they cannot directly copy or use your words to do so.

It is worth noting here that there is no copyright in titles. You can, if you wish, develop and produce a film and call in *2020 – A Space Odyssey*. Whether or not you should is another matter. Names, titles, slogans and short phrases are not generally considered unique or substantial enough to be covered by copyright law. In the USA you may be permitted to trademark a title but will need to prove that it is a genuine brand first. For example, J.K. Rowling has trademarked the title *Harry Potter* to protect not only her work, but also those who consume it. If you see a book, film, play or series with the words *Harry Potter* in the title, you (the consumer) have a right to expect it to have been created by her.

The US Patent and Trademark Office states that a trademark protects words, symbols, designs and logos, identifying the source of the goods and distinguishing them from others. Pepsi is protected and so is the Nike tick. But unlike copyright, which is automatic, if you want to register a trademark you must apply for the right to do so. And your application may not be successful.

LENGTH OF COPYRIGHT

For all literary, dramatic, musical or artistic works the length of copyright is seventy years after the death of the author (or the longest living author if the copyright is shared). To be more precise it is actually seventy years from the end of the calendar year in which the last surviving author of the work died. If the work was published posthumously then it will be seventy years after publication. For films, copyright expires seventy years after the end of the calendar year that saw the death of the last principal director, author or composer who is credited as a creator of the work.

It is important to remember this, as some writers live a long time after their work is first published. J. D. Salinger published *Catcher in the Rye* in 1951 when he was a relatively young man of thirty-two. But he did not die until January 2010, when he was ninety-one. So *Catcher in the Rye* will remain in copyright until the end of 2080, 130 years after it was first published.

The length of copyright may be different for other forms of work. For example, some photographs, magazines and musical scores may only be in copyright for fifty years. So it is important to check precisely before assuming that copyright has expired. Infringement of copyright is serious, and authors have every right to seek redress from production companies and producers if they think this has occurred.

FAIR USE

The concept known as 'fair use' refers to limited and clearly defined circumstances when copyright material may be used without first obtaining the permission of the original authors. It is also sometimes known as 'fair dealing', and, if the rules are followed, it will not necessarily be considered an infringement of the copyright. Unfortunately there is no statutory definition of what exactly constitutes fair use, nor the percentage of the original work which that be quoted or used 'fairly'. Cases will be judged on the extent to which the copyright has been infringed (how much was used) or the context in which it was used. One major criterion will be whether the use has negatively impacted on the sales of the original work, or if the author is likely to have lost potential revenue as a result. But fair use may apply in the following circumstances:

- If the work is being used solely for private study, educational or research purposes. For example, sections from a film might be shown to a class of students to educate them on style or technique. Or a student may be permitted to photocopy a chapter from a published work for their own research purposes.
- For criticism, review and news reporting. For example, if a clip is shown when reviewing a film during a broadcast programme, or during a news story about the making of that film or one of the actors appearing in it. However, this use may not be considered 'fair' when applied to the inclusion of a still photograph in a report.
- Format shifting, or back-up of a work you own for personal use.
- Time shifting: in other words, recording of broadcasts for the purposes of listening to, or viewing, at a more convenient time.
- Caricature, parody or pastiche: meaning that it might be OK to use someone else's material, provided you use it in a way that is clearly for satirical or artistic purposes. For example, if the popular long-running NBC television series *Saturday Night Live* broadcasts a sketch that is a parody of an episode of *Friends*, this is fine, provided it is short and clearly intended as comedy or parody.
- Homage: where a film or television drama explicitly and obviously references an earlier work. Like parody, homage depends on 'intent'. If you openly acknowledge the influence of Alfred Hitchcock or Stanley Kubrick on a particular sequence, you are not stealing their work but paying tribute to it, and this counts as fair use. Martin Scorsese does this in *Shutter Island*, and Mathew Weiner does the same in *Mad Men* when he slyly reworks Douglas Sirk and other iconic films from the 1950s and 1960s.

WHAT NEXT?

If you know that the author of the published work has been dead for seventy years or more, you still have a few more things to check before planning your production. There are circumstances where copyright belongs to the company who commissioned the work, and not to the author him- or herself. If a writer was 'on staff' or employed by a company when he or she wrote it, then they may not be the owner of their own work. They may have signed a contract agreeing that all work created during this period of employment belongs to the company who hired them. This could apply to work written by staff journalists at a newspaper or magazine, the creators of comic strips and cartoon characters, or to writers working as employees of a production company.

In 1937 F. Scott Fitzgerald was broke, disillusioned and in debt. He signed a contract with Metro-Goldwyn-Mayer Films to become a staff writer, and turned up every day at their studio for two and a half years to write for them. Very little of this work ended up on screen, but it is still the property of the studio, whose assets and film library are now owned by Warner Brothers. Although Fitzgerald died in December 1940 and most of his novels and short stories came out of copyright in 2011, the work created for MGM does not form part of his literary estate and remains their property 'in perpetuity' – in other words, forever.

It may also be useful for you to undertake research into any previous film versions based on the original novel or play, and assess whether or not there is anything in them that may be considered in some way 'definitive' and that you should avoid copying. So far there have been seventeen screen versions of Jane Austen's *Pride and Prejudice*, including the 1940 version starring Greer Garson and Laurence Olivier, a Bollywood musical version, *Bride and Prejudice*, and one with Zombies. However, the BBC television adaptation released in 1995 was the first to reveal Mr Darcy, in the form of Colin Firth, emerging semi-clad from a swim in his own lake wearing a dripping wet white shirt. This scene is not in the book and comes from the imagination of the screenwriter Andrew Davies. If you chose to include it in your own adaptation you could be accused of stealing another filmmaker's ideas.

If the work that has inspired you is still in copyright, then the next step for you to take is to find out who now owns it. In many cases this will be the living author, and he or she will almost certainly have a representative appointed to deal with his or her work. This is normally a literary agent. To find out who represents your author is relatively easy, and a quick internet search should reveal it. If not, then your best next step would be to contact the publishers' rights department and ask them. If the author is dead, you may find yourself dealing with a literary estate manager. This could be a lawyer or agent, but in some cases may be a living relative of the author, who has inherited the estate on the author's death.

When an author dies the rights to his or her work will pass on as part of their estate. In most cases this will be to their husband or wife, children and grandchildren, but the author may have written a will bequeathing the rights to someone else or to an institution. For example, when J. M. Barrie died he left the rights to his play *Peter Pan* to Great Ormond Street Hospital. GOSH benefited significantly from the income this bequest generated until the copyright expired in 2007. George Bernard Shaw left the rights to his estate to be shared equally between the British Museum, the National Gallery of Ireland and the Royal Academy of Dramatic Arts (RADA). As an aside, it is worth mentioning that the greatest benefit these three institutions have earned from the Shaw estate derive from the film musical *My Fair Lady* rather than any theatrical productions of his plays.

There may also be circumstances in which a living author no longer owns or controls the rights to their own work, usually because they have already signed them away. In February 2018, author Margaret Atwood revealed in an interview that she had not benefited from any profits from the hugely successful Hulu adaptation of her novel *The Handmaid's Tale* or any sequels to it, because she sold the rights for a film adaptation over thirty years ago to MGM, who produced a film based on the book in 1990. The ten-part series for Hulu was produced by MGM Television who still control the rights, and they were not obliged to pay the original author any

Peter Pan sculpture by artist Diarmuid Byron O'Connor, standing at the entrance to Great Ormond Street Hospital. Until 2007, the hospital held the rights to the play.

more money or royalties. Atwood has made money from new sales of her original book and was apparently paid as a consultant to the series.

The normal procedure, once you have located the copyright owner, is to ask them to grant you an option on the work.

WHAT IS AN OPTION?

Acquiring an option over a literary work effectively grants you, the producer, the exclusive rights to develop a project for the screen based on that work. The option means that you are the only person, or company, who has the right to develop the work into a television drama or film, at least for as long as you hold on to these rights. An option enables you to minimize the development costs because you don't have to pay the full price of the work until later when you 'exercise' the option, normally on the first day of principal photography of your film or drama series. It also means you don't waste time or money developing a project only to find out later that you don't have the right to make it.

Without any agreement the producer is infringing the author's copyright and stealing their work. Any reputable organization you approach for development or production funding will ask to see proof that you own or control the rights before advancing any money to the project.

The agreement under which rights are acquired is called the 'option agreement'. This is an important document and must cover certain points clearly and unambiguously. But provided all the points are covered, the agreement can remain fairly simple and you may not necessarily have to pay a lawyer to draw this up for you. An agreement that is not clear about the exact rights to be acquired, or the amounts to be paid for these rights, may be only an agreement to agree and therefore not enforceable.

The main points, which should be clearly set out and agreed by both parties in the contract, are as follows.

How long is the term of the option?

Normally the first option period – that is, the period during which the producer has the exclusive right to adapt and develop the work – will be for a year from signature of the option agreement, though you may be able to persuade the author or their agent to agree to grant you an option for eighteen months. Try to get the longest period you can. As we have established, development can take a long time.

How much is the option fee?

As a rule of thumb the option fee will normally be between 5 and 10 per cent of the price agreed to acquire the rights in the literary work. So if you have agreed a final price of £40,000 for the rights, the option will be between £2,000 and £4,000. It may be much less, or almost nothing at all, if you are optioning a short story, an article or something written by a friend. A 'notional' fee of £1 is sometimes agreed in this case, but you are still advised to draw up a simple option agreement to make the arrangements clear and transparent.

Is the option fee set against the agreed final price?

It is customary (but by no means an absolute rule) for the first payment under the option agreement to be treated as an advance against the final price payable if the producer exercises the option. So if you agreed to pay £40,000, and paid an option of 10 per cent or £4,000, then the sum due when the option is exercised will be £36,000.

Can the option be extended for a further period, and if so, on what terms?

Producers should always negotiate from the outset for the right to extend the first option period by another year or eighteen months, on payment of an additional fee. There is nothing more frustrating than to find yourself almost at the point of having your film fully financed only to discover your option is running out and cannot be renewed.

Is the extension fee set against the agreed final price, or in addition to this?

When a producer acquires an option that can be extended, it is not unusual for the payment due for that extension to be treated as a separate payment, which is not set against the final price. So in the example above, if an extension is agreed and the option is subsequently exercised, the total amount payable would be £4,000 for the first option, £4,000 for the extension, and £36,000 when exercised, making a total of £44,000.

What is the final agreed price for exercising the option and acquiring all rights to the literary work?

The final agreed price means the total amount you will pay for the full and exclusive rights to make your film or series based on the existing literary work, and to distribute that work throughout the world in perpetuity. There are no rules about what this sum might be as it is driven entirely by the marketplace and the popularity of the author and their work. A relatively unknown author, or one who has fallen out of fashion, may accept a modest amount for their work.

Some authors view money from film and television as 'gravy' or 'frosting', and expect to make their living from advances and royalties for selling copies of their novel or e-book fees. Anything else is an unexpected but pleasant bonus. Other authors have higher expectations and may ask larger fees. You should expect the price to be higher if the author's previous works have been best sellers or adapted into successful films or series. Don't imagine J. K. Rowling is going to accept £25,000 as the final price for the rights to her next novel.

Many books are optioned or sold even before publication. Development producers and production companies keep their ears open about new works coming out, about which a buzz has been created. Events such as the Frankfurt and London book fairs generate a lot of noise around certain titles, and authors and agents try hard to sell film and television rights early. For new and emerging producers, it is often worth looking at publishers' back catalogues and out-of-print lists. Many great titles are still available ten or more years after they were published, including some that have been optioned for film or television but were never produced, so the rights have reverted back to the author.

When does the final agreed price become payable?

It is customary for the purchase price for the rights to be paid on the first day of principal photography, but this can be negotiable. For the producer, the exercise of the option becomes a line in the final budget of the film, and this will be shown in the cash flow. If additional rights are being acquired these might be paid for later, when the film is completed and delivered. It is sometimes the case that the agent for the author of the original work tries to negotiate further payments for their client if the final budget for the film or series turns out to be substantially higher than expected.

This is a difficult area for producers, who must tread a fine line between keeping costs down and being fair to the original talent. Clearly, if you acquired the rights to a work and told the author you were planning to make a low budget British film costing around £2m, and then delivered a £200m studio blockbuster, the original author would have a genuine grievance, but probably not a very strong legal case against you. You would have to decide what a future relationship with them was worth to you. Literary agents may also ask for their client to have a share of the 'net profits' of the film. Again, this may be a reasonable request, but be aware that this is probably going to end up coming out of the producer's share of the net profits.

Exactly what rights are being acquired?

The option agreement must set out clearly exactly what rights are being acquired by the producer:

- As a minimum, you will want the right to adapt the work for film, television and online streaming. At this moment you don't know where exactly your project is going to end up. This will probably be described in the agreement as the right to 'exploit the work by all audiovisual media', which covers you for any new media that is not yet invented. You should specify that you have acquired these rights 'in perpetuity'.
- You will also want to acquire the right to commission and authorize adaptations in the form of

synopses, treatments and scripts based on the work. Without this clause you can't ask a writer to start working on the adaptation.

- You will need the right to submit the script or treatment to third parties who may be interested in the further development, production or exploitation of the film or series based on the work. Without this you can't raise funding for your project.
- You may wish to specify or negotiate something in the agreement relating to sequels, spin-offs, remakes or other future works featuring the same characters. As a producer you don't want to work hard on developing and delivering a successful drama only to find the author selling their next book in the franchise to another company.
- You need to specify which other rights are included in the final purchase price, or which may be available to you on a first refusal basis at the point you exercise the option. For example, you may wish to ask for certain ancillary rights such as computer games or merchandise derived from the characters.

Exactly what rights are excluded from the agreement and retained by the author?

The author may request that certain rights are excluded from the deal. It is quite normal for the author to seek to retain the rights for talking books, radio and stage adaptations. They will also want to retain the right to publish extracts from their original work in newspapers or magazines. You may be able to ask them to agree to 'hold back' the stage rights until after your film has been exhibited. You may want the stage rights yourself, and agree to an additional sum later to acquire these.

What is the mechanism for extending the option?

The mechanism for extending the option will usually be a simple notice in writing sent to the author's agent. But make sure you make a diary note of when this has to be done. In the midst of development it's painfully easy to miss these deadlines and accidentally lose rights or upset your author.

What is the mechanism for exercising the option?

The mechanism for exercising the option will be more complicated, and will most likely involve a longer contract, which should be drawn up by lawyers. This document will go into much more detail about possible net profits as well as marketing, promotion, credits and so on.

Does the author have any right to be consulted during the development or production of the film?

This is perhaps the most difficult area to negotiate, and will be different for all authors. Some will show absolutely no interest in how their work is adapted for the screen, will politely take the money, sit at home and may ask to come to the premiere and meet the stars. Other writers will start the negotiations by asking to write the script. Be wary of this. Novelists are not all natural screenwriters. Although some turn out to be extremely good, they are the exception, not the rule.

Others will ask for 'approval' over the choice of writer, script, director and even casting. Say 'no'. This may seem harsh, but by the time you have raised all the funding for your film, you will probably have half a dozen people with approvals already. It will be hard enough pleasing them, without also having to go back to the writer of the novel. Instead you can offer them 'consultation'. This is a standard industry contractual term, although it is largely unenforceable. Nevertheless, you should do your very best to stick to the spirit of consultation, and offer the author opportunities to be involved in the evolution of the project. Some of his or her ideas may turn out to be invaluable.

CREATING DRAMA BASED ON REAL STORIES AND PEOPLE

Another possible source for your film project may be a true life or real story, which you decide can be fictionalized. As with copyright, different circumstances will apply depending how old the material is and whether the persons featured in your drama are alive or dead.

Basing a film on a story from the past may seem simple, but there are some factors to bear in mind. Under English and Welsh law the dead cannot be libelled, so theoretically you can say whatever you like about them and they cannot answer back. This law has been tested by journalists and newspapers many times over since the death in 1997 of Diana, Princess of Wales, who has been the subject of a number of books and articles and film and television productions.

However, when dealing with stories from the recent past, it is important to research whether anyone featured in your drama is still alive and, more importantly, whether or not they may object to the way you represent them. Have you accidentally or intentionally interpreted the facts of their life in a way with which they could disagree, or put words into their mouth they can prove they never said? This can include living family members, or descendants and children of those in your film, especially if they appear in the drama and you knowingly or accidentally say something that offends or upsets them and which they can prove is untrue.

In 2017, the US cable channel FX transmitted an eight-part drama series produced by Ryan Murphy. *Feud* tells the story of the legendary battle between Bette Davis and Joan Crawford during and after the production of their film *Whatever Happened to Baby Jane*. Davis and Crawford are both dead, as are all the other key figures featured in the drama – except one. On 30 June 2017, two days before her 101st birthday, and shortly after being made a Dame of the British Empire, Olivia de Havilland filed a lawsuit in the Los Angeles Superior Court against the *Feud* producers. She sued them for 'infringement of common law right of publicity, invasion of privacy and unjust enrichment'.

De Havilland claimed that the series characterization of her had damaged her 'professional reputation for integrity, honesty, generosity, self-sacrifice and dignity'. She requested that she be awarded both damages and any profits gained from the use of her likeness, whilst also seeking an injunction to prevent FX from using her name. The case was closely studied by filmmakers because it threatened their ability to portray real events with fictionalized elements. Although the first time the case was heard the argument was upheld, it was referred to the Court of Appeal, who threw it out in March 2018. The court upheld the view that fictional representations are protected by the First Amendment. Justice Anne Egerton wrote:

> Whether a person portrayed in one of these expressive works is a world-renowned film star — 'a living legend' — or a person no one knows, she or he does not own history. Nor does she or he have the legal right to control, dictate, approve, disapprove, or veto the creator's portrayal of actual people.

Another area to be aware of is the source of your material. Are the facts about this person 'in the public domain' and available to all? Ultimately, a fact is a fact, and if it is in the 'public domain' you can use it, especially if it has appeared in more than one published source. This could be as simple as two or three different journalists or newspapers publishing the facts of the case. Historical film biographies such as *The Darkest Hour* may not need to credit a biography of Winston Churchill because there are already so many accounts of his life and work.

However, if there is only one definitive authorized biography of the person at the centre of your film, the situation may be different. Has someone spent years researching the subject and then published this in the form of a book or academic paper? If so, you may need to consider either optioning this work, or offering the historian a role as a paid consultant to your film or series. A decision to base your film on opinion or unpublished research should be considered very carefully, and if you have any doubts you should take legal advice.

Legal advice may also be required if you are planning a campaigning documentary or docudrama that challenges the public account of events or the outcome of a trial. Television film treatments of *The Murder of Steven Lawrence*, *Three Girls* or

Hillsborough cannot get a release or permission from the senior public figures they are accusing of incompetence or cover up. So they will often take the risk of being sued for libel, in the hope that the individuals will not want to risk further publicity and exposure, nor have their actions examined under oath in a courtroom. Ultimately this decision will come down to the broadcaster, and their own 'in house' legal team will have the final say, whichever way the producer argues.

There is also a danger of injunctions against a programme being made or broadcast, because the burden of proof is less exacting than a libel trial. But injunctions can't happen after the event, only before. So genuinely controversial documentaries or docu-dramas tend to keep their sources, scripts and footage closely under wraps during the production process to avoid this possibility.

COMMISSIONING THE PROJECT

Whether your project is an original idea, an adaptation, or based on fact, you have now arrived at the moment when you must enter into a contractual arrangement with your screenwriter, or with the screenwriter you hire to adapt the work. In the first instance you will need to open negotiations with their agent.

AGENTS

Most experienced writers will have an agent to represent them, and the same is true of directors, crew members and cast. This is a good practice, as it means you can discuss the dirty business of fees and money with someone else, and not directly with the person you will be working with. As a producer you will need to negotiate the best terms for the project, without underpaying or undervaluing the contribution of the talent you want to make it happen. Remember that agents are working for the best interests of their client, and earn most of their salaries from a percentage of their fee: the more their client earns, the more they themselves are paid. So it is obviously in their interest to get them the best possible deal.

That said, literary agents do know the market very well, and have a good understanding of what is fair for a particular project and what is not. They know better than anyone what the 'going rate' is for a particular kind of drama, and how much they can ask for their client's services.

The agent is also responsible for negotiating the finer details of the deal, which will be written down in the form of a contract, signed by all parties. This will include not only how much the writer earns, but also a schedule of when these payments fall due, and how long each different stage of the writing process should take. The contract should also deal with arrangements if the project fails to go into production or is abandoned, terms for any sequels or spin-offs, how the writer should be looked after if they are asked to travel for work, credits, and whether the writer is entitled to receive any net profits.

SCREENWRITER CONTRACTS

In the UK there are standard minimum terms that have been agreed between the industry's formal negotiating bodies, in this case PACT (Producer's Alliance for Cinema and Television) and WGGB (the Writers Guild of Great Britain). Details of the latest agreements and sample contracts can be found on the WGGB website.

In the USA, the Writers Guild of America is a very powerful organization with the ability to call strikes, close down productions, and black list anyone who breaks their rules. In the UK the WGGB does not have the same power, and membership is optional. Many screenwriters will not be members of the guild, but it is still advisable to adhere to their guidelines and minimum terms when commissioning a new project.

The PACT/WGGB agreement identifies the following different types of production, and sets out minimum payments and conditions for each one:

- Feature films budgeted at over £2m;
- Feature films budgeted between £750,000 and £2m;

- Television films budgeted over £750,000;
- Films budgeted below £750,000;
- Television series and serials with a format provided other than by the writer.

PAYMENTS TO WRITERS

Your agreement with the screenwriter will contain a schedule of payments setting out what is due, and when. The normal schedule, and the one approved by PACT/WGGB, is as follows:

- Payment on commencement of treatment;
- Payment on acceptance of treatment;
- Payment on commencement of first draft script;
- Payment on delivery of first draft;
- Payment on commencement of second draft script;
- Payment on principal photography.

These six payments add up to the total minimum payment due under the contract.

There are also further payments due to the screenwriter for advance purchase of certain use fees. This means paying 'up front' for the right to show the film more than once (repeat fees), or to buy the rights to show it in certain foreign territories.

The contract should also state clearly how long each part of the process will take. For example, you may wish to set a date by which the treatment must be delivered, and also make it clear how long you have to consider it and get back to the writer with notes or to confirm acceptance. The term 'acceptance' can sometimes be open to interpretation, especially later in the development period. Make sure it is clear when a script or treatment is accepted by doing so in writing, and if you feel further work is needed, ask the writer to make the changes first.

There will also be cut-off points in the contract should the two parties not agree on how to proceed with the project. If, on receiving the treatment from your writer, you decide not to carry on to the script commissioning stage, what happens to the project will depend on whose original idea it was. If you approached the writer with an idea, the copyright in the idea remains yours. But if they approached you with an idea, it will remain theirs, and they will be free to take it to another producer.

TURNAROUND

Turnaround is the term used to describe the arrangements when an option lapses and the rights revert to the original copyright holder. This may be the screenwriter, if the project was their idea in the first place, or it could be the producer or a production company if they initiated the project and invited the writer to become involved. Sometimes turnaround can be 'invoked', and sometimes it simply depends on the passage of time. Sometimes turnaround will involve a repayment of development costs, and sometimes it won't.

Normally, in any development or option agreement between a writer and a producer (or a production company) and a broadcaster or studio, some provision is made for turnaround. Typically this will include an opportunity to 'buy back' the project after a certain period of time (anything from six months to two years). Or, after a longer period of time (typically two to five years), the option lapses and the rights simply revert to the writer or producer for free.

But there are complexities. For example, the BBC develops a ten-part murder mystery, and pays for some scripts, a series bible and future storylines. But when the crunch comes, the channel controller decides to pass on the series. The independent producer offers the project to ITV, who say 'yes' and immediately 'green light' the series for production. Depending on the turnaround provisions of the original contract, the BBC can get all its development costs back immediately, or repayment can be deferred to the first day of principal photography, or until the show is eventually broadcast. Or, the BBC can get their costs plus a share of any future profits from worldwide sales. Or, the BBC can get nothing at all.

Much the same applies when a writer puts a project into turnaround at the expense of a producer. So there can be friendly turnarounds and hostile turnarounds, but unless you want to just sit out the option, turnaround usually involves a negotiation. Sometimes one of the parties takes a hard line to stop the other profiting. But normally, some fair agreement is reached, not least because you will probably want to work with the writer, producer, broadcaster or studio again.

TREATMENTS AND SCRIPTS

The standard way to commission a screenwriter in our industry is to begin with a treatment. This document can be quite short or very long, and will vary enormously depending on how the writer likes to work and whom you need to show it to. The Guild agreement defines a treatment quite broadly as:

> An outline or synopsis in narrative form of an entire story indicating the fuller structure and development and characterization of the plot.

It's important to remember that the treatment is a working document for the screenwriter and you. It is entirely different from a sales pitch or selling document, which will usually be no more than one A4 side and is designed to attract funders. (There is more on writing proposals and pitch documents in Chapter 5 'Raising Production Finance'.) What you need from a treatment is a clear sense of what the film or series is. You need a beginning, a middle and an ending. You want to understand the characters, their arcs and journeys through the drama, and you need an idea of structure and some exciting moments. If your project is a comedy, a joke or two might be useful. If it's a thriller, some heart-stopping, page-turning moments are a must.

Writers have their own way of plotting and planning their stories before they commence the script. This interim work might include documents such as a 'beat sheet', a 'scene by scene' or a 'step outline'. This will all be useful to you as the producer, but it is part of the work in progress, and not usually shown to anyone outside the core development team.

When you receive the first draft of the treatment you can start to give feedback or notes. If there are differences between what you expected and what the writer is focusing on, then this early stage is an important time to discuss them and come to an agreement on the direction of the project.

Once you have a treatment with which you are happy, you may wish to start trying to raise development money for the project and applying to funding institutions. But development funds are increasingly limited, and you may need to ask your writer to do more work, including writing a first draft script (depending on their experience and reputation).

WORKING WITH WRITERS

A multitude of books has been published on screenwriting practice and theory, and what constitutes a good script. This is not one of them. But I do suggest you read at least one or two of those listed in the bibliography at the end of this book.

As a producer, you must have experience of what works and what doesn't work in a script, know what questions to ask, and be able to offer suggestions for changes and improvements. This knowledge can best be gained by watching a wide variety of films and programmes, and reading as many scripts as you can lay your hands on. There are plenty of places to find scripts on line, a few of which are listed in Useful Websites at the end of this book. If you haven't seen the film, read the script first before you watch it. This is a much more useful way to understand what works and what doesn't.

Giving notes to writers can be a delicate business and must be done with tact and diplomacy. Good writers will respect your input and welcome the collaborative nature of development. But they may also be fiercely protective of their work and reluctant to change something they like and think is working.

Writers dislike notes that are too vague or too general, and find these unhelpful. Comments along the lines of:

> This script needs to be more dramatic…
> 26 per cent funnier …
> Needs twice as much jeopardy …

A new beginning, middle and end…..
I hate both the lead characters

won't be 'the beginning of a beautiful friendship'.

Writers like notes that are clear and specific, so they know where, and how, to begin a rewrite. What you think works, and what you want them to keep, is often as important as what you may be asking them to change.

Writers also like honesty. If you have a note from an investor or a broadcaster, be frank about it and don't try to pass it off as your own.

Try to avoid telling your writer what and how you think they should write. It is better to say an element or scene is not working, and let them propose a solution.

Legendary film and television producer, Tony Garnett, famously only ever gives one note on a first draft script, and it runs something like this: 'You lost me in scene 16 on page 21.' And according to writers, it works every time.

Remember that every successful relationship between a producer and a writer is a unique collaboration with one thing in common. Somehow, the producer has enabled the writer to create their best work.

Together you want to make a film. You have a script you both believe in. It is time to think about exactly how you are going to achieve that objective.

FURTHER PROJECT DEVELOPMENT

Development of a project is not only about the research and writing process. It also includes fundraising, scheduling and budgeting, which are all discussed in detail in the following chapters. During this time you may also need to attach some other talent to make the project more attractive to investors and commissioning editors before you launch it into the marketplace. The main person you need to find is a director, but you may also want to attach some principal cast as well.

FINDING A DIRECTOR

The process of finding a director is more or less the same as the one you already went through when you were looking for a writer. You should conduct intensive research by watching shorts, series episodes and feature films. Most working directors have an agent to represent them, so look on the main agents' websites and IMDb for credits.

When you have drawn up a shortlist, start checking availability, and talking to other producers who have worked with the names on your list. When you have narrowed it down to two or three names, contact their agents and ask if they would like to read your script. If they say yes, and like it, you then arrange a meeting. Some agents will ask if you are meeting anyone else, or if their client is the only person you are considering. You should be honest about this, as they will probably find out if you are not. Except when approaching really 'big name' directors, it is quite fair to say you are meeting more than one person.

You may decide to involve the screenwriter in this meeting and invite them along, too. This can be a good idea, as the relationship between writer and director is important. But in some cases, it may be preferable to have a first meeting with a potential director alone, and then introduce the writer later. At the first meeting you want to find out what the director thinks of the script, how many substantial changes they want to make to it, and get an idea of how they would like to cast it. If you have been developing your project as a low budget feature and the director starts talking about helicopter shots, action sequences and star casting, they may not be the person you want.

You should also be alert as to how much the director wants to change the script. Of course they will have ideas and suggestions, and these are always welcomed. But be cautious if they start talking about major character and plot changes and appear to want to make a different film.

When you have found the director you want to work with, you need to reach an agreement with them. At this stage you cannot normally sign a contract since you don't have funding or confirmed dates for the production. A more flexible arrangement is a 'letter of intent', in which the director confirms their interest in the project, subject to their availability at the time, a deal being negotiated, and other considerations. The letter of intent is not legally binding, but its purpose is to show commissioners and investors that the director is committed to the project and genuinely wants to make it with you. The letter is normally drawn up and issued by the director's agent and signed by him or her.

ATTACHING CAST

Once you have a director on board, your next step may be to attach one or more main cast to the project. Many investors, sales agents and distributors want to know who is playing the key roles before they will commit funding to your project. It is usually quite difficult to attach actors without a director.

You can approach actors directly through their agents, but in many cases the best way to talk to them is by engaging a casting director now. Casting directors are a vast resource of knowledge and experience, and can really help you get your script read by those you want to meet. For new or inexperienced producers, they are essential. Normally casting directors receive a fee for casting the whole project. If you involve one at this early stage they may accept an advance, set against the final fee they will receive when the project is green lit and the full budget is available. Alternatively they may agree to be paid a daily rate for a certain number of days to help you with casting the lead roles.

The producer, director and casting director meet to discuss a wish list for the two or three main roles. The casting director then approaches the agents for these actors and asks if they will read the script and meet the director. In some cases the agent may want to know if the meeting is an 'offer'. The process of offers is explained fully in Chapter 6 'Pre-Production', but essentially it means that the actors won't come in for an audition or meeting unless it is understood that the part will be offered to them if they want it.

If the meeting goes well, and the actor decides they want to play the part, you then need to attach them. In some cases this can involve a similar 'letter of intent' to the one you have already obtained from the director. In other cases the actor's agent or manager may wish to make a more formal agreement with you, and will ask for a contract. This is difficult if you don't yet have all the funding. Sometimes the agent will ask for a 'pay or play' commitment from the producer. This commits you to paying their client the agreed fee even if the film does not go ahead or the actor is not engaged on it.

There are some exceptions, such as 'force majeure' or the artist breaking the agreement, but any decision to agree to 'pay or play' has significant financial consequences and must be very carefully considered. In most cases agents will agree that 'pay or play' doesn't come into force until the film is green lit, and that it is paid on the start of principal photography. This ensures their client gets the part and can't be replaced, but means the producer isn't liable to pay them until the film is fully financed and ready to shoot. Although 'pay or play' may appear onerous to the producer, it protects the actor against turning down other work and then not being employed on the film.

MOVING FORWARDS

You now have all the elements of your creative package. You have a contract to show that you own or control the 'underlying rights' in the original material. You have a contract with your screenwriter, and a first or second draft script you like and agree on. You have attached a director and some principal cast. Now you need to move on to the more practical considerations. First of all, how much will the film cost, and where will you raise the money to make it?

A scheduling stripboard with coloured strips. This is how all scheduling was done before new software became available.

3

SCHEDULING AND BUDGETING

The development of any film or television project is much more than just the research, commissioning and scriptwriting process. Before you go out to raise the money for your project you need to know how much it is going to cost to make. You most definitely don't want to find yourself in a much awaited and sought after meeting with a commissioning editor, sales agent or film funding institution and be unable to answer their questions about the budget. And in order to get a reasonable idea of the cost of production, you first need to produce a schedule. So, whether you are working as a producer or as a line producer, it is vital that you understand the complexities of scheduling and how to budget your film or series.

SCHEDULING THE WHOLE PROJECT

In the UK and the USA, the final shooting schedule is produced by the first assistant director during pre-production. But as a producer you must know and understand the principles of scheduling and how to use the software generally employed to do this. You will want to understand why the first AD has arrived at certain decisions, and to be able to discuss the schedule in detail with him or her and the rest of your heads of department. And you need at least a rough schedule to accurately budget your short, feature film or series.

Before looking in detail at shooting schedules, it is important to emphasize once more that the shooting period is only part of the production. You must also plan how much time is needed for fundraising, and how many weeks are required for pre-production, post-production and delivery. The

number of weeks that each member of your cast and crew will be working on the project is one of the biggest variables in your budget.

A simple timeline or monthly calendar is a useful tool to keep on track. If you are planning a crowd funding campaign you might find it helpful to have a separate planner just for this activity. For larger projects, including television series and documentaries, there may also be a complex writing or research schedule to plan as well. You will also need to schedule the post-production and delivery of multiple episodes.

The production schedule chart shows one example of a schedule for a six-part television drama series. In this example the series shoots in three 'blocks'. Each block represents two episodes, which are scheduled together for more efficient use of locations and cast. The three blocks each have a different director, but many members of the shooting crew will work across all the episodes. From commission to delivery of the last episode takes a year. The delivery of new treatments, scene × scenes and script drafts is scheduled to allow time for reading each one and making notes. Slightly longer is allowed between delivery of the first episodes and transmission to provide time for publicity and on-screen promotion and to send out review copies.

From the producer's point of view, the week beginning 27 September will be the worst week. Block one is in the final week of its shoot and must complete filming on time. Block two is in the later stages of pre-production, and recces will be taking place in this week. Block three is about to start full pre-production, and the shooting script needs to be locked.

In all cases I like to work backwards from the delivery or transmission date. This is the one fixed

Timeline for Production and Delivery

A sample timeline for production and delivery of a single film.

Week begins	
29-Oct	Deliver to Distributor / Sales Agent
22-Oct	Final Deliverables and paperwork
15-Oct	Final Deliverables and paperwork
08-Oct	Sound Mix
01-Oct	Sound Edit 5 / Titles and end roller
24-Sep	Sound Edit 4 / Music recording / ADR
17-Sep	Sound Edit 3 / ADR / Foley
10-Sep	Sound Edit 2 / VFX / Grade
03-Sep	Sound Edit 1 / VFX
27-Aug	Picture Lock
20-Aug	Edit 5 - Fine Cut
13-Aug	Edit 4
06-Aug	Edit 3 - Director's Cut
30-Jul	Edit 2
23-Jul	Edit 1
16-Jul	Shoot 4
09-Jul	Shoot 3
02-Jul	Shoot 2
25-Jun	Shoot 1
18-Jun	Pre-production 6
11-Jun	Pre-production 5
04-Jun	Pre-production 4
28-May	Pre-production 3
21-May	Pre-production 2
14-May	Pre-production 1 / Shooting Script Lock
07-May	Location Scouting and Casting
30-Apr	Script Draft 4
23-Apr	
16-Apr	Script Draft 3
09-Apr	
02-Apr	
26-Mar	Script Draft 2
19-Mar	
12-Mar	
05-Mar	Script Draft1
26-Feb	
19-Feb	
12-Feb	
05-Feb	
29-Jan	
22-Jan	Revised Treatment
15-Jan	
08-Jan	Treatment

An example of a production schedule for a six-part television series from development to delivery.

Week	Block One		Block Two		Block Three	
	Episode 1	Episode 2	Episode 3	Episode 4	Episode 5	Episode 6
12-Apr						
19-Apr	Sc x Sc	Sc x Sc				
26-Apr						
03-May			Treatment	Treatment		
10-May	Draft 1	Draft 1				
17-May						
24-May			Sc x Sc	Sc x Sc		
31-May					Treatment	Treatment
07-Jun	Draft 2	Draft 2				
14-Jun			Draft 1	Draft 1		
21-Jun					Sc x Sc	Sc x Sc
28-Jun						
05-Jul	Draft 3	Draft 3				
12-Jul			Draft 2	Draft 2		
19-Jul	Shooting	Shooting			Draft 1	Draft 1
26-Jul	Prep	Prep				
02-Aug	Prep	Prep				
09-Aug	Prep	Prep	Draft 3	Draft 3		
16-Aug	Prep	Prep			Draft 2	Draft 2
23-Aug	Prep	Prep	Shooting	Shooting		
30-Aug	Prep	Prep	Prep	Prep		
06-Sep	**Shoot**	**Shoot**	Prep	Prep		
13-Sep	**Shoot**	**Shoot**	Prep	Prep	Draft 3	Draft 3
20-Sep	**Shoot**	**Shoot**	Prep	Prep		
27-Sep	**Shoot**	**Shoot**	Prep	Prep	Shooting	Shooting
04-Oct	Edit	Edit	Prep	Prep	Prep	Prep
11-Oct	Edit	Edit	**Shoot**	**Shoot**	Prep	Prep
18-Oct	Director Cut	Director Cut	**Shoot**	**Shoot**	Prep	Prep
25-Oct	Edit	Edit	**Shoot**	**Shoot**	Prep	Prep
01-Nov	Fine Cut	Fine Cut	**Shoot**	**Shoot**	Prep	Prep
08-Nov	Picture Lock	Picture Lock	Edit	Edit	Prep	Prep
15-Nov	FX / Grade	FX / Grade	Edit	Edit	**Shoot**	**Shoot**
22-Nov	FX	FX	Director Cut	Director Cut	**Shoot**	**Shoot**
29-Nov	FX	FX	Edit	Edit	**Shoot**	**Shoot**
06-Dec	Sound Edit	Sound Edit	Fine Cut	Fine Cut	**Shoot**	**Shoot**
13-Dec	Sound Edit	Sound Edit	Picture Lock	Picture Lock	Edit	Edit
20-Dec	Christmas	Christmas	Christmas	Christmas	Christmas	Christmas
27-Dec					Edit	Edit
03-Jan	Sound Edit	Sound Edit	FX / Grade	FX / Grade	Director Cut	Director Cut
10-Jan	Sound Edit	Sound Edit	FX	FX	Edit	Edit
17-Jan	Sound Mix	Sound Mix	FX	FX	Fine Cut	Fine Cut
24-Jan	Deliver	Deliver	Sound Edit	Sound Edit	Picture Lock	Picture Lock
31-Jan			Sound Edit	Sound Edit	FX / Grade	FX / Grade
07-Feb			Sound Edit	Sound Edit	FX	FX
14-Feb			Sound Edit	Sound Edit	Sound Edit	FX
21-Feb			Sound Mix	Sound Mix	Sound Edit	Sound Edit
28-Feb			Deliver	Deliver	Sound Edit	Sound Edit
07-Mar	Transmit				Sound Edit	Sound Edit
14-Mar		Transmit			Sound Edit	Sound Edit
21-Mar			Transmit		Sound Mix	Sound Edit
28-Mar				Transmit	Deliver	Sound Mix
04-Apr					Transmit	Deliver
11-Apr						Transmit

A sample page from a shooting script showing the generally accepted layout.

4   EXT.   HARBOUR PROMENADE.   DAY   4

A young woman is walking a dog on a lead along a seaside
promenade. This is AMY. She is wearing sunglasses. AMY
stops at one of the numerous outdoor cafés and sits down at
one of the tables. She loops the dog's lead around the leg
of her chair, opens her bag and takes out a book.

5   EXT.   SEASIDE TOWN. STREET. DAY   5

A car is hurtling down the street, going faster than it
should on this steep, narrow road. At the bottom of the
hill the driver mounts a mini-roundabout and makes a sharp
left hand turn into the harbour.

6   EXT.   HARBOUR PROMENADE. DAY   6

A middle aged WOMAN jumps back as the speeding car mounts
the pavement and skids to a halt.

7   EXT.   HARBOUR CAFÉ.   DAY   7

A WAITER approaches AMY to take her order.

                         AMY
                A skinny flat white and a
                large glass of tap water
                please.

                       WAITER
                Anything to eat?

                         AMY
                No thanks.

The WAITER bends down to pat the dog before turning back
into the café.

8   EXT.   HARBOUR PROMENADE. DAY   8

A young man, SAM, leaps out of the car, slams the door and
starts to run along the promenade towards where AMY is
sitting.

9   EXT.   HARBOUR CAFÉ.   DAY   9

AMY looks up and recognizes SAM racing towards her.

                     AMY (shouts)
                Sam!! What the ...

point in your calendar and cannot change under any circumstances. It is useful to start here and work back to see when each stage needs to be completed in order to meet this target.

SCHEDULING THE SHOOT

Most professional screenwriters like to use Final Draft®, a scriptwriting software that includes a number of standard templates and helpful formulae. However, there are other cheaper and free alternatives available online.

Before you can start work on your schedule there are a few things in the script you need to check and may need to amend first.

SCENE HEADINGS

First, check the scene numbers. Has the writer accidentally skipped a number or repeated one? Or possibly not numbered the scenes at all? You need every scene to be correctly and consecutively numbered before you can begin your schedule.

Next, they must be identified as taking place either inside or outside – INT(erior) or EXT(erior). If it says 'INT' is it actually an interior scene, or is it partly outside as well? If the character is coming through a door, will the exterior be partly visible as well as the interior? At this point you may decide to split a scene into two or more shorter scenes, reflecting where they *actually* take place, and must renumber the following scenes accordingly. Remember that it is quite likely the interior and exterior of a particular set could be shot in two entirely different locations, and weeks apart. Car scenes can be particularly tricky ones to decide. Is the scene taking place inside the car, outside the car, or both? To help make your decision, think about where the camera will be placed.

Next, you must check the set description. Especially on series with multiple writers there can be inconsistencies and overlaps. For example, INT MOLLY'S BEDROOM might be the same as INT CHILD'S BEDROOM; or EXT PARK might be the same as EXT CHILDREN'S PLAYGROUND. Go

through and ensure these are consistent throughout the whole script or all the series scripts. This will avoid wasting time looking for locations you already have. To make things easier you can decide on an overall description for each set and then add any subdivisions of that set afterwards, for example:

EXT. WESTWOOD GENERAL HOSPITAL. CAR PARK
EXT. WESTWOOD GENERAL HOSPITAL. AMBULANCE BAY
INT. WESTWOOD GENERAL HOSPITAL. CORRIDOR
INT. WESTWOOD GENERAL HOSPITAL. OPERATING THEATRE

Now look at the time of day the writer has given the scene. This should be either DAY or NIGHT. Anything else is misleading. I have never read a script in which at some point the writer doesn't describe a scene as taking place at dusk, dawn, evening, morning, sunrise or sunset. However, this is generally unhelpful. The opportunity to shoot at dusk or dawn is no more than twenty minutes on a clear day – or, put more simply, you will only have time to attempt the shot once. Sunrise or sunset may be a fraction longer. Anything described as 'morning' should be renamed DAY. A scene described as EVE depends on the time of year you are shooting: in the UK in winter it might be dark at 3pm, and in early summer it will still be light at 9pm. Later in prep you might add actual times of day, but for now make sure you identify if the lights need to go on, or if the sun is out.

BREAKING DOWN THE SCRIPT

Your next task is to go through the script again and mark or highlight everything that is unusual or may require special equipment, additional labour or production resources, or may have health and safety implications. Here is a list of some of the things you should be looking out for, but there may be others, depending on the project:

```
        4    EXT.    HARBOUR PROMENADE.  DAY                    4

             A young woman is walking a dog on a lead along a seaside
             promenade. This is AMY. She is wearing sunglasses. AMY
             stops at one of the numerous outdoor cafés and sits down at
             one of the tables. She loops the dog's lead around the leg
             of her chair, opens her bag and takes out a book.

        5    EXT.    SEASIDE TOWN. STREET.  DAY                 5

             A car is hurtling down the street, going faster than it
             should on this steep, narrow road.  At the bottom of the
             hill the driver mounts a mini-roundabout and makes a sharp
             left hand turn into the harbour.

        6    EXT.    HARBOUR PROMENADE.  DAY                    6

             A middle aged WOMAN jumps back as the speeding car mounts
             the pavement and skids to a halt.

        7    EXT.    HARBOUR CAFÉ.   DAY                        7

             A WAITER approaches AMY to take her order.

                              AMY
                    A skinny flat white and a
                    large glass of tap water
                    please.

                              WAITER
                    Anything to eat?

                              AMY
                    No thanks.

             The WAITER bends down to pat the dog before turning back
             into the café.

        8    EXT.    HARBOUR PROMENADE.  DAY                    8

             A young man, SAM, leaps out of the car, slams the door and
             starts to run along the promenade towards where AMY is
             sitting.

        9    EXT.    HARBOUR CAFÉ.   DAY                        9

             AMY looks up and recognizes SAM racing towards her.

                              AMY (shouts)
                    Sam!! What the ...

        Under the Sun/Draft 4                          - 2 -
```

(handwritten annotations: "Distance from water?", "SA?", "Café Customers?", "Passers By?", "SA?")

An example of a 'marked up' script page with highlights to show items requiring special consideration or additional resources.

Children (actors under eighteen years old)
Animals (including domestic animals such as dogs and cats)
Stunts (anything potentially dangerous to your actors or crew)
Crowd scenes (large numbers of extras)
Visual or special effects (for example rain, smoke and fire, as well as CGI and green screen)
Live music or performances
Vehicles (including bicycles, cars, vans, trains)

Guns or firearms of any kind
Insert material (computer or TV screens)
Additional equipment (Steadicam, low loaders, drones, cranes)

This information will all need to be transferred on to the breakdown sheets, which are the starting point for creating your schedule.

At the same time you should be double-checking exactly who is in the scene. Normally all

A Movie Magic
Scheduling
stripboard.

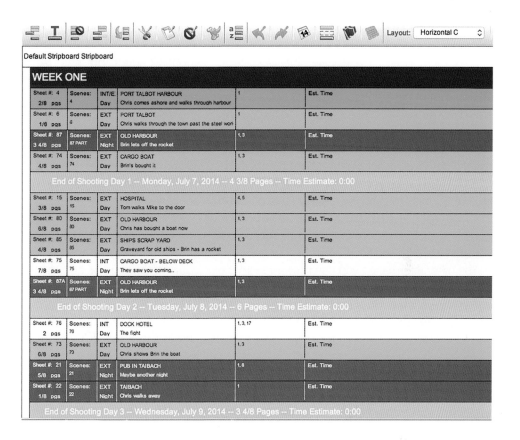

Layout:	Horizontal C					

Default Stripboard Stripboard

WEEK ONE

Sheet #: 4	Scenes:	INT/E	PORT TALBOT HARBOUR	1		Est. Time
2/8 pgs	4	Day	Chris comes ashore and walks through harbour			
Sheet #: 6	Scenes:	EXT	PORT TALBOT	1		Est. Time
1/8 pgs	6	Day	Chris walks through the town past the steel work			
Sheet #: 87	Scenes:	EXT	OLD HARBOUR	1, 3		Est. Time
3 4/8 pgs	87 PART	Night	Brin lets off the rocket			
Sheet #: 74	Scenes:	EXT	CARGO BOAT	1, 3		Est. Time
4/8 pgs	74	Day	Brin's bought it			

End of Shooting Day 1 — Monday, July 7, 2014 — 4 3/8 Pages — Time Estimate: 0:00

Sheet #: 15	Scenes:	EXT	HOSPITAL	4, 5		Est. Time
3/8 pgs	15	Day	Tom walks Mike to the door			
Sheet #: 80	Scenes:	EXT	OLD HARBOUR	1, 3		Est. Time
6/8 pgs	80	Day	Chris has bought a boat now			
Sheet #: 85	Scenes:	EXT	SHIPS SCRAP YARD	1, 3		Est. Time
4/8 pgs	85	Day	Graveyard for old ships - Brin has a rocket			
Sheet #: 75	Scenes:	INT	CARGO BOAT - BELOW DECK	1, 3		Est. Time
7/8 pgs	75	Day	They saw you coming..			
Sheet #: 87A	Scenes:	EXT	OLD HARBOUR	1, 3		Est. Time
3 4/8 pgs	87 PART	Night	Brin lets off the rocket			

End of Shooting Day 2 — Tuesday, July 8, 2014 — 6 Pages — Time Estimate: 0:00

Sheet #: 76	Scenes:	INT	DOCK HOTEL	1, 3, 17		Est. Time
2 pgs	76	Day	The fight			
Sheet #: 73	Scenes:	EXT	OLD HARBOUR	1, 3		Est. Time
6/8 pgs	73	Day	Chris shows Brin the boat			
Sheet #: 21	Scenes:	EXT	PUB IN TAIBACH	1, 8		Est. Time
5/8 pgs	21	Night	Maybe another night			
Sheet #: 22	Scenes:	EXT	TAIBACH	1		Est. Time
1/8 pgs	22	Night	Chris walks away			

End of Shooting Day 3 — Wednesday, July 9, 2014 — 3 4/8 Pages — Time Estimate: 0:00

members of the cast will appear with their character name in capital letters in the script – but check that none has been missed out. If someone doesn't speak it doesn't mean they are not present. If in doubt, double check with the writer, who should be there. It is both costly and insulting to call someone for a scene and then realize they are not needed and send them away. But it is equally bad not to have someone on set who should be there, and is relaxing at home or working out at the gym instead.

In the UK and USA, the industry standard software for scheduling in film and television is Movie Magic Scheduling from Entertainment Partners. For short films you can easily create a schedule using Excel or another spreadsheet software package, but for anything longer or more complex it is really helpful to understand how to use the specialist software. In the past, shooting schedules were created using a stripboard on which

every scene was painstakingly written out by hand on different coloured strips, and then arranged and rearranged on the board as the schedule was built. Now, thankfully, we have a computer program to help. But despite its advantages, Movie Magic won't actually produce the schedule for you, and you still have to do some of the work. I have laid out here some of the basics to get you started with scheduling and using the software. For more advanced information there are numerous online tutorials and forums to help.

If the script you are scheduling is already in Final Draft®, the first part of the process of creating your schedule will be a little easier, since you can start by 'importing' the script directly into Movie Magic. This action will instantly create what is known as a 'breakdown sheet' for each scene of the script for you. This is where you will add further details about all the individual components, or 'elements', of that scene.

Breakdown Sheets

BREAKDOWN SHEET PART ONE: FIELDS

The top half of the breakdown sheet contains what are known as 'fields'. These should remain constant, and mainly include information directly imported into the breakdown sheet from the scene headings in the script. They should include the scene number, INT or EXT, the set description, and whether it is DAY or NIGHT. By this time you will already have checked this information at least once so it should be correct, but this is another chance to make sure that before you start you add additional notes of your own.

The other information you can now add into the fields section will include the following: pages, timing, synopsis, story days and location – these are described below.

PAGES

Scripts are traditionally broken down into sections of ⅛ of a page. The page count may have come through automatically when you imported the script, but you should still double check it is correct. Look at the scene in question on the page and decide if it is ⅖, ⅝, or 2⅝, and so on. At this stage this can be an estimate.

TIMING

'Timing' is the estimated length the scene will play in the final edited version of the film. In pre-production the script supervisor will provide you with accurate scene timings for the final shooting script, but it is useful to have a rough timing now. There is a commonly held belief that each script page is a minute long, and that therefore a sixty-page script will produce a sixty-minute programme. But this is simply not true, and a page of snappy dialogue between two characters talking fast could be no more than thirty seconds on screen, whereas a page of action description could end up as five minutes in the final edit.

Timing each individual scene is important and can only really be done one way. I suggest you shut yourself away somewhere private, take out your stopwatch or set your mobile phone accordingly, and start reading aloud and walking through the action. Then make a note of the time of each individual scene. When you have worked through the whole script this way you will know how long it will play on screen. If you are aiming for a short film – say, under fifteen minutes, and your timing comes out at thirty minutes – then you know at this point that you need to go back to your writer to discuss script revisions.

SYNOPSIS

In this section you will have to write a brief description of the content of the scene so that it can be easily identified. It needs to be short and to the point and does not require much description or

An example of a breakdown sheet in Movie Magic Scheduling.

too many emotions. For example, 'Sam walks over the bridge' or 'Mary and John argue over dinner'.

STORY DAYS

Script or story days must be identified in the shooting script and given a number. A story day means a new day in the story of the film. As most films and series do not have the luxury of shooting sequentially, marking the story days is an important way of ensuring continuity. For example, your film may take place over a seven-year period but only contain fifteen story days. On the first story day your two main characters may meet for the first time. On Day 2 they may have their first date. Story Day 3 could be six months later when they get engaged, and so on. For more information on story days *see* Chapter 6, 'Pre-Production'.

LOCATION

At this point in time you probably won't know the location where the scene will be shot, but if you do, you can enter it here. It is important to note the difference between the 'set', which is the fictional place (The Old Oak Pub), and the 'location', which is the real place you are filming (The Red Lion, 27 The High Street).

BREAKDOWN SHEET PART TWO: CATEGORIES AND ELEMENTS

The bottom half of the breakdown sheet is where you can now add various categories. These will normally include as a minimum the cast, stunts, special effects, extras, additional labour, special equipment and vehicles. You can add any others you want according to the demands of the particular project. Within each category you can then add what are known as 'elements'. These are the different types of additional people, equipment, props and other elements you will need when you come to shoot this particular scene. They are the items you highlighted when you marked up your script earlier. So refer back to the marked script and start adding any animals, stunt arrangers, drones, cranes and so on here.

CAST

MMS will automatically allocate each character in the script a number based on the order of their first appearance in the screenplay. You can decide to keep these numbers or can overwrite them and allocate your own chosen number to each character. This is advisable for a number of reasons. The main one is that your lead actors will want to have the highest numbers – 1, 2, 3 and so on. It is also helpful to group characters who frequently appear together. So a family of two adults and two children might be 6, 7, 8, 9.

One additional thing to be aware of with cast is whether there is more than one actor playing a particular character, and when the actor changes. For example, if you have a character who ages from ten to seventy years old during the film, you may have three or more actors playing the part. These need to be identified from the script as MARY 1 (sixteen to twenty-two), MARY 2 (forty to fifty) and MARY 3 (eighty plus), and be given three different cast numbers.

SUPPORTING ARTISTS

Supporting artists are non-speaking parts. They used to be known as 'extras', and on many shoots (and occasionally in this book) are still referred to as this. Sometimes they are also described as 'crowd' or 'background artists'. Almost every exterior scene will require at least some supporting artists to make the place appear busy and inhabited. But they are an expense, as they will need to be paid a daily fee, fed, clothed, and possibly made up and transported.

As you go through the script, try to work out how many extras might be required for each scene and then add them here, identifying who they are and what they could be doing. For example, '6 × passers-by', '15 × customers', '2 × waiters', and so on. Bear in mind that the writer may not have written any crowd members into the script, and use your own judgement to decide how many could be required. It will only be an estimate at this stage.

STUNTS

A stunt is any kind of on-screen action requiring special planning and training, and which could potentially endanger a member of the cast or crew. Whether something is a stunt or not varies greatly, but at this stage it is safest to assume it will be a stunt if you are in any doubt at all. The details will be discussed later, and it is always best to assume the worst or most expensive option. The kind of actions to consider are fight sequences, falls, punches or hits, riding bicycles or horses, jumping, extreme sports, anything involving water or diving, and so on.

Depending on the age of the actor and the precise nature of the action, it may be safe for them to perform the action themselves. Or you may need to hire a trained stunt performer to undertake the action on their behalf. Often the middle course of action is to have a professional stunt arranger on set for a particular scene. They then rehearse the action with the actors and supervise how it can be safely carried out on the day of filming.

VEHICLES

Vehicles are another area needing discussion and planning. Normally actors will not be insured to drive any vehicle used in filming. In any case it is dangerous to allow them to perform scenes and speak dialogue whilst at the same time being in control of a car. There are a number of alternatives. One will be to hire what is known as an 'action vehicle driver' who is specially trained to drive and perform certain driving actions such as accelerating at speed, emergency stops, and turns. This is a good solution if you are filming action sequences, shooting on long lenses, or can't clearly see the driver's face.

However, if the scene in question involves characters driving together and talking, you may instead decide to mount the car on a low loader, which is then towed behind another vehicle containing the director, camera operator and first AC. The actors are pretending to drive the car but are not in control of it, and can focus instead on remembering their dialogue and giving a performance. Another alternative might be to film the actors in a stationary car and add moving backgrounds later in post-production. But at this stage, just make a note that vehicles will be involved in the scene, and mark it for further discussion.

PROPS

I would recommend only adding props to the breakdown sheet if they require additional special consideration. For example, I would note any guns or firearms since you will need to have an armourer on set for these scenes. I would definitely include any animals, and I might also note boiling liquids or hot food requirements. But I would not list things such as briefcases or umbrellas.

ADDITIONAL LABOUR

If anything in the scene might require extra help from someone not normally working as part of the daily crew, you should make a note here. This may be additional electricians if it is a night scene with a lot of lighting, or it may be extra costume assistants if there is a very large number of extras. It could be a specialist such as an animal trainer or handler, or it might be a chaperone or tutor who accompanies a child actor to the set.

VFX AND SFX

Visual effects (VFX) and special effects (SFX) should always be noted on the breakdown sheet. Visual effects will normally be done in post-production, and are discussed in more detail in that chapter of this book, but they may still require some special considerations during the actual shoot. For example, you may need to use a green screen at a window if you intend to change the view from the window later.

Special effects are those created mechanically on set during the shoot. They can be as simple as an effect achieved solely with the use of camera movement and lenses, or they may be much more complex. They often involve creating a particular kind of weather, such as rain, wind, smoke or snow. They might involve pyro-technics, fireworks, explosions, gunfire or something much simpler, such as a bonfire. In many cases specialist help will be needed to produce the effect.

IMAGES

It is possible to add pictures to the breakdown sheet. This can be useful if you have a rough sketch or storyboard for a stunt sequence, or a photograph of a set or location.

ELEMENT LINKING

It is also possible to link certain elements together. For example, you can link a particular cast member to a particular prop so that each time one appears, the other will be there too.

NOTES AND RED FLAGS

Finally you can add further notes about the scene, and 'red flags' to alert you to a particular restriction or scheduling conflict.

Once all your breakdown sheets are complete and you have one for every scene in the film, you should save this version and name it as 'Schedule Script Order'. It may be useful to refer to this document again in future.

The First Draft Schedule

Your next task will be to start working on your first draft schedule. This is done in what is known as the 'Stripboard Manager'. To begin I suggest you save the breakdown sheets once again as a new file and name it Schedule Draft 1. I also recommend keeping each and every version of your schedule and saving each variation with a new number and the date it was created. This will avoid any confusion later.

STARTING THE SCHEDULE

Now that you have recorded all the many different elements you can begin to work on the actual schedule. Replicating the old manual stripboard system, Stripboard Manager shows a summary of the key information from each breakdown sheet and displays it as a 'strip'. You can now start moving these 'strips' around and organizing them into logical sequences to begin building your shooting schedule. To do so you simply drag the strip up or down the schedule. Clicking on a strip displays the whole breakdown sheet.

In the first instance I suggest grouping all the scenes at one set together. Then divide these into day scenes or night scenes.

SHOOTING WEEKS, DAYS AND HOURS

An important decision now is how many days or weeks you need to shoot your project. This will have a major impact on your budget. Most low budget films will aim to shoot between three to five minutes per day. Television productions may be expected to shoot a higher ratio (six to eight minutes is not unusual), and action films will be a lot less. Short films often work with much smaller shooting crews and therefore shoot less material each day.

The normal working day is eleven or twelve hours. This is split into two halves of five (or five and a half) hours each, with a break in the middle of an hour for lunch. The meal break is customarily referred to as 'lunch' whatever time it is called, so if your shooting hours are 11am to 10pm and the break comes at 4pm, it will still be described as lunch.

It is becoming more common on some shoots to now work what is known as a continuous day (also known as 'French hours'). This means shooting for ten or eleven hours straight through without a formal break for lunch. In practice a meal is still provided for the cast and crew, but the time it is taken is varied. For example, whilst the director rehearses a scene privately on set with the cast, the lighting and camera crew may take time to eat their lunch. Then, when they return to light the set, the director and cast can have their meal.

There are a number of advantages to working this system. The first is that it reduces the overall working day by an hour so everyone can leave earlier. The second is that it avoids the need for everyone to stop working at the same time, travel back to the unit base and then stand in a queue waiting to be served lunch. I've been on many shoots where lunch has effectively taken an hour and a half or even longer, and this can be a tremendous strain on completing the day's work in a particular location. Third, you may be shooting in a location where stopping for lunch will make completion of that day's filming impossible, such as a beach where the time between tides is only six hours.

There are no hard and fast rules about precisely when a shooting day must start, and the time will depend on the number of day and night scenes to be completed, and the time of year you are shooting. It is preferable to avoid working full nights wherever possible. Night shoots are tough on everyone, and they are expensive, since a day off must be given at the end of a period of night filming. Instead you should try to schedule what are known as 'split days'. For example, if you are filming in November when the days are shorter and it is dark from around 4pm, you could make the start time 12 noon and the wrap time 11pm. This means the unit will wrap before midnight, and the cast and crew can travel home and sleep during the hours of darkness, which is much healthier. In this case you might schedule some interior scenes for three hours at the start of the shooting 'day', and then move outside to set up and film night scenes for the remaining seven hours.

In the UK, working practice requires a minimum eleven-hour rest period between wrap and call time. Different rules apply to cast working hours, particularly if you have any actors who are members of the Screen Actors Guild of America. You can vary the call time provided you maintain this eleven-hour break. So if Monday's call time is 12 noon, on Tuesday you can call the unit at 11am, on Wednesday at 10am, and so on. This is a good way to pull back from late starts to earlier ones.

The number of days worked each week is also flexible. Many productions work what is known as an 'eleven day fortnight'. This means a variable working week, which alternates between five and six days. So a typical film might shoot for five weeks as follows:

Week One: six days; **Week Two:** five days; **Week Three:** six days; **Week Four:** five days; **Week Five:** six days

This results in a total of twenty-eight filming days, which for a 100-minute feature is an average of 3.5 minutes per day. On a short shoot of five weeks this is a perfectly acceptable working schedule. It is less popular on much longer shoots of, say, twenty weeks. This is why some television productions prefer to work a five-days-a-week working schedule throughout. So, for example, a drama series for commercial television would shoot each 42-minute episode in a two-week block of five days each (or ten days), with an average of 4.2 minutes per day. Children are not allowed to work for more than five days a week under any circumstances.

As you start to work with your strips and create the perfect schedule, you will need to take all the different elements into consideration. Inevitably there will be conflicts to resolve, and just at the moment you think you have everything correctly balanced you will notice something that throws it all out again. The factors that will inform your decision making are described below.

Location Availability

Are there any restrictions on the locations you may be using? For example, if you are filming in a pub you may need to complete by 5pm so that they can open in the evening. If you need to film at a restaurant they may insist it is on a day of the week they are closed – normally Mondays. Or if you wish to film at a court, you may only be able to shoot there at the weekend. And if it's a church scene you might have to choose a midweek day when there are no services.

Set Dressing and Redressing

Is any redressing required between particular scenes? Or does one set need to be struck in order to build another in the same place? I once produced a series that took place over more than fifty years about a family who lived in the same house for most of this time. The rooms needed to be redressed for four different historical periods, so the shooting crew had to go away and film scenes elsewhere to allow the art department to redecorate and redress the sets.

Cast Availability

Are all your cast members available for every day of your shoot? If not, what restrictions do they have? Are they working on another production whose dates overlap with yours, or performing in the theatre and need to be released by 5pm on certain days? Can you afford to pay them for the whole shoot, or is it more economical to schedule all their scenes together over three to four days and then release them?

Working Hours

Depending on where in the world you are planning to shoot, there may be formal union agreements that relate to the daily working hours and whether overtime is permitted or not. You are advised to check these before making any assumptions about the standard working day, as described above.

There are also strict rules about the number of hours children below the age of eighteen are allowed to work. These must be adhered to, and are a major consideration when scheduling for them. You should also remember that any children still in full time education must be tutored or schooled. More information about the laws concerning working with children is included in Chapter 6, 'Pre-Production'.

Time of Day

Is it essential to film a scene at a particular time of day? We have already noted that it is helpful to be as flexible as possible and to avoid definite times, but this may be unavoidable.

Special Equipment

Do you need special equipment, such as cranes or drones, for particular scenes? If so, it will always be cheaper to group these together and hire the equipment for one or two consecutive days, rather than spread them around and hire it for longer. Unfortunately this is not always possible.

Stunts

Stunts require additional time and planning. You may need stunt performers on set, and you will almost certainly have to have a stunt co-ordinator or stunt arranger to choreograph the action. It will always be cost effective to schedule stunt scenes together where possible, and thus avoid paying your stunt arranger a whole day's fee to be on set for just one short scene. It is also recommended not to schedule stunts in the first week to enable the crew to get used to working together effectively before tackling anything very complex.

Weather

In most cases it is impossible to factor in weather conditions when scheduling, as it is generally too unpredictable. But if a specific scene is weather dependent, or if you are recreating snow or rain using some kind of physical effect, you should take this into account.

Supporting Artists

It will be cheaper if you can group together scenes with large numbers of extras into one or two days. Even if the scenes are different parts of the story, extras can be redressed and rearranged, and no audience will ever notice that they are appearing more than once.

Tides

Filming on or near beaches can mean checking local tide tables.

Lighting

Will the scene require a particularly complicated lighting set-up? Do you need to build a lighting tower, or to rig black-out curtains? If so, it may be more economical to send in a pre-lighting crew to prepare a particular set, rather than have crew standing around waiting to film.

MAKE-UP AND COSTUME CHANGES

If an actor requires a major costume or make-up change, you should allow time for this to happen and arrange the shooting day to accommodate such changes.

NUDITY OR SEX SCENES

It is best to avoid shooting scenes involving nudity or sex at the start of the shoot. These are always difficult for cast and crew, and should be scheduled in Week Two or later, after everyone has

109	109	INT	SAVOY GRILL Picasso sees Curtis Bidwell sitting in the restaurant	Night	3/8	pgs.	2, 54

--- END OF DAY 7 -- 19 Nov 2001 -- 2 3/8 pgs.

08.00-19.00 Base

106	106	INT	HEADQUARTERS BEAUSOLIEL'S OFFICE Beausoliel refuses Borne permission to do any deals	Day	2 2/8	pgs.	1, 2, 3
173	173	INT	HEADQUARTERS BEAUSOLIEL'S OFFICE Borne tells Moon that he is taking him off Ray du Barriatte	Day	2 5/8	pgs.	1, 2, 4, 7
179	179	INT	HEADQUARTERS BEAUSOLIEL'S OFFICE Borne and Sparks tell Beausoliel about the ship	Day	1 5/8	pgs.	1, 3, 4
205	205	INT	HEADQUARTERS BEAUSOLIEL'S OFFICE Beausoliel tells Borne that he will set up Harwich	Day	3/8	pgs.	3

--- END OF DAY 8 -- 20 Nov 2001 -- 6 7/8 pgs.

08.00-19.00 Base

89	89	INT	HEADQUARTERS CORRIDOR Beausoliel won't talk to Borne, Borne won't talk to Sparks	Day	5/8	pgs.	1, 3, 4
91	91	INT	HEADQUARTERS CORRIDOR Borne asks Moon if Khan is with him	Day	1/8	pgs.	1
93	93	INT	HEADQUARTERS CORRIDOR Borne tells Moon to get on with it	Day	2/8	pgs.	1, 4
181	181	INT	HEADQUARTERS CORRIDOR Moon confronts Borne about being taken off the Du Barriatte case	Day	1 1/8	pgs.	1, 7
107	107	INT	HEADQUARTERS BORNE'S OFFICE Picasso tells Borne she is having dinner with agent Bidwell	Day	3/8	pgs.	1, 2
2	2	INT	HEADQUARTERS SQUAD ROOM Borne details the drug drop to the squad	Day	4/8	pgs.	1, 2, 4, 5, 6, 7, 8, 9, 10,
5	5	INT	HEADQUARTERS SQUAD ROOM Borne tells the squad of the plan to arrest Fairey	Day	1 5/8	pgs.	1, 2, 4, 5, 6, 7, 8, 9, 10,
105	105	INT	HEADQUARTERS SQUAD ROOM Sparks tells the squad about Benny Luck	Day	1 6/8	pgs.	1, 2, 4, 5, 6, 10, 51

--- END OF DAY 9 -- 21 Nov 2001 -- 6 3/8 pgs.

08.00-19.00 Base

8	88	INT	HEADQUARTERS SQUAD ROOM Borne briefs the squad : they go through their options	Day	3	pgs.	1, 2, 4, 5, 6, 7, 8, 10, 5
129	129	INT	HEADQUARTERS SQUAD ROOM Picasso tells the squad about Arrango	Day	2 5/8	pgs.	1, 2, 3, 4, 7, 51

--- END OF DAY 10 -- 22 Nov 2001 -- 5 5/8 pgs.

08.00-19.00 Base

176	176	INT	HEADQUARTERS SQUAD ROOM Borne wants to nail Arrango	Night	3	pgs.	1, 2, 4
178	178	INT	HEADQUARTERS SQUAD ROOM Sparks finally gets the name of the ship	Night	2/8	pgs.	4
256	256	INT	HEADQUARTERS SQUAD ROOM They find out what will happen when the ship arrives at Harwich	Night	2	pgs.	1, 2, 3, 4, 7
258	258	INT	HEADQUARTERS SQUAD ROOM The listen to Luck arranging for the money to be collected	Night	1	pgs.	1, 2, 3, 4

--- END OF DAY 11 -- 23 Nov 2001 -- 6 2/8 pgs.

An example of a finished stripboard schedule.

become acquainted. I would also discuss with the actors and director the best time of day for these scenes. Some actors ask if sex scenes can be scheduled first on the day's schedule, so that they can get them out of the way and not have to think about them any more for the rest of the day.

EMOTIONAL JOURNEYS

It is unfortunately very rarely possible to film any production in sequence. However, having taken all the above into consideration, it is still helpful if you can consider the emotional journey of key characters when scheduling. This may be especially

--- END OF DAY 4 -- 14 Nov 2001 -- 3 5/8 pgs.							
08.00-19.00 Studio							
60	60	INT	MOON'S CAR PECKHAM FLATS Moon and McLeod each have a hand on the money bag	Night	1/8	pgs.	7, 46
44	44	INT	MOON'S CAR PECKHAM FLATS Moon shows McLeod how to count the money	Night	5/8	pgs.	7, 46
15	15	INT	MOON'S CAR PECKHAM FLATS Moon tells Borne he's in position	Night	1/8	pgs.	7
50	50	INT	MOON'S CAR PECKHAM FLATS Moon tell McLeod to make the call	Night	2/8	pgs.	7, 46
42	42	INT	MOON'S CAR PECKHAM FLATS Moon shows McLeod the money	Night	3/8	pgs.	7, 46
25	25	INT	MOON'S CAR PECKHAM FLATS Moon listens to the call	Night	1/8	pgs.	7
71	71	INT	MOON'S CAR PECKHAM FLATS Moon answers his mobile	Night	1/8	pgs.	7, 46
73	73	INT	MOON'S CAR PECKHAM FLATS Moon hands over the money	Night	1/8	pgs.	7, 46
17	17	INT	MOON'S CAR PECKHAM FLATS Moon tells Borne Crowe's is covering Khan	Night	1/8	pgs.	7
143	143	INT	CAR BOOT Crowe reaches for the jack	Day	1/8	pgs.	9
140	140	INT	CAR BOOT Crowe loses consciousess again	Day	1/8	pgs.	9
135	135	INT	CAR BOOT Crowe regains consciousness	Day	2/8	pgs.	9
--- END OF DAY 5 -- 15 Nov 2001 -- 2 4/8 pgs.							
08.00-19.00 Location							
96	96	INT	BARKING PS CUSTODY AREA Spanish and D'Eye discuss who they are going to interview	Day	4/8	pgs.	5, 6
150	150	INT	BARKING PS CUSTODY AREA Deck and O'Rouke are brought in	Day	3/8	pgs.	5, 51, 55, 56
103	103	INT	BARKING PS INTERVIEW ROOM Spanish starts to interview McLeod	Day	4/8	pgs.	5, 46
52	152	INT	BARKING PS INTERVIEW ROOM O'Rouke starts to talk	Day	1 3/8	pgs.	7, 56, 63
197	197	INT	BARKING PS INTERVIEW ROOM Moon interviews Deck	Day	1 2/8	pgs.	7, 55
156	156	INT	BARKING PS OFFICE Moon thinks that O'Rouke will talk if he thinks that Crowe is dead	Day	3/8	pgs.	7, 8, 9
--- END OF DAY 6 -- 16 Nov 2001 -- 4 3/8 pgs.							
08.00-19.00 Location							
153	153	INT	SAVOY RECEPTION Arrango leaves the hotel	Day	2/8	pgs.	2, 5, 6, 51, 57
151	151	INT	SAVOY RECEPTION Picasso asks to speak to the manager	Day	3/8	pgs.	2, 58
154	154	INT	SAVOY CORRIDOR Picasso and Silver are let into Arrango's room	Day	2/8	pgs.	2, 51, 58
124	124	INT	SAVOY CORRIDOR Picasso tells Bidwell the name of Raphael Arrango	Night	1 1/8	pgs.	2, 54

The finished stripboard includes daybreaks, dates and banners.

important for scenes with younger children, who can find it easier to understand their character's motivation if the shooting sequence mirrors that of the script. Similarly, I would rather not ask two actors who have barely met to film a passionate lovemaking scene on the first day.

DAYBREAKS AND BANNERS

Once you are reasonably happy with your first schedule you can insert the daybreaks. There is a facility for inserting automatic daybreaks in Movie Magic, but they will be exactly that, automatic, and won't reflect the realities of each filming day. Banners can also be added to provide information such as WEEK ONE, REST DAY, UNIT MOVE, and so on.

Within Movie Magic Scheduling there are ways to change the layout, format and colours of different strips. Most schedulers use four basic colours and assign different ones to INT NIGHT, INT DAY, EXT NIGHT and EXT DAY scenes. Bear in mind that the schedule will probably need to be copied at some point in black and white, so avoid background colours that are too dark and hard to read.

Much later, you can insert real dates into your schedule using the Calendar Manager function.

Creating a shooting schedule for your project is absolutely the best way of getting the film and its complexities firmly into your head. However well you think you know the script, it is only when you start scheduling that you really understand the balance of characters, the amount of night filming, the number of stunts, special effects, and so on. This is why I always prepare a schedule for every one of my projects myself. I may never show it to anyone else, but having done it, I know everything I need to know in order to move on to the next stage and begin the budget.

BUDGETING

There are numerous ways you can decide to lay out your budget, and there are software packages that can help. Movie Magic Budgeting (MMB) is part of the group of software distributed by Entertainment Partners, and if you have already created your draft schedule using their Movie Magic Scheduling software, it may speed up some of the processes. But you can also design your own budget template using Excel or similar programs. I would not recommend purchasing MMB unless you know you are going to have a lot of complicated budgets to produce. It is expensive, and it can take some time to become familiar with how it works. For short films, a simple Excel template will be sufficient, such as the one shown in this chapter.

It cannot be overstated how important it is to estimate correctly the cost of production. Underestimating the costs will result in you running out of money and being unable to complete the filming or post-production. Keep checking, and rechecking, that you have not left out anything important. At this early stage it is far better to overestimate than to underestimate. Once you have your first budget you can start to take things away or reduce them.

Before you begin your budget there is some key information that you must get together; this will include most of the following:

- How many days or weeks is the shoot;
- How many weeks pre-production will you need;
- How many weeks should be allowed for editing and post-production;
- Cast breakdown – how many days or weeks for each member;
- Location breakdown;
- Stunts breakdown;
- Additional labour breakdown;
- Special effects breakdown.

Budgets are generally presented as a 'top sheet', followed by the detailed budget breakdown showing each different category or 'line', and itemizing everything you may spend within each account.

At the top of the sheet it is customary to include some key information about the project such as

Budget Template
Short Film

RIGHT AND OVERLEAF: A template for a short film budget using Excel.

Title :		
Director :		
Producer :		
Format :		
Length:		
1 Script, Development and Underlying Rights	£	-
2 Producer/Line Producer/Production Mangement	£	-
3 Director	£	-
Director's expenses	£	-
4 Cast - payments - list all	£	-
Travel and expenses to cast if any	£	-
5 Extras and crowd - list numbers	£	-
Travel and expenses to extras if any	£	-
6 Stunts and stunt doubles if any - no of days	£	-
7 Crew - payments - list all with rates of pay	£	-
Travel and expenses to crew if any	£	-
8 Production equipment itemised as		
Camera	£	-
Sound	£	-
Lighting	£	-
Editing	£	-
Grip	£	-
Other	£	-
9 Art Department equipment and materials	£	-
including any prop hires, construction, action	£	-
vehicles, action props, firearms, SFX etc	£	-
10 Costumes, wigs and make up materials	£	-
11 Studios and location hire and costs	£	-
itemise each item and each location plus any	£	-
additional location expenses	£	-
12 Transport costs (if not paid as expense allowance)	£	-
include costs of recces, minibus hire,	£	-
artist transport, taxis etc	£	-
13 Accommodation and living costs, include	£	-
lunches, catering, hotels etc	£	-
14 Film stock and processing (if required)	£	-
15 Edit facilities picture - grade, picture post-	£	-
production, visual effects etc	£	-

Budget Template
Short Film

16	Sound editing and mixing incl crew, studio etc	£	-
17	Music - including copyright clearance and original composed music and musicians	£ £	- -
18	Insurance - must include equipment, employers and public liability insurance cover	£ £	- -
19	Other costs, eg. Festival entry, publicity etc.	£	-
20	Contingency - 5-10% of total budget	£	-
	TOTAL BUDGET	**£**	**-**

the title, production company, length, format, producer, director. It is also very helpful to include the budget version number, the date, and the name of the person who has prepared it.

The rest of the top sheet shows the total amount of money that you will be spending in each 'line' or category of the budget – for example 'costumes', 'production equipment' or 'production management'. You can add or delete any categories that apply to your project.

All budgets are divided into two main categories, known as 'above the line' and 'below the line'. There is sometimes a third category, which includes some fixed costs such as publicity and finance fees.

'Above the line' refers to the fees that are due to the talent involved. It may be helpful to think of this as those individuals whose names might appear above the main title on the finished film. It will normally include the writer, director, producers, executive producers and principal cast. It may also include the cost of acquiring any rights, and the reimbursement of any other development costs. If you are the line producer these figures will be given to you by the producer, and you will not be able to change them as they are fixed costs.

'Below the line' refers to the costs involved in actually making the film or series. In other words, everything else. This is where flexibility and financial juggling come into play.

All the different elements of the production are given a 'line' in the budget. This line may be sub-divided into different categories. For example the 'Production Management' line is subdivided into the cost of the salaries paid to the production manager, the production co-ordinator, the production assistant and so on. Some sample budget pages are shown to illustrate different (non-sequential) areas of the complete budget.

As you work through the budget you can begin to insert more information and detail, and to think about how you plan to make the film. When will the second AD come on board? How many weeks prep will he or she need? How many unit cars and drivers will be required? How many supporting artists? What budget will you assign to the costume department? How much will the weekly camera rental package cost? And so on.

In your first pass at the budget many of these figures will be estimates, which will have to be revised up or down as more information becomes available. If you are using a budgeting package that has built-in formulas, you can amend a figure within a particular account and the totals will automatically update. You can also assign what are known as 'globals'. For example, you can say that the shoot will be twenty-eight days long, or that post-production will be ten weeks. This means that if you decide to cut a week from the post-production and make it only nine weeks, everything related to that 'global' will automatically be amended to the new figure.

SALARIES: CREW

In the first pages of the budget most of the entries will be related to what you are paying individual members of your crew. The level of fees or salaries will vary enormously according to the scale of your production. Experienced line producers and production managers know the 'going rate' for each job for low budget films, television dramas and documentaries. There may be considerable variations, but it is my advice to try where possible to stick to certain 'bands' and keep all fees and salaries within these.

For example, you may decide that heads of department such as the editor, the first AD and the production designer should all be paid the same amount per week, and this will be Band A. The next group, Band B, may include the production co-ordinator, the second AD and the art director. Band C may include the production office runner, the floor runner and the art department runner. This means those doing comparable jobs are paid the same, and this is the fairest way to run a production. Whether you like it or not, crew will talk about their salaries, and if they find out they are receiving different wages for broadly the same hours and responsibility, there will be a lot of unhappiness and unrest.

The way in which your crew are contracted will depend where in the world you are working, and the specific regulations relating to that country. There is considerable variation between the USA, the UK and the rest of the world. When working abroad you are advised to work with a co-producer who understands the local system, or take advice from a local employment lawyer.

Most crew engaged on productions filming in the UK will be freelance. That is to say, they will be employed on a project by project basis on a short contract for the duration of the film, often no more than a few months. The UK government has published regulations about which members of the crew may be treated as 'self-employed'

and which must be contracted on a PAYE basis. Details can be found on the UK.GOV. website. The difference is that self-employed workers are paid a gross salary and are responsible for their own tax and National Insurance payments, whereas those on PAYE (pay as you earn) contracts have their tax and NI deducted at source by their employer, which in this case is the production company.

In production budgets these additional percentages, which must be added to the basic rate, are known as 'fringes'. For example, in the UK the current National Insurance (NI) rate is 13.8 per cent. This is noted on relevant salaries at the end of each entry. Rates change with new government legislation, so it is advisable to check the current rate. Most crew will also be working on short-term contracts of less than a year, and are therefore unable to take any holiday during the period of their engagement. This makes them eligible for what are known as 'holiday credits' (HC). What this means is an additional payment to compensate them for the holiday entitlement they cannot take. Currently this is calculated at 12.1 per cent of basic pay, excluding any overtime.

Occasionally some members of the crew may be employed through a company. This normally applies only to individuals who include their equipment in the deal. For example, a director of photography or camera operator may hire him or herself to the production along with their camera, lenses and other equipment. In this case they will still be in the budget, but will be included as a 'package' fee, and NI and HC will not apply.

In the UK, value added tax (VAT) must be added to goods and services if the provider has a turnover of more than £85,000 per annum or has voluntarily registered for VAT. Other European countries have a similar tax with different registration limits and different names. If your production company is registered for VAT it can reclaim the VAT it pays to suppliers by completing a quarterly VAT return. If you are not registered for VAT, then this becomes an additional cost to the production.

UNDER THE SUN

100 mins Digital HD
Prep – London & Wales – 6 weeks
Shoot – London (4 wks) & Wales (1 wk)
28 days (5 weeks)
Post-production – London x 10 weeks

Producer – Sue Austen
Writer – A.N. Other
Director – TBC
Budget No.1 / 31.12.17
Prepared by S.Austen

An example of the top sheet of the budget for a low budget feature film.

OPPOSITE AND OVERLEAF: Examples of detailed pages from a full budget. These pages are not sequential but are selected to illustrate different 'lines' within the complete budget.

Acct#	Category Title	Page	Total
10	Story, Script and Development	1	£53,000.00
11	Producers	1	£51,000.00
12	Director	1	£35,500.00
14	Above the line cast	1	£112,000.00
	Total Above the Line		**£251,500.00**
20	Production Management	2	£116,351.00
21	Assistant Directors	3	£28,685.00
22	Crew - Camera	3	£53,803.00
23	Crew - Sound	4	£16,232.00
24	Crew - Editing	4	£27,194.00
25	Crew - Lighting	5	£30,072.00
26	Crew - Art Department	5	£90,815.00
27	Crew - Wardrobe	6	£23,964.00
28	Crew - Make Up	6	£13,960.00
29	Casting	7	£13,000.00
30	Below the line cast	7	£43,415.00
31	Stand ins/Stunts/Crowd	8	£49,002.00
32	Materials - Art Department	8	£80,000.00
33	Materials - Costumes/Wigs	9	£13,500.00
34	Production Equipment	9	£77,250.00
35	Studios and offices	10	£13,675.00
36	Location Facilities	10	£52,600.00
37	Travel and Transport	11	£84,400.00
38	Hotel and Living	12	£60,625.00
39	Special Effects	12	£50,000.00
40	Post Production Picture	13	£71,000.00
41	Post Production Sound	13	£45,000.00
42	Music	13	£40,000.00
43	Other Production Costs	14	£17,250.00
44	Fringes	14	£32,008.00
	Total Below the Line		**£1,143,801.00**
50	Publicity	15	£12,000.00
51	Insurance	15	£22,500.00
52	Finance and Legal	15	£75,000.00
53	Industry Fees	15	£10,250.00
	Total Other		**£119,750.00**
	Total Above the Line		£251,500.00
	Total Below the Line		£1,143,801.00
	Total Other		£119,750.00
	Total		**£1,515,051.00**
	Contingency 5%		£76,752.55
	Total Budget		**£1,591,803.55**

It may be time-consuming to be VAT registered, but it can save you money. This is something you should discuss with your accountant and seek their advice on. VAT is currently 20 per cent in the UK, and can add a significant amount to your budget if you cannot reclaim it. For example, if your camera package rental is £4,500 per week, adding 20 per cent VAT of £900 to this amount will raise the cost to £5,400. And over the course of a five-week shoot, this will be £4,500, or an extra week's rental.

Acc no	Description	Amount Units	x	Rate	Subtotal	Total
20	**Production Management**					
20.01	Line Producer					
	Prep	7 weeks		1400		
	Shoot	5 weeks		1400		
	Wrap	2 weeks		1400		
						19,600
20.02	Production Co-Ordinator					
	Prep	6 weeks		950		
	Shoot	5 weeks		950		
	Wrap	1 weeks		950		
						11,400
	NI @ 13.8%					1,573
20.03	Production Secretary					
	Prep	6 weeks		600		
	Shoot	5 weeks		600		
	Wrap	1 weeks		600		
						7,200
	NI @ 13.8%					994

Acc no	Description	Amount Units	x	Rate	Subtotal	Total
20.04	Production Office Runner					
	Prep	5 weeks		400		
	Shoot	5 weeks		400		
	Post	10 weeks		400		
						8,000
	NI @ 13.8%					1,104
20.05	Production Accountant					
	Prep	7 weeks		1200		
	Shoot	5 weeks		1200		
	Post - full time	2 weeks		1200		
	Post - part time	8 weeks		600		
						21,600
20.06	Assistant Accountant					
	Prep	3 weeks		750		
	Shoot	5 weeks		750		
	Wrap	2 weeks		750		
						7,500
	NI @ 13.8%					1,035
20.07	Location Manager					
	Prep	8 weeks		1200		
	Shoot	5 weeks		1200		
	Wrap	1 week		1200		
						16,800
20.08	Locations Assistant					
	Prep	3 weeks		750		
	Shoot	5 weeks		750		
	Wrap	0.5 weeks		750		
						6,375
	NI @ 13.8%					880

continued overleaf

Acc no	Description	Amount Units	x	Rate	Subtotal	Total
29	**Casting**					
29.01	Casting director	fee		12,000		12,000
29.02	Casting expenses	allow		1,000		1,000
	Account total					**13,000**
30	**Below the line cast**					
30.01	Mike	3 days		1000		3000
30.02	Tom	2 weeks		1500		3000
30.03	Jack	1 wk + 1 day		2000		2000
30.04	Mary	1 week		1250		1250
30.05	Graham	1 wk + 1 day		1750		1750
30.06	Dorien	1 week		1500		1500
30.07	Sharon	1 day		550		550
30.08	Estate Agent	1 day		550		550
30.09	Rhian	1 day		550		550
30.1	Andy	1 day		550		550
30.11	Jeff	2 days		550		1100
30.12	Frank (stunt man?)	1 day		550		550
30.13	Mick (stunt man?)	1 day		550		550
30.14	Holly (child)	3 days		100		300
30.15	Rachel (child)	3 days		100		300
	total cast					17500
	NI @ 13.8%					2415
30.07	ADR	allow				5000
30.08	Rehearsals/read through/fittings	allow				1,000
	Account total					**43415**
31	**Stand Ins/Crowd/Stunts**					
31.01	Stand Ins	5 weeks	2	450		4500
	NI @ 13.8%					621
31.02	Chaperones	6 days		120		720
	NI @ 13.8%					99
31.03	Crowd	300 days		80		24000
	NI @ 13.8%					3312
31.04	Stunts					
	Stunt co-ordinator					
	Prep and recces	5 days		350		1750
	Stunt performers	20 days		550		11000
31.05	Voice Coaching	allow				2000
31.06	Boxing Coaching	allow				1000
	Account total					**49002**

Acc no	Description	Amount Units	x	Rate	Subtotal	Total
32	**Art Department Materials**					
32.01	Sets, set dressing and props	allow				50,000
32.02	Graphics	allow				5,000
32.03	Art Department consumables	allow				3,000
32.04	Action Vehicles - incl drivers	allow				20,000
32.05	Animals - incl handlers	allow				2,000
	Account total					**80,000**
33	**Wigs and Costumes**					
33.01	Costumes hire and purchases	allow				10,000
33.02	Costume Dept consumables	allow				1,000
33.03	Wigs	allow				1,500
33.04	Make Up Supplies	allow				1,000
	Account total					**13,500**
34	**Production Equipment**					
34.01	Camera package	5 weeks		5,000		25,000
34.02	Additional camera equipment	5 weeks		1,000		5,000
34.03	Grip equipment	5 weeks		1,000		5,000
34.04	Additional hires for vehicles etc	5 weeks		300		1,500
34.05	Cranes and towers hire	allow				5,000
34.06	Sound Equipment	5 weeks		600		3,000
34.07	Sound consumables /batteries	5 weeks		100		500
34.08	Walkie Talkies	5 weeks		200		1,000
34.09	Lighting package	5 weeks		3,200		16,000
34.1	Additional lighting for nights etc	allow				2,500
34.11	Lighting consumables and gels	5 weeks		500		2,500
34.12	Generator and fuel	5 weeks		650		3,250
34.13	Editing Equipment / storage	12 weeks		1,000		12,000
	Account total					**82,250**
35	**Studios and Offices**					
35.01	Production Base - Wales	13 weeks		400		5,200
35.02	Cutting Rooms - London	15 weeks		200		3,000
35.03	Post Production Office - London	12 weeks		300		2,400
35.04	Props Store	10 weeks		100		1,000
35.05	Rehearsal Rooms - Wales	1 week		200		200
	Office equipment hires	25 weeks		75		1,875
	Account total					**13,675**

Jan 19, 2016
6:41 AM   **Day Out of Days Report for Cast Members**

Month/Day	07/07	07/08	07/09	07/10	07/11	07/12	07/13	07/14	07/15
Day of Week	Mon	Tue	Wed	Thu	Fri	Sat	Sun	Mon	Tue
Shooting Day	1	2	3	4	5	6		7	8
3. BRINLEY	SW	W	W	W	W	W		W	
12. DOUG						SW			
16. ANDY									
9. HOLLY				SW					
2. ELAINE					SW	W		W	W
17. FRANK			SWF						
1. CHRIS	SW	W	W	W	W	W		W	W
5. MIKE		SW			W	W			
7. MARY				SW					
4. TOM		SW							
8. GRAHAM			SW	W					
13. RHIAN					SWF				
15. SHARON									
10. RACHEL				SW					
18. ESTATE AGENT									
11. HARRY						SW			
6. JACK				SW					
14. DORIEN									

An example of a 'Day Out of Days', showing when particular cast members will be required to work.

SALARIES: CAST

In the UK, actors are represented by the union Equity. In the USA they are represented by the Screen Actors Guild (known as SAG). There are agreements in place that regulate the minimum fees and conditions for all actors employed on film and television productions, and these must be followed. This includes short films and student films. More information on this may be found at Equity. org.uk.

There are different ways in which actors may be contracted for the shoot. If they are leading players and will be called most days, you will want the flexibility of engaging them for the whole shoot. But there will be other cast members who appear in only a few scenes whom you can book for a week or even for just a day.

One of the functions within Movie Magic Scheduling allows you to produce a document known as a 'Day Out of Days'. This shows all the times a character will need to be called to work throughout the shoot. SW stands for 'start work', W means 'work' and WF stands for 'finish work'. In the example shown, you can see that the actor playing Frank will be working for only one day, whereas the actor playing Chris will be engaged for the whole shoot. Scheduling actors to complete their performance within a shorter time is a good way to save money, but can put pressure on the schedule and may conflict with location choices.

In addition to their standard daily or weekly rate, actors are also entitled to further payments when the finished film or series is shown or broadcast in other territories, or when it is repeated (shown again). In some cases it may be most cost effective and efficient for the production to 'buy out' all the different uses in advance, and show that the film is 'cleared' for distribution throughout the world. In other cases, especially for low budget films, the producer may decide only to pay up front for those rights that he or she knows are definitely needed. Further payments can then be made to the cast as and when they become due. These additional cast payments are known as 'residuals'. Make sure you check with any distributor or broadcaster what rights they expect you to have bought out before negotiating cast contracts.

Sample Budget: Line by Line

Using the Top Sheet shown earlier, below is a brief summary of what will be included in each line of this budget and some accompanying notes. You may also find it helpful to refer to the job descriptions for members of the crew in the following chapter.

STORY SCRIPT AND DEVELOPMENT

In this line you should include all payments to screenwriters. Break these down episode by episode if this is a series. You should add any payments due for underlying rights, options already paid, and for exercising the option on principal photography. On series there may also be payments to the original writer if he or she is due any format fee. Include here any other development costs not included elsewhere in the budget. There could be fees due to be paid back now for development finance. Script editor payments and fees to development producers may also be included here.

PRODUCERS

In this account you will include all fees to producers, executive producers and co-producers, but not to line producers. If there are any producers' expenses already incurred and approved that are not covered elsewhere in the budget they should also go here. There may also be production company fees and overhead payments.

DIRECTOR(S)

Include here all fees and payments to the director or directors if multi-episode.

'ABOVE THE LINE' CAST

These are payments and fees to your principal performers and main cast, including any buy-outs or residuals.

PRODUCTION MANAGEMENT

In this line you should include all payments to the crew from this department: this includes the line producer, production manager, production co-ordinator, production assistants and production office runners, location manager and assistants, production accountant and assistants, and post-production supervisor. The detailed pages shown earlier give an illustration of this account.

CREW: ASSISTANT DIRECTORS, CAMERA, SOUND, EDITING, LIGHTING, ART DEPARTMENT, WARDROBE, MAKE-UP

This includes payments to everyone employed on your crew, department by department. Include any fringe payments for NI or holiday credits here.

CASTING

The casting director will normally have agreed an overall fee for the job, rather than a weekly rate. Within this account you may also include payments to any casting assistants and any casting expenses.

BELOW THE LINE CAST

This is where you list all the other parts, their weekly rate, and their estimated engagement.

STAND-INS/STUNTS/CROWD

These are all together in the same part of the budget because they are all associated with 'on-screen' performance.

Stand-ins are extremely useful, even on low budget films, and can save you time. Major Hollywood stars sometimes have their own personal stand-ins, but most productions will hire an additional runner to stand in when required for eyelines or blocking. If you have a lot of children in your production, stand-ins will be invaluable to enable you to rehearse and light scenes without calling the children to the set and wasting valuable hours. Stand-ins are also useful for the same reason if you have a lot of hair and costume changes.

Stunt performers and arrangers are members of the actors' union Equity. They are paid a minimum amount per day. Although many stunt personnel work as both arrangers and performers, they are not allowed to perform both functions in the same scene. If you need to engage a stunt performer, you also need a separate stunt arranger on set to supervise the action.

The cost of paying supporting artists can be considerable. Directors will want to fill certain scenes with a lot of people, all of whom have to be paid, costumed and fed. Negotiating the number of extras is always a challenge for producers, but you may have to be quite firm about what the budget can support and what it cannot. Outside large cities you may be able to find local extras willing to work for a lower rate for the novelty or experience of appearing in a film. But in London and the major production centres, you will normally be calling professional extras who expect to be paid the going rate for a day's work.

If supporting artists are asked to do anything other than be part of a crowd or walk by, they may be deemed to be 'special extras' and earn additional payments. It is generally accepted that supporting artists may say a few words before the part becomes classed as that of an actor. For example, a waiter could say 'Are you ready to order?' But they are not trained actors and should never be asked to replace them.

MATERIALS: ART DEPARTMENT, COSTUMES AND WIGS

At this early stage you can only estimate how much should be allocated to each department for materials, but try to be as accurate as you can. The largest sum will always be for the art department who have the most expenditure. Once the script is locked and the production designer is on board, he or she will be expected to provide detailed costings for everything. Their budget can then be revised upwards or downwards accordingly. Art department materials include all wood used for set construction, all set dressings including practical lights and practical plumbing in some cases, all props, vehicles and action vehicles, graphic design and signage, greenery, animals and animal handlers.

Unless your film has a lot of wigs or prosthetics, the sum for make-up and hair is likely to be quite low. The costume budget will depend on the size of the cast, how many extras there are, and whether it is period or contemporary.

PRODUCTION EQUIPMENT

This account will include your estimate for all the equipment you will need to hire in for the production, and the number of days or weeks you need it. This includes the camera package, lenses, grip equipment, lighting, sound, editing equipment, and special equipment such as cranes. This account will also include some smaller items of production equipment that you will be buying rather than renting, such as gels, batteries and hard drives. These are known as 'consumables', and the detailed pages shown earlier give an illustration of this account.

STUDIOS AND OFFICES

This account will normally include the cost of renting studios and production offices. Remember to include the cost of an office during post-production, too. You should also budget for any additional costs such as council tax, electricity, heating, lighting and internet services.

LOCATION FACILITIES

In this account you will include location fees, unit base fees and other location costs such as permits, road closures, marquees, extra parking charges and green rooms.

TRAVEL AND TRANSPORT

Travel and transport is a large item on most production budgets. If you have worked on a film shoot and seen the size of an average film unit you will understand why. Many members of the crew will need hire cars or vans to get to and from locations or for picking up and returning props and equipment. Props, lighting, camera and grip will each need a van for the duration of the shoot. Costume and make-up may need special 'buses' kitted out as changing rooms and with make-up chairs and mirrors, washing machines, tumble driers and more. You may also need a dining bus and accommodation, or 'trailers' for actors to rest between scenes.

Within this account you will also need to budget for any flights or train travel for cast members who may normally live elsewhere or abroad. If your production base for all or part of the shoot is far away, you may need to pay for the whole crew to travel there and back.

On most films and series actors are not expected to make their own way to and from set. The production hires a number of 'unit drivers' and cars to pick up the cast and take them home after completion of the day's work. This will certainly be true for any leading players. Avoid any demands by actors or their agents for dedicated drivers: this means having someone standing around all day who can't be called on to collect other performers. Instead opt for 'pool drivers' who can take anyone, anywhere. Also try to ensure that everyone except the biggest stars is prepared to share transport, and not insist on solo trips.

Within this account include the drivers' wages, but do not include any 'on-screen' or action vehicle drivers, who come under art department. You should also include petrol for all these different vehicles, as well as any additional costs such as congestion zone fees or road tolls.

HOTEL AND LIVING

In this account include any accommodation costs for crew and actors. Remember to include overnight accommodation if this is required for recces during pre-production, or if actors have to be recalled for automated dialogue replacement during post-production.

You should also budget for all the catering during the shoot. It is normal practice for productions to pay for breakfast and lunch, and to provide tea, coffee, water and snacks during the day. If you are filming late and outdoors at night you may also provide soup or hot snacks. Specialist location catering companies normally charge a set amount per head per day to cover all food and drink requirements. They bring their own catering staff, mobile kitchens, cutlery and plates. You have to provide a dining space, which could be a room, a bus or a marquee.

In this account you may also wish to include an amount to cover entertainment, such as the wrap party or refreshments at the read-through, or cast and crew screening. I would normally also put in a sum to cover coffees and lunches during meetings and post-production.

If you are filming for any period of time away from the nominated production base, you may need to offer everyone from the cast and crew a 'per diem' to cover their evening meal. In this case it is assumed you are already paying for breakfast and lunch, so the amount reflects this and is normally £10 to £15.

SPECIAL EFFECTS

Depending on the nature of the special effects you need to create, you may need to hire in additional labour, equipment or a specialist company. It is advisable to seek more than one quote and to look for the most competitive price. Send the relevant pages or scenes from the script so they understand the effect you are trying to achieve and can quote accordingly. Ask for examples of previous work, and check websites for reviews and experience. Make sure it is clear exactly what the SFX company will provide, and what they expect you to have available already. This applies to both equipment and personnel.

POST-PRODUCTION PICTURE

In this account include all elements of the post-production process relating to picture. This will include the costs of grading and any visual effects shots or sequences. If you are shooting on film there may be costs involved in creating digital copies of the final picture. You may wish to commission a title sequence or end roller from a graphic design or animation company. You may also have some other on-screen subtitles or headings. (See also Chapter 8, 'Post-Production'.)

POST-PRODUCTION SOUND

In this line you should add all the elements required to create the finished soundtrack in post-production. This will include the cost of hiring a sound editor, Foley artists, ADR studios, and the final sound mix or 'dub'. (See also Chapter 8, 'Post-Production'.)

MUSIC

Include here the costs of clearing any existing music or tracks. Also include the composer's fee for all music created specially for your film, as well as payments to any musicians, singers or orchestras required to produce it.

PUBLICITY

You will need to create a publicity pack to promote the film. You will definitely need a stills photographer for some days during the shoot, and you may want to pay a freelance unit publicist and should include their fee here. Other costs might include someone to design a poster or image to represent the film. On larger productions there may be someone employed to create an EPK (electronic press kit), including filmed interviews with the main cast, director, heads of department and writers.

Insurance

Insurance is a very important part of all film production. There are companies who understand the particular challenges of the film industry you can approach to obtain a quote. You may need a number of different kinds of insurance, and you should take advice about which of the following you must provide:

- Public liability insurance (to cover accidents to members of the public, location damage, and so on);
- Employers' liability insurance (to cover accidents to members of your cast and crew);
- Equipment insurance (to cover damage to any hired-in equipment whilst you are using it);
- Travel insurance (to cover delays or medical expenses if someone is taken ill whilst they are abroad);
- Production insurance (this may cover you for reshoots if you have to abandon filming for any reason);
- Errors and omissions insurance (this may pay your legal costs if someone brings an action against your production, for example for breach of copyright).

There is a more detailed account of the different types of insurance you will require in Chapter 6, 'Pre-Production'.

Finance and Legal

You will inevitably have to pay for some legal advice, and for someone to draw up contracts connected with the financing arrangements of your film. There can be a lot of work involved if there are a number of investors, and these fees can mount up very quickly. You should also include here any finance fees, such as loans, bank charges and interest.

Industry Fees

In some circumstances you may be expected to pay a levy or charge to an industry body in the country where you are filming. In the UK, companies are asked to contribute 0.5 per cent of the production's UK core expenditure to the Skills Investment Fund (SIF). This applies to all high-end television, games, animation and films that are wholly or partly produced in the UK. The money earned in this way is used to directly support the next generation of talent.

Contingency

A contingency is an amount added to the final budget to cover any unexpected costs. Some investors and funders will not allow contingencies, believing that accurate budgeting of each account should cover all eventualities. Other investors will be happy to see a notional amount included here. The lower the budget, the more likely it is that you will need a contingency. I would definitely recommend adding it to short film budgets where possible.

Revising your Estimates

After completing every section of the budget you may be shocked and surprised by the total you reach. The first pass budget is always higher than expected, but this is a good thing. It is far better to have everything included and then begin taking things away, than to have forgotten something you really need. Over the ensuing weeks and months you will be able to amend many of the figures as more accurate information becomes available.

4
PRODUCTION TEAMS BY DEPARTMENT

As the producer, and the person in overall charge of the whole production, it is important that you know precisely what everyone else is there to do. You must understand their role, and how each member of the crew interacts and works with others.

This chapter will briefly explain who makes up each different department, who reports to whom, and what each person does. You will need this knowledge in order to prepare your budget and to work out how many people to pay, and how long each person will be engaged. On short films some of these jobs may be doubled up, and one person may take on two or three different roles.

PRODUCTION DEPARTMENT

The production office is the producer's closest team, and the following are some of the people with whom you will have most contact on a daily basis. The production office team is made up of the following people.

LINE PRODUCER AND/OR PRODUCTION MANAGER

The line producer will be one of the first people to be employed, and will be with you throughout pre-production and the shooting period. Depending

Writer Director Line Producer Production Manager Production Co-Ordinator **Production Assistant** Office Runner Script Editor Production Accountant and Assistant **Actors** Casting Director Supporting Artists First Assistant Director Second AD **Third AD** Floor Runners Location Manager Production Designer Art Director **Assistant Art Director** Production Buyer Petty Cash Buyer Standby Art Director Property Master **Dressing Props** Standby Props Construction Manager Painters Carpenters **Riggers** Plasterers Assistant Location Manager Unit Manager Director of Photography **Camera Operator** Focus Puller Clapper Loader Script Supervisor Best Boy **Electricians** Genny Operator Nurse Chaperone Tutor **Animal Handler** Home Economist Make-Up Designer Make-Up Artists Costume Designer **Wardrobe Supervisor** Sound Recordist Boom Operator Stunt Arranger Stunt Performers **Caterers** Unit Drivers Editor Assistant Editor Sound Designer **Composer** Colourist Footsteps Artists Dubbing Mixer Special Effects Supervisor **Unit Publicist** Stills Photographer

The producer must understand everyone's job.

on the scale of the production you may have a line producer, a production manager, or both. The roles are similar, with the line producer being the more senior and more highly paid. On very low or micro-budget films, the producer may take on some of these duties and may employ a production manager to support them. On larger budget films or long drama series you may need both a line producer and a production manager.

The LP or PM manages the production office and is responsible for the budget. Your LP must keep you informed of each department's spending throughout the shoot. This is done through weekly cost reports, which are prepared for them by the production accountant.

The term 'line producer' refers to the 'line' drawn in the budget indicating those items 'above the line' and those which are 'below the line'. 'Above the line' items include all the talent fees, such as payments to writers, director, producers and major cast. 'Below the line' items are almost everything else and are the actual costs of making the film. The line producer is responsible for everything below the line.

Line producers hire the crew and issue their contracts. They negotiate deals with facilities companies and suppliers, manage these arrangements, and ensure that the production has everything it needs on a daily basis. They are also responsible for some aspects of health and safety and risk assessment, and for arranging appropriate insurance cover and dealing with any claims.

They will usually not remain on the production for the post-production period, although they may arrange some of the post-production deals. Normally the production office team has a two- to three-week wrap at the end of the shoot, and then moves on to another production.

PRODUCTION CO-ORDINATOR

The production co-ordinator is the LP or PM's right hand. He or she reports directly to the LP or PM and is chosen by him/her. Successful partnerships frequently work together from one production to the next. The PC will set up the production office and organize equipment, supplies, cleaners and repairs. They will schedule the production meetings, book rehearsal and audition space, and make the arrangements for cast and crew transport, flights, accommodation, travel and any visas.

It is the production co-ordinator's job to issue script revisions and any changes to the daily shooting schedule, and to produce and issue the daily call sheet in consultation with the second AD. They are the key point of contact for everything, and all requests should go through them for approval by the LP. During the shoot they will also prepare and circulate daily progress reports. They will normally have a two-week wrap at the end of the shoot.

PRODUCTION ASSISTANT

The production assistant (PA) reports to the co-ordinator. The PA's job is to support the production team. They may take responsibility for sending out script amendments and the daily script pages, known as the 'sides'. They may be helped during the later stages of prep and throughout the shoot by a production office runner.

PRODUCTION ACCOUNTANT

Production accountants are responsible for making all payments during pre-production, production and post-production. They will set up accounting systems and must approve all purchase orders, run the payroll, and manage any individual petty cash accounts. They should supervise the production's cash flow, and make sure that there is enough money in the bank account each week to settle all the payments. They may need to file VAT returns or make arrangements for foreign currency transactions.

The production accountant will have a direct relationship with financiers and investors who control the cash flow. They must ensure that all legal requirements are met, and that information is gathered for tax accounting purposes. During the shoot they will produce a weekly cost report detailing the exact financial position of the production, and forecasting any projected over-spends or under-spends in particular accounts or lines in the budget.

The production accountant will normally work full time from the start of pre-production to set up systems and manage the budget. In some cases they may become part-time during post-production. After the film is delivered, the production accountant prepares a statement of account detailing all the income and expenditure. This document will be delivered to all the investors and financiers, and is required by government agencies before any tax credit can be applied.

Depending on the scale of the production, they may be supported by one or more assistant accountants.

LOCATION MANAGER

The location manager and any location assistants or unit managers are part of the production department, and will usually appear in this line in the budget. But they must also work closely with the director and with the art department. The location manager is responsible for finding all the locations, and may start work on a project some weeks before it is green lit. Experienced location managers use their local knowledge and research to suggest the best places to film. They start by showing locations to the director and production designer, and offering suggestions as to how the space might work for a particular scene. Once the choice is approved they will then negotiate the terms and conditions of use with the location owner, and obtain any filming permits from local authorities or private landowners.

An important part of the location manager's job is to find a suitable unit base and sufficient parking for the large number of trucks and vehicles that make up a modern film unit. They may need to liaise with local police over temporary road closures, or make them aware of any stunts or dangerous filming activities, and provide risk assessments. The location manager organizes the technical recce, which takes place at the end of pre-production.

During the shoot, the location manager and their team will be the first people on set and the last to leave at the end of the day. They must check that the location has been left exactly as it was found, including removing any rubbish. They are also responsible for ensuring that any equipment is safely and securely locked up for the night. The location manager also prepares a daily movement order to be issued to all cast and crew. The movement order gives precise details of how to find the location, including maps and driving directions. It should also list any special conditions, such as whether high visibility vests must be worn, and the location of emergency exit routes. They may put out signs along the route to show the crew where to go.

The location manager, or their assistants, will prepare and distribute letters to local residents, informing them that a film crew will be in the area. They may also need to knock on doors to ask if curtains can be drawn or lights switched on and off. They are usually on set for most of the day to ensure the shooting day runs smoothly.

ASSISTANT LOCATION MANAGER/ UNIT MANAGER

Depending on the size of the production, there may be one or more assistant location managers or a unit manager. They support the location manager and may help in the preparation of movement orders. They will be involved in making sure that the unit moves around freely, and that the unit base is properly organized, and will instruct drivers of vehicles where to park. They may supervise the arrangement of catering, toilets and other facilities at the unit base. They will help with clearing up at the end of the day.

ASSISTANT DIRECTORS DEPARTMENT

FIRST ASSISTANT DIRECTOR

The first assistant director is one of the most important people on any shoot. A good first AD can ensure a smooth-running and happy set, while a bad one will do exactly the opposite. The first AD's main role is to assist the director. They manage the rest of the assistant director's department and form an important link between the production office and the set.

The first AD will normally start work four weeks before filming; their first job is to create the shooting schedule. During production the first AD is in charge on the set, and they control its discipline. Their overriding responsibility is to keep filming on schedule by driving it forwards, and ensuring that everything the director needs is ready and waiting to be cued. They usually direct the background artists, and are normally the one to call 'action' when everyone is ready. One of their most important duties is to be responsible for health and safety on the set. They have the right to stop or change an activity or shot if they believe it is unsafe to continue. They also ensure that children's working hours are not exceeded.

The first AD supervises the preparation of the daily call sheet, deciding on the next day's filming schedule and what additional information should be included.

Second Assistant Director

The second AD works directly to the first. They usually spend the shooting day at the unit base, rather than on the set. It is their job to make sure that all actors are picked up to arrive at the base in good time, and to manage the cast transport arrangements. They liaise with costume, hair and make-up departments to estimate how long each cast member needs before they are ready to perform. They make sure everyone knows their 'call time', including cast, extras and crew. They prepare the next day's call sheet for approval by the first AD and the production office. On most productions the second AD will also be responsible for sourcing extras, and approving their time sheets.

Third Assistant Director

In the USA the third AD is known as the second second AD. They work on set alongside the first

AD to whom they report. They are responsible for co-ordinating the extras on set, and preparing and cueing the background action. They may have to keep members of the public out of shot and off the set. They are normally assisted in these duties by one or more floor runners.

Floor Runner

Becoming a floor runner on a professional shoot is a first step for many people who want to enter the film and television industry. Being part of an efficient working crew is a great learning experience for anyone planning a career in production. Runners may be asked to do anything from getting teas and coffees for the cast, to standing in during lighting set-ups and blocking. Their tasks will vary enormously, depending on the scale of the

The Mitchell camera that was used to shoot the original British film *The Italian Job* in 1969.

production, and most days will be different. Runners need to be quick and efficient. In most cases a driving licence will be essential.

CAMERA DEPARTMENT

DIRECTOR OF PHOTOGRAPHY

The director of photography is one of the most important creative roles on any film. They are chosen by the director, and in collaboration with the production designer, play a crucial part in deciding the visual style. The DoP may start discussing the lighting and look of the film with the director many months before the shoot, but they may not become a full-time part of the team until mid-way through pre-production. They will choose the rest of the camera team as well as the gaffer. Some DoPs also decide to take on the role of camera operator.

During prep, the DoP decides on the choice of camera, lenses, lights and filters. They may test different film stocks and try out different aspect ratios before selecting which to use, and which best suits the particular project and director's vision. During the shoot the DoP works closely with the director in rehearsals and blocking, discussing the camera moves and the lighting for each scene. At the end of the day the DoP will usually view the rushes with the director. In post-production the DoP attends and contributes to the digital grading.

CAMERA OPERATOR

The camera operator is, quite literally, the person who operates the camera. They work closely with the director of photography, the director and the grip, and also manage the first AC, the second AC and any camera trainees. They normally start work two weeks before the shoot.

During the shoot, after the director and DoP have rehearsed and blocked a scene, the camera operator will be involved in discussing the precise camera positions and moves. Camera operators also work closely with the actors, letting them know what the camera can see and what it can't, and guiding them to their marks.

Camera operators are responsible for making sure that the camera, lenses and other equipment is prepared and ready for the next set-up or shot. They make sure the camera is working correctly at all times, and oversee the work of the first and second ACs. Some camera operators have specialist skills, such as operating a steadicam. On larger productions there may be a second camera operator for all or some of the scenes.

FIRST AC (ASSISTANT CAMERA)

The first AC used to be known as the 'focus puller', and it is a highly skilled and difficult job. The first AC is responsible for focusing and refocusing the camera lens during each shot. They need precise timing and judgement, as it is usually impossible to see whether the focus is sharp until the rushes are screened, by which time it may well be too late to do anything about it. The first AC is also responsible for preparing and looking after the camera equipment and lenses, making sure they are correctly cleaned, put away and stored after use, and for assembling the camera and its component parts for different shots.

SECOND AC (ASSISTANT CAMERA)

The second AC used to be known as the 'clapper loader'. Their job is to work with the camera operator and help them to position and move the camera. It is their responsibility to load and unload film magazines, charge the camera batteries, change lenses and fill out the camera sheets, noting how much stock or storage has been used. They also get to operate the clapperboard before each take, which identifies the slate number and allows the editor to synchronize the sound and picture. If you are using film stock rather than digital cards, they should regularly check stock levels and inform the production office if it is running low and a new order needs to be placed.

They should also mark up the film cans at the end of each shooting day to be sent to the laboratory with the camera sheets. During blocking and rehearsal of scenes the second AC will mark the actors' positions on the floor so that the first AC can work out when to change or pull focus.

DIT OR DIGITAL IMAGING TECHNICIAN

The DIT is a relatively new role on film sets, but one that is becoming more and more essential. A DIT will only be required if you are shooting on a sophisticated digital camera, such as the Arri Alexa or Red Epic. They are not required if you are shooting on film stock. They help the camera operator to check the camera settings are correct. Once the shots have been taken, the DIT is responsible for ensuring the footage is properly backed up across a number of storage drives. Because digital footage is usually shot 'raw', the DIT will apply an LUT ('look-up table') to give an impression of what the footage would look like when it has been graded or coloured. This allows the DoP and director to check the shot for image quality.

GRIP

The grip works with the director and camera team to make sure that any movement of the camera can be achieved smoothly. It is a skilled and physically demanding job. They push the dolly (a wheeled platform that carries the camera and the camera operator), and design, build and lay any tracks. They may advise on how to achieve complex set-ups, such as 360-degree movements, and they will be involved in fixing camera mounts on cars, rigging low loaders and crane shots. They look after all the camera support equipment, and may supervise additional grips if they are required on certain shooting days.

SCRIPT SUPERVISOR

The script supervisor is part of the camera department, although their role involves them working closely with many other people including the actors, the director, production office and editor. The script supervisor job used to be known as 'continuity'. They are principally there to make sure that each shot scene can be edited together into a coherent sequence.

During pre-production the script supervisor times the script, checks for inconsistencies, and marks the story days. During the shoot they are on set all the time. They check the actors are delivering the correct lines from the shooting script, and may prompt them if they make mistakes or change any words. They should check there is adequate coverage of each scene, and mark each set-up and take on their script. Their continuity sheets are sent to the editor at the end of each day so that he or she can see which shots cover which sections of the action. The script supervisor also notes which takes are preferred by the director, the DoP and the camera operator, and conveys this information to the editor. They will also time each take, and note this on their daily reports.

They keep detailed notes and take reference photographs to check against for subsequent scenes or any pick-ups. For example, they will check the level of liquids in a glass, how many buttons are done up on a jacket, the exact position of a scarf or hat, and so on. The script supervisor's paperwork includes daily continuity reports, log sheets for the editor, and daily production reports. They report any missing shots to the production co-ordinator and second AD, who make sure these are not overlooked and are rescheduled.

On most professional shoots there will usually also be either a camera assistant or camera trainee in the department.

SOUND DEPARTMENT

PRODUCTION SOUND MIXER OR SOUND RECORDIST

The production sound mixer is responsible for all sound recording on set. They normally start two weeks before shooting to discuss the sound style of the film with the director, and should take part in the technical recce.

Clean dialogue tracks are essential, and sound is often overlooked at the expense of picture. But

Sound-recording equipment.

order, and carrying out minor repairs where necessary.

Boom operating can be a physically demanding job, involving standing for long periods and holding the heavy boom above the head. The boom operator must work closely with the camera operator at all times to make sure there are no shadows, and that the boom never comes into shot.

Depending on the size of the production there may also be one or more sound assistants or trainees.

LIGHTING DEPARTMENT

GAFFER

The gaffer is normally chosen by the director of photography. He or she is the chief electrician and manages the rest of this department. The DoP consults with the gaffer over the lighting plan and the positioning of all the lights on set. The gaffer then executes this plan. The gaffer must be a trained electrician and is responsible for checking that all the lighting equipment and the electricity supply comply with health and safety requirements.

The gaffer will be expected to provide a budget for all the lighting equipment and lighting crew, and to stay within this. This may include additional electricians or extra lights for certain days of the shoot.

On most shoots the department will consist of a 'best boy', who is the gaffer's main assistant, and a number of trained electricians, who are always known as 'sparks'. There may also be a genny operator (generator operator) if a large mobile generator is required.

ART DEPARTMENT

PRODUCTION DESIGNER

The production designer is a key role on every production. He or she is the person responsible for the overall look of any film, television drama, music

this is a mistake, which will always cause problems when you get to post-production. The production sound mixer must make decisions about where to place microphones for optimum sound quality, and so must work collaboratively with many other departments including lighting, art department and locations. They also need to work closely with the costume department to discuss the placing of microphones on the actors. After each take they should check the quality of the track, and if necessary, ask for another one.

They manage the rest of the members of the production sound department, including boom operators and trainees. If live or recorded music is required on set they will normally set up the playback and direct its operation. They should also record any atmospheres or wild tracks that may be needed later in post-production to enrich the final sound track.

BOOM OPERATOR

The boom operator assists the production sound mixer and operates the boom microphone, which is either hand-held or mounted on a dolly. If radio microphones are required, the boom operator positions them correctly around the set or location, or on actors' clothing. Boom operators are also responsible for all the sound equipment, ensuring that it is in good working

Set model created by the production designer.

video or commercial project. They must combine visual storytelling and a strong artistic eye with practical skills, budgeting and team management. They will translate the writers' and directors' vision into real physical sets, and must do so on an absurdly tight schedule without breaking the bank.

The production designer will be one of the first people to join the team in pre-production, and over the following weeks will add more and more staff to their department. The art department will normally be the largest department on any film or television shoot, with the highest budget to spend.

The production designer works closely with the director, producer, line producer and director of photography as well as with wardrobe and locations. They should spend some of their time in early prep researching the period or the background to the story. They are integral to key decisions about the look and colour palette of the film.

The PD must have excellent team management skills as well as being an artist. In the run up to shooting, they will be managing a large team, prioritizing their work schedules and ensuring everything will be ready in time. During the shoot they may be working on the sets for tomorrow and the day after, and will leave the daily decisions on set to their art director. The PD will normally have a two-week wrap.

ART DIRECTOR

The art director reports directly to the production designer, and his or her job is to support and

execute their instructions. On larger productions there may be more than one art director, and in this case the most senior is known as the supervising art director and more junior personnel are assistant art directors. Production designers deliver their designs with instructions for atmosphere, colour and texture to the art director, who will then oversee the production of any technical drawings and models. The art director will work closely with the location manager to know when a location will be available for their team to go in and begin dressing it. They will be closely involved in decisions about the sourcing of vehicles and props.

PRODUCTION BUYER

The production buyer works closely with the production designer and the art director and is responsible for sourcing, purchasing or hiring all the set dressing and props for each set. They will issue all the orders and keep a close check on how long each prop is out on hire, any damage, and when it must be returned. Additional hires can be expensive. They have the important job of managing the art department budget, and must stay on top of all the costs at all times. They should produce a weekly cost report for the production accountant. They may also have an assistant who is known as a 'petty cash buyer'.

PROPERTY (PROP) MASTER

The property master is head of the props department and reports to the production designer and art director. He or she is responsible for storing, delivering and returning all props, whether purchased, made or hired. They work closely with the production buyer, and may assist them in researching and sourcing particular props, especially for period films. They organize all the prop pick-ups from suppliers and prop houses, and arrange for them to be delivered at a designated time to the location or set. They manage the prop store, which is usually divided into individual set areas. They must make sure all props are labelled correctly.

They may supervise or commission the making of some props and discuss how particular hand props work with the director or actors. For location shoots the props department has its own truck, and it will be the responsibility of the props master to ensure that everything required for the day's filming is safely loaded on to it. After the end of the shoot, the props master will be in charge of all prop returns and may also organize the sale or disposal of anything that was specifically purchased for the film.

CONSTRUCTION MANAGER

The construction manager reports to the art director. He or she is responsible for all the set construction, and the execution of the design department's plans. The construction manager is in charge of a team of people including carpenters, plasterers, painters, joiners and scenic artists. He

or she is responsible for ordering all the building materials and ensuring the sets are ready on time and delivered on budget. The construction department may also be required to build larger items to be installed on locations, such as platforms and stages, balconies or towers.

DRESSING PROPS

The dressing props and the props storeman take delivery of the props required to dress sets or locations. They will execute the art director's instructions, and dress all the sets and locations to meet the design brief. This may include hanging curtains, laying floors and carpets, installing kitchens and bathrooms with working plumbing, carrying

The production design department may be asked to create sets.

Sets may be constructed on location as well as in a studio.

The construction team builds the façade of a row of period houses.

The finished street on location.

large items of furniture, and setting up practical lights. On smaller productions without a greensman they will also deal with foliage and plants at exterior locations.

Normally there will be a minimum of two dressing props on a shoot to enable them to carry heavy props and equipment. They work ahead of the shooting crew, preparing sets in the days before they arrive. When filming is completed and rushes clearance has been given, they return to strike sets and restore locations to their original state.

STANDBY PROPS

There will normally be two standby props on most productions. During the shoot the standby props work with the standby art director and are responsible for looking after all the hand props. They may be called on to explain how specific props work. They are responsible for the continuity of props between takes, and may be asked to reset them or return them to their starting place for subsequent takes.

STANDBY ART DIRECTOR

After a set has been dressed and approved, the art director will normally move on to supervise the construction or dressing of the next one. The standby art director's main duty is to be their representative on set throughout the filming day, and make sure all elements of design appearing on camera are precisely the way the production designer and art director decided they should be. During filming the standby art director is usually close to the video playback monitor to see what the camera is shooting and check continuity of props during different takes. They might be required to refill glasses, replace food, wipe marks, remake beds and so on. Sometimes the standby art director has worked during prep as an assistant art director, or they may join the shoot shortly before principal photography begins.

OTHER DEPARTMENT ROLES

Normally in the art department there will also be an art department assistant and an art department runner. If it is a large department there may also be an art department co-ordinator. Depending on the scale and demands of the production there may be other specialist members of this department, such as concept artists, draughtsmen/women, specialist researchers, graphics artists, a home economist (to prepare any food needed in shot), a greensman/greenswoman to supply and care for plants, an armourer to look after any weapons, animal handlers and others.

COSTUME DEPARTMENT

COSTUME DESIGNER

The costume department is also commonly referred to as 'wardrobe'. The head of the department is the costume designer, and he or she is responsible for selecting and providing all the costume for the full cast as well as all the supporting artists. Some of these may be specially made for the production, either by the costume designer themselves or, more likely, they will be commissioned from a freelance costume 'maker'. Depending on the scale of the production, the costume designer will normally have four weeks prep. For period films or science fiction they will need longer. The costume designer will use a number of different sources for all the costumes on a production, including buying, hiring from specialist companies, and making. They are given a budget by the producer or line producer, and must account for how this is spent on a weekly basis.

The costume designer works closely with a number of other departments, including production design. There must be good communication between them to avoid situations where an actor arrives on set in a dress that matches the sofa or wallpaper. They will also help the sound department with the placing of microphones on costumes; they must avoid materials that create too much rustling. They may need to provide 'repeat' costumes for scenes involving stunts or special effects. They look after all the costumes during the shoot, including laundry and repairs.

The costume designer is assisted by a wardrobe supervisor and wardrobe assistants. On days when there are a large number of supporting artists they may also have additional daily assistants (dailies) to help.

HAIR AND MAKE-UP DEPARTMENT

HAIR AND MAKE-UP DESIGNER

The designer leads the make-up department, which includes hairdressing. Their job is to design the make-up and create different hair styles for each actor and member of the cast. They may also be required to create special make-up effects including wounds, skin conditions and facial hair. In some cases they will also commission prosthetics and wigs. During pre-production they may work with the camera department on test shoots to see what make-up looks like under different lighting conditions.

The make-up designer is assisted by a number of make-up artists and hairdressers, depending on the size of the cast and the demands of the production. They work longer hours than most other departments as they are usually required to arrive very early in the morning to prepare actors for the first scenes of the day. At least one member of the department will be required to stand by on set during the shooting period to make any last minute adjustments, and to check continuity between shots.

EDITING DEPARTMENT

EDITOR

The editor is another important creative role. Normally they are chosen by the director. They start work on the first day of principal photography by setting up the cutting room. They receive all the material shot each day, known as the 'rushes'. The pictures are then 'synced-up', with the sound recording by the assistant editor. During the shoot the editor assembles the film using the selected takes, and according to instructions received from the set through the camera and sound sheets and continuity reports. They will report back to production details of any missing shots, poor quality images or sound, and other technical issues. They also note the length of shot sequences for comparison with the estimated timings. By the end of the shoot the editor will have a complete rough assembly to show to the director.

During the first stage of post-production, the director and editor work together in the cutting room to create the finished film. This is a highly creative process and the end product may be quite different from the screenplay. The first version is known as the 'director's cut', which is shown to the producers and some executives. Taking into account any notes, the next version is known as the 'fine cut'. When everyone's approval has been given, the film is then 'picture locked'. The editor normally remains involved during the next stage of post-production to supervise the sound editing, music and track laying. They will normally attend the sound mix and the grade.

ASSISTANT EDITOR

The assistant editor takes charge of the day-to-day running of the cutting room, leaving the editor free to edit the film. They liaise with other departments, including production, camera and sound. If shooting on film they may need to be in touch with the laboratory about processing. During filming the assistant editor will check the camera sheets when the rushes arrive, and then sync them up with the sound. On some shoots the assistant editor may be required to work different hours from the editor, sometimes overnight, so that the rushes are already synced when the editor arrives as the cutting room.

Assistant editors are normally employed from the first day of principal photography until picture lock, but on low budget films they may finish earlier.

POST-PRODUCTION SUPERVISOR

The role of the post-production supervisor varies according to the type of film and the budget. The post is almost always a freelance position, and some P-P supervisors work on multiple productions at the same time. They will normally be recruited during pre-production for occasional days to advise on the post-production schedule, and will be consulted on the hiring of post-production personnel, and facilities such as title designers, sound editors, grading suites and so on. They may be more involved at this early stage if the production requires a lot of CGI or VFX shots.

During post-production they report to the producer, and also work closely with the production accountant, supplying them with information for the weekly cost report. The supervisor works alongside the editor, making sure that each different stage of post-production is correctly planned and managed, and that it stays on schedule. They remain involved until all the various elements of the film have been delivered to the broadcaster or distribution company, including all the post-production paperwork. This may be many weeks after everyone else involved has finished.

OTHER POST-PRODUCTION ROLES

There are many other specialist personnel involved in the post-production process, including sound editors, footsteps artists, composers, musicians, music supervisors, sound mixers, colourists, and visual and special effects supervisors. These roles are discussed in more detail in Chapter 8, 'Post-Production'. Most of these people will be employed on a freelance or fee basis. When budgeting these areas it is customary to include a single lump sum for 'music', 'special effects' or 'grading'.

PUBLICITY DEPARMENT

Stills Photographer

Having good quality and professionally produced marketing materials is essential for all film productions, including short films that hope to get into festivals. Stills photographers are normally hired on a daily basis for an agreed daily fee, including their equipment. It is not necessary (and it is expensive) to have a photographer on set every day. On a low- to medium-budget feature the stills photographer may be on set for between ten and fifteen days.

Producers should decide which scenes are likely to be visually interesting sets or locations, or choose those featuring key actors, and book a photographer to cover these days. The stills photographer should make suggestions for set-ups, and may ask for time to take a photograph at the end of a particular scene. They should then supply copies of all the day's shots, from which an agreed selection will be made.

Unit Publicist

Normally the unit publicist will begin working with the producer during pre-production. They may be asked to issue press releases, or to provide information to the trade press. During the shoot, the unit publicist arranges for selected journalists to visit the set and interview actors or members of the crew. They should ensure articles are prepared ready for the film's release. The unit publicist will normally also prepare and write the press pack, or will commission a journalist to write it. They work closely with the stills photographer, and on larger shoots may also supervise the production of an electronic press kit (EPK). They are normally engaged on a fee to cover all their work on the production.

More details of the contents of the press pack, and information on marketing materials, are included in Chapter 9, 'Marketing, Festivals and Distribution'.

OTHER PERSONNEL

In addition to the specialist departments already listed, there may be a number of other teams and individuals employed on the production, either for the whole shoot or for selected days. These may include the following:

- Caterers: the team engaged to cook and serve food for the cast and crew;
- Transport captain: in charge of all the unit drivers and arranging their schedules;
- Facilities manager: in charge of the facilities provided at the studio or unit base and their daily operation;
- Animal handlers (or 'wranglers'): in charge of any animals and their welfare;
- Stunt arrangers and performers;
- Action vehicle drivers;
- Tutors and chaperones: to educate and supervise children and minors;
- Nurses and paramedics: to stand by on set during dangerous sequences;
- Armourer: required for any scenes involved firearms;
- Riggers: may be employed to construct scaffolding towers or large black-out tents;
- Voice and dialogue coaches: may be required to help actors with specific accents;
- Choreographers: to arrange dances and teach the cast dance steps;
- Second unit: a separate small unit that may be sent off to shoot pick-up shots, establishers, or material not involving the main cast.

Deciding between a studio build or location shoot has an impact on the budget.

5
RAISING PRODUCTION FINANCE

Movie-making is the process of turning money into light. All they have at the end of the day is images flickering on a wall.

John Boorman, Director
(*Deliverance, The Emerald Forest, Hope and Glory*)

Raising production finance is one of the most critical duties of the producer, and it is important for all producers to really understand the benefits and possible disadvantages of each different form of investment. In this chapter we will examine some of the types of funding commonly used in the film and television industries, and explain the vocabulary surrounding them. We will also look at what information and documents you may need to put together a funding application, whether for a short film, a full length feature, or a television series. And we'll explain what you need to launch your project into the marketplace.

FEATURE FILM FUNDING

THE MAJOR STUDIOS

If you are fortunate enough to have acquired or developed the kind of film preferred by the major Hollywood studios you can skip most of the rest of this chapter. Hollywood is a 'one stop shop'. The large studios – known as the 'majors' – will develop, finance, distribute and market their films, and invest vast sums of money into each of these different stages. Paramount Pictures, 21st Century Fox, Warner Bros Pictures, Universal Pictures, Walt Disney Studios and Sony Pictures Entertainment are the six major film studios dominating American cinema and the global movie business. The proposed acquisition of the 21st Century Fox Company by Disney will bring this select group down to five. The average studio film costs in the region of $65m to produce, and around $35m to promote and distribute. Many cost much more than this.

THE 'MINI' MAJORS

On the next rung of international film production and distribution are the so-called 'mini' majors; these include Lionsgate, who enjoyed a huge worldwide hit with *La La Land* in 2017, Studio Canal, Pathe and eOne Entertainment. They sit in the dangerous middle ground of medium-budget films, which could mean production costs of anything from £5m to £35m or more. An example of this kind of film is the sci-fi success *Arrival*, which cost $45m to produce. Medium-budget films are often the hardest to get funded as they need to do well at the box office to make a decent return, but are not as easy to sell to audiences as the lucrative franchise films. Mid-budget films may also secure much of their funding from a single source.

An important new player in the funding of medium- and low-budget films is the online platform

Netflix. Netflix has announced plans to release eighty new feature-film titles on its platform in 2018, with budgets ranging from $1m to $90m. This is almost as many new titles as all six major studios combined: in 2017, Disney, Fox, Paramount, Sony, Universal and Warner Bros collectively released 106 films under their major labels, and more under their subsidiary divisions. Netflix is not the only newcomer in the feature-film funding business, but it is becoming one of the most important. It not only fully funds new projects up front, but is also aggressively acquiring titles at film festivals and markets such as Sundance, Berlin and Cannes.

But most films are not made this way. The majority of low- and medium-budget films are funded from a number of different sources, and can have as many as a dozen different organizations putting in money. The most common types of funding are described below. When referring to 'low-budget films' in this book we mean films with a total budget between £1m and £5m, or $1.3m and $6.5m. Films under £1m are referred to as 'micro-budget' films.

NATIONAL FILM FUNDS

Almost every country in the world has a national film fund. The main exceptions are the USA and Russia. In the UK the British Film Institute is the national fund, and receives its income from The National Lottery. The BFI invests directly into the development, production, distribution and exhibition of feature films, as well as supporting UK filmmakers attending festivals abroad, managing the annual London Film Festival and the BFI Southbank and BFI IMAX cinemas, and supporting educational and training programmes and the National Film Archive. It has special funding streams to support first features and documentaries. Other similarly constituted national funds include the Centre National du Cinéma et de l'Image Animée – CNC – in France, Telefilm Canada, the Danish Film Institute and Screen Australia.

National film funds are primarily paid for directly by governments or through government-sponsored schemes, as in the UK. They are designed to support and encourage local talent. Many apply what they call a 'cultural test' to all potential projects, which is usually a points-based or tick system. To qualify for funding the project must obtain sufficient points or ticks. These are applied to areas such as the nationality of the key talent including writer, director, producer, lead actors, director of photography and composer. Other factors taken into account may be the cultural heritage of the project, the original source material, filming locations, music, who is doing the special effects and so on. To pass the cultural test for a UK film, a project must achieve eighteen of a possible thirty-five points.

From the cultural test table it is possible to see what criteria are applied, and in most countries these are broadly the same. For example, in A1 – which is a film set in the UK or EEA – four points are awarded if the whole film is set in the UK or another EEA state. If 75 per cent of the film is set in the UK or an EEA state, three points are awarded; if it is 50 per cent, two points are awarded; and for 25 per cent it is one point.

In A2, four points are awarded if all the lead characters are UK or EEA, but if there were only one UK or EEA lead and only 50 per cent of the supporting characters were UK or EEA, then the film might receive only two or three points.

Section B, the cultural contribution of the film, is particularly important. Additional new guidelines have been introduced to ensure that diversity is better represented in all BFI-supported films. The full cultural test guidelines are available on the BFI website.

National Film Funds invest in local filmmakers to support their own industry and talent. They are very unlikely to be the majority funder in any single project, and will tend to spread their funds thinly across as many qualifying films as possible. Although they hope to see a return on their investments, this may not be the primary motive for supporting a particular film. For this reason this kind of public funding is frequently referred to as 'soft money'.

	UK CULTURAL TEST	POINTS
A	**Section A - Cultural Content**	
A1	**Film set in the UK or EEA**	**4 points**
A2	**Lead characters British or EEA citizens or residents**	**4 points**
A3	**Film based on British or EEA subject matter or underlying material**	**4 points**
A4	**Original dialogue recorded mainly in English or UK indigenous language or EEA language**	**6 points**
	Total Section A	**18 points**
B	**Section B - Cultural Contribution**	
B1	**The film demonstrates British creativity, British heritage and/or diversity**	**4 points**
	Total Section B	**4 points**
C	**Section C - Cultural Hubs**	
C1	**(a) At least 50% of the principal photography or SFX takes place in the UK**	**2 points**
	(b) At least 50% of the VFX takes place in the UK	**2 points**
	(c) An extra 2 points can be awarded if at least 80% of principal photography or VFX or SFX takes place in the UK	**2 points**
C2	**Music Recording/Audio Post Production/Picture Post Production**	**1 points**
	Total Section C (Maximum 4 points in total in C1)	**5 points**
D	**Section D - Cultural Practitioners (UK or EEA citizens or residents)**	
D1	**Director**	**1 point**
D2	**Scriptwriter**	**1 point**
D3	**Producer**	**1 point**
D4	**Composer**	**1 point**
D5	**Lead Actors**	**1 point**
D6	**Majority of Cast**	**1 point**
D7	**Key Staff (lead cinematographer, lead production designer, lead costume designer, lead editor, lead sound designer, lead visual effects supervisor, lead hair and makeup supervisor)**	**1 point**
D8	**Majority of Crew**	**1 point**
	Total Section D	**8 points**
	Total all sections (pass mark 18)	**35 points**

The cultural test table shows how points are awarded to qualify as a British film. A minimum of eighteen points is required.

REGIONAL FUNDS

Some countries also have regional funds and film offices that can support local filmmakers. These can fall into a number of different categories and types of support. For example, in Canada and Australia, each province and state has a regional fund (British Columbia, Quebec, Queensland and so on). In the UK, the regional agencies include Creative Scotland, Film Cymru Wales and Northern Ireland Screen, each with a budget for local production. In Germany, each of the different states or Länder has its own film fund, while in Spain there are funds to support Catalan and Basque projects, as well as those from Galicia and Valencia.

In some of the larger countries, these funds will invest significant amounts of money into a production that culturally supports the local region or language, or one that will be filmed there. In smaller regions the support may be more limited, and may include the local film office negotiating lower or no payment for locations or cast accommodation, providing cheap flights, or offering other forms of sponsorship, preferential rates for equipment hire and 'support in kind'. Like national funds, regional funding may be viewed as 'soft money'.

CREATIVE EUROPE

One of the largest regional funding organizations is Creative Europe, the European Union's financial support programme for the creative, cultural and audiovisual sectors in Europe. It is the successor to the previous Culture and MEDIA programmes, and was launched on 1 January 2014. Creative Europe has a budget of $1.46 billion to be spent between 2014 and 2020. Its specific remit is to support European projects with the potential to travel and find audiences beyond their national borders – in other words, it actively promotes co-production between companies from two, three or more European countries.

Creative Europe runs a series of programmes and initiatives with regular funding deadlines. There are currently around eighteen Creative Europe funding opportunities (often called 'schemes' or 'strands'), each focusing on a specific sector or type of activity.

EQUITY INVESTMENT

Private equity investment differs from public funding in that it will always be 'recoupable' – that is to say, the investor wishes to see a return for their money. Not only do they want to get back their original investment, they also hope to make a profit as well. As with everything else in film funding, there are as many different kinds of equity investors as there are film projects, but the bottom line is the same: the investor is asking the question: 'Will putting my money into this film make me richer?'

Some investors may treat part of their funding as recoupable equity and part as another form of investment, such as a pre-sale or distribution advance.

PRE-SALES AND DISTRIBUTION AGREEMENTS

Pre-sales are sales made in advance of shooting your film. Securing pre-sales may be essential to help you cash flow your production, and almost all independent films need to obtain some kind of pre-sale funding in order to be made. There are various different types of pre-sale deals, including foreign pre-sales, negative pick-ups, co-production, television pre-sales and VOD (video-on-demand) distribution. These deals may be negotiated directly by the producer or by an intermediary such as a sales agent who is acting on your behalf.

If you pre-sell a territory or a group of territories to a distributor you receive an 'advance' or a 'minimum guarantee' calculated on the expected receipts from that territory. This is like an advance in publishing, an agreed sum that you receive before publication, but not necessarily all that you will ever get from this territory. Once the contract has been signed, the advance is paid in one sum or in a series of smaller sums or 'tranches' at agreed points during the production.

So, for example, if you agreed to 'pre-sell' the Italian language rights to your film to a distributor for 15 per cent of the budget, you could receive this money up front, or at least could receive a binding contract that you can use to borrow money. On a film with a budget of £2m this would be around £300,000. If the film wins awards and does very well, the Italian distributor might make back the advance and more, in which case he will pay 'overages'. The overages go into the 'pot', to be later distributed amongst all the investors. If the film does badly and doesn't make back its advance, the Italian distributor takes the hit and makes a loss.

When you secure a pre-sale it could be a territory, a language, a means of delivery, or a combination of any of these. You could pre-sell the DVD rights worldwide, or for part of the world. You could pre-sell all the French language rights (including French-speaking Canada) comprising cinema ('theatrical'), DVD, VOD, cable and television. Scandinavian rights are often sold as a package: Norway, Sweden, Denmark, Finland and Iceland. It is complicated, and can become even more so when worldwide DVD rights go in one direction, and then someone wants to pre-buy all rights in one territory including the DVD release.

SALES AGENTS

Because of all these complicated negotiations, producers often appoint a sales agent to work with them, who can steer them through the deals in return for a percentage of the sum raised on each individual contract. Sales agents attend all the major markets such as Cannes, the American Film Market (AFM), the European Film Market (Berlin) and the Toronto Film Festival (TIFF), and can offset the considerable costs of being there across a number of different projects. To secure pre-sales for your project the sales agent will want a package that will include, as a minimum, the script, details of the director, the approximate budget, and some idea of the cast. Typically the percentage paid to a sales agent on each individual sale they secure might be between 10 and 20 per cent, or more.

For the producer, selecting a sales agent or sales company will always be an important decision. You should conduct careful research into their reputation, experience and relationships.

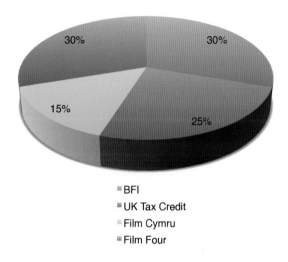

Low Budget Feature £1.6m

- BFI
- UK Tax Credit
- Film Cymru
- Film Four

Chart showing how a low-budget British feature might be financed.

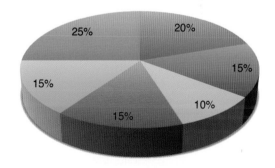

Low Budget Feature £3.5m

- National Film Fund 1
- National Film Fund 2
- National Film Fund 3
- Creative Europe
- Pre-Sales
- Tax Credits

Chart showing a possible funding model for a European co-production.

Ask other producers they have worked with, and look at the company or individual's previous successes, and even their taste in films. If they have a track record of selling comedies and horror titles, they may not necessarily be the best company to look after your LGBT art house title. Your research should include looking at recent similar titles to your film, who sold them, and how well these titles did in the international market. How many titles does the agent already have on their slate? Too many may suggest a 'pile it high, sell it cheap' approach; too few may suggest other producers have lost faith.

Before committing to a sales agent, they should be asked to provide you with a set of sales estimates, drawn up specifically for your project. The sales estimate lists each territory with an 'asking price' and a 'settling price'. If possible you should try to find out how accurate their previous sales estimates have proved to be – how often they have achieved close to the asking price, and how often and how far they fell below it.

Another question may be whether the sales agent will offer any advance, and if so, how much? This may help you to decide their level of interest and commitment to your film.

Lastly you have to decide whether you like and trust them – and perhaps more importantly, how committed to and enthusiastic they appear to be about your project. Nobody can sell a film they don't like or don't believe in.

Co-Production

A co-production partner is a company or individual with whom you should always aim to have a genuinely collaborative relationship. The dictionary definition of 'co-production' is 'together', 'jointly' or 'mutually', and this is a good thing to remember when entering into a co-production deal. Co-producers don't want to be seen as sleeping or passive partners. Most countries have formal co-production treaties with a number of others, and information about these treaties can be found on the national funding bodies' websites. The BFI currently has bi-lateral co-production treaties with twelve countries, as well as being a signatory of the European Convention on Cinematographic Co-production, which enables it (at the time of writing) to co-produce with all the countries in the European Union.

Usually both parties benefit from a co-production arrangement. Good co-producers often work together on successive projects. Sometimes producers seek a co-producer in the place they want to film because they need help in an area they are unfamiliar with. A co-producer can use their local knowledge to propose or advise against crew members, local suppliers and facilities, or can arrange insurance. Importantly, you always need a co-producer if you wish to access local tax credits.

Broadcasters

Television companies are frequently one of the major investors in feature films, as well as in other types of programme. The BBC, Channel Four, ZDF, RAI and ARTE are all key players in this market. Cable examples include HBO and Canal+ (Studio Canal). These broadcasting companies offer another form of pre-sale. They are pre-purchasing the right to show your film at an agreed time in the future, normally after it has enjoyed a theatrical (cinema) and DVD release in their territory. In most cases you will agree a number of showings over a limited number of years. After this elapses the broadcaster may purchase additional showings, or the rights will revert to the production company and can be sold again to someone else.

Video on Demand

Video-on-demand services are growing in number and popularity, and have become an important component of all film and television funding in recent years. Many more are entering the market. There are two types of model: the first are transactional video-on-demand services, which charge users for each film they watch. Examples include Apple iTunes, BFI Player and Curzon Home Cinema. As a general rule these services are more likely to purchase films after they are completed, rather than as a pre-sale.

TERRITORY	ACCEPT	ASK
ENGLISH SPEAKING		
USA/ Canada	400,000	750,000
Australia/New Zealand	75,000	125,000
South Africa	25,000	75,000
Airlines	75,000	150,000
Sub-Total English Sp.	**575,000**	**1,100,000**
EUROPE		
Benelux	75,000	150,000
France (FST)	200,000	350,000
Germany	200,000	300,000
Switzerland (Theatrical)		
Greece/Cyprus	25,000	75,000
Iceland	5,000	10,000
Italy	75,000	150,000
Portugal	25,000	75,000
Scandinavia	75,000	125,000
Spain	65,000	90,000
United Kingdom	300,000	750,000
Sub-Total Europe	**1,045,000**	**2,075,000**
LATIN AMERICA		
Pan Latin America		
Argentina/Par/Uru/ Chile	50,000	100,000
Brazil	50,000	85,000
Central America	10,000	20,000
Colombia	10,000	20,000
Mexico	50,000	120,000
Peru/ Ecuador/ Bolivia		
Venezuela	10,000	20,000
Sub-Total Latin America	**180,000**	**365,000**
ASIA		
Pan Asian Pay TV		
China	25,000	75,000
Hong Kong / Macao	15,000	25,000
India	20,000	35,000
Indonesia	20,000	35,000
Japan	100,000	175,000
Malaysia	15,000	25,000
Philippines	20,000	30,000
Singapore	20,000	30,000
South Korea	50,000	85,000
Taiwan	20,000	30,000
Thailand	10,000	20,000
Sub-Total Asia	**315,000**	**565,000**
ASIA MINOR		
Israel	25,000	50,000
Middle East	75,000	150,000
Turkey	30,000	75,000
Sub-Total Asia Minor	**130,000**	**275,000**
EASTERN EUROPE		
Bulgaria	10,000	20,000
CIS/Baltics	85,000	125,000
Croatia/Slovenia/ Serbia	10,000	20,000
Czech & Slovak Rep.	10,000	20,000
Hungary	20,000	50,000
Poland	25,000	75,000
Romania	10,000	20,000
Sub-Total East Europe	**170,000**	**330,000**
TOTAL	**2,415,000**	**4,710,000**

Sales estimates are provided to the producer by prospective sales agents. The chart illustrates the minimum and maximum prices accepted.

The second type of video-on-demand service charges a monthly subscription. This gives the user access to a wider amount of content, chosen to appeal to their taste. Examples include Netflix, Amazon Prime, MUBI, Hulu and Now TV. As previously stated, in the past year Netflix has become a major player in purchasing and pre-purchasing film titles for its service. It may fully finance films before shooting, or buy rights later at festivals and film markets. Amazon Prime has a wide selection of older titles, acquired when it bought the Love Film catalogue. It is also investing in new content, but this is more often television series. MUBI is a channel for film lovers, which presents a small selection of new titles each month for just thirty days.

CROWDFUNDING

Crowdfunding has become an important source of finance for short films, television pilots, documentaries and micro-budget features. For films, Kickstarter and Indiegogo are the most frequently used platforms. They provide the space for producers to launch their projects and seek financial support for them. It is important to understand the difference between reward-based crowdfunding for individual projects, and platforms such as Crowdcube, who are seeking equity investors in small businesses or venture capital schemes.

Veronica Mars still holds the record as the most successful crowdfunded feature film. When the popular teen show was cancelled after its third season, screenwriter Rob Thomas decided to bring his characters back in a feature seven years later in 2013. With an established fan base already, the campaign reached its initial target of $2m in less than ten hours. The final amount raised was $5.7m. The campaign was also significant for raising this sum from a huge number of small donations and minimum pledges. A total of 91,585 backers invested in the film – also a Kickstarter record.

Rewards-based crowdfunding campaigns rely heavily on social media to get the word out, and the most successful campaigns achieve a reach far beyond the immediate network of the individual or company who has posted it. The platform will take a percentage of the money raised, or a fee for collecting donations on your behalf. However, different platforms operate with different rules, and it is important to understand these before launching any campaign. For example, Kickstarter only collects and pays out the money if the campaign reaches its target. Unsuccessful campaigns on Kickstarter get nothing, whereas on Indiegogo the money raised (minus any fees) is paid to the project whether it reaches its initial target or not.

When considering any crowdfunding strategy, preparation is critical. Before launching you should first carefully research the rules of the platform you choose. It is also advisable to join the platform ahead of your launch and make small donations

Studio 'back-lot' sets.

Deciding where in the world to shoot can have an impact on how a film is financed.

(£1 to £5) to other projects that interest you and are similar to your own. This will help to build your contacts and followers when you launch your own campaign.

It is also vital to think carefully about the rewards you offer, and avoid making these too complicated. There is no point in receiving a lot of £10 donations and promising each one a poster, DVD or signed copy of the script if it costs you £5 or more to produce these, and sending them all out individually takes someone you have to pay to do it, a week. Remember that many crowdfunders are friends, family and colleagues of those who have created the campaign, and don't expect much in return apart from a credit on the end roller.

You must also plan the campaign itself like a military operation, and prepare as much material as you can before launch. Individuals who have raised significant amounts of money through crowdfunding describe it as some of the hardest and most intense work they have ever done. You will need an appeal film to begin, you must add regular updates and news throughout the campaign, and you need to make full use of all social media platforms such as Facebook, Instagram and Twitter.

Despite the hard work, the advantages to the producer of crowdfunding investment are considerable. Money raised through rewards-based crowdfunding is treated as a donation, and donors do not expect a return on their investment, other than the rewards promised. So, after any platform fees (normally 5 per cent), credit card charges, campaign costs and rewards promised, the producer retains 100 per cent of the balance raised and does not have to share profits from this investment in the film with anyone else.

A second advantage is that a market for the series or film is established. The producer has already made contact with a wide group of people who have shown a demonstrable interest in their product and can be invited to view it online or in cinemas. In the case of television pilots, this helps to show future commissioners that there is an audience out there waiting for more episodes.

TAX CREDITS

Many countries offer producers a tax credit system to incentivize production in their country or region. In the UK, the tax credit applies to feature films, children's programming, animation, and high-end television programmes with a budget over £1m per hour. The UK tax credit is 25 per cent of the qualifying spend – that is, the amount spent in the UK on areas of the budget that qualify. In reality the amount that most productions receive is normally closer to 20–22 per cent. It is possible to apply for the UK tax credit for a short film, but only if all the criteria are met, including paying members of the cast and crew, passing the cultural test, and proving that your film is 'intended for theatrical release'.

If you film partly abroad and spend a portion of your budget there, you may be able to apply for tax credit on the spend in that region. The following is an example:

Your film is budgeted at £5m. You have a UK writer and producer and lead actress. The director and lead actor are Canadian. You plan to build the interiors in the UK and shoot all the exteriors in Canada. Post-production is in the UK, but special effects will be done in Canada. The total qualifying UK spend is £3m. The total qualifying Canadian spend is £2m. You can therefore claim the UK tax credit of 25 per cent on the £3m UK spend and reclaim £750,000, and (depending on where in Canada you film) in the region of 35 per cent of the £2m Canadian spend and reclaim a further £700,000. And if you are doing the special effects in Canada there may be a further 16 per cent you could claim on the amount this represents in your budget. So if all the SFX costs amount to £400,000 you might reclaim another £64,000.

Therefore, a film with a budget of £5m, which qualifies for these tax credits, would be able to reclaim £1.514m and only need raise the balance of £3.486m from other sources. As will be evident, this is a significant help to any fundraising effort.

When considering where in the world to film, taking into account what tax credits are available may be a key component of your fundraising strategy. Tax credits are offered by governments to encourage economic activity, inward investment and employment. Since the UK government first introduced the tax credit for feature films in 2007, production spend in this country has increased each year. The film industry had lobbied for tax credits for many years, and they were finally introduced because so many high-budget movies were choosing to film abroad. Since their introduction, UK studios at Pinewood, Shepperton, Leavesden and Cardiff are full, and the creative industries are one of the few growth sectors in the UK economy.

You may not need any cultural elements at all to qualify, but you will need to spend money, employ crew, and use facilities. If you are planning to build sets in a studio, and there is a good level of skilled craftsmen and women and technical services, you can be creative in where you choose to film.

In 2017, UK-based filmmaker Terence Davies directed a film about the American poet Emily Dickinson. The film was entirely set in New York and starred Cynthia Nixon as Dickinson. It was filmed in the Flanders region of Belgium, partly on studio sets and partly on location. At the time it was filmed, the local regional economic fund, Screen

Flanders, was offering producers a tax shelter of up to 66 per cent of their eligible audiovisual spend in the Flanders region. This means that for a film with a budget of £2m, the tax credit would be up to £1.32m and the producer would only need to raise a further £680,000 from pre-sales and other forms of funding to go into production.

GAP FINANCE

Gap finance is a last resort for producers. After the enormously hard work and months involved in developing the project, attaching key talent and raising investment, you may find yourself with a 'gap' in your finance plan of 10–15 per cent of the budget. Securing this last funding is often the difference between going ahead with the project or postponing the shoot, sometimes indefinitely. And it may not be possible to get all the pieces of the puzzle back together again – ever. This is why many producers turn to gap financiers in these circumstances, and take out a loan to cover the shortfall.

There are specialist film finance investors who will plug the gap and lend you the money to make your film. The loan is normally against any unsold larger territories, for example France, Germany or Japan. Their terms vary, but they often charge a high interest rate for the money you are borrowing. They may also seek preferential terms above other financiers, including asking for their loan to be recouped in 'first position' before the other equity investors.

PRODUCT PLACEMENT

Successful franchise films can attract serious money from product placement. The *James Bond* films are well known to have secured millions of dollars in this way. Product placement involves the subtle advertisement of products, which may give them status or popularity by association. For example, if Bond drinks a particular brand of beer or drives a certain kind of car, this makes the product attractive to others. The regulations regarding product placement in television production are stricter than in films, especially in programmes made for the national broadcaster, the BBC. However, in January 2018 the UK's main commercial channel, ITV, announced that its flagship soap opera *Coronation Street* had signed product placement deals with Costa Coffee and the Co-op, who will both be opening stores in the iconic Manchester street.

For the low-budget filmmaker, product placement is unlikely to be a major source of finance because brand managers are largely interested in reaching a guaranteed wide audience.

COMPLETION GUARANTEES

In some cases financiers and investors in films may ask the production company to provide a completion guarantee or 'bond'. The purpose of the bond is to make sure that the film or series will be completed and delivered, and not left in an incomplete and therefore valueless state. The bond company provides an assurance that the investors will not be responsible for any production overspend or overages, but may insist on a 10 per cent contingency to mitigate any potential losses. There are a few specialist companies that provide these bonds, most notably Film Finances Limited based in London and California, who provide bonds for productions across the world.

DEFERMENTS

Deferment of fees is another way some producers try to close the gap between the money actually raised and the production budget. It is not good practice, and is often a way of paying crew less than the market rate for the work they are doing. If you are asked to sign an agreement deferring part of your agreed fee or wages, think hard about doing so. In most cases deferred fees are never paid, and essentially you are agreeing to work for a reduced amount.

TELEVISION FUNDING

For a long time television funding followed a very different pattern from feature-film funding, but recently the models have become much more similar. Very few projects are now fully financed by broadcasters in the way they used to be. The exceptions are domestic dramas (soaps), current affairs, some entertainment, comedy and reality shows, sport and news – in other words, programmes that are mainly targeted towards a local audience within the broadcaster's country and are unlikely to have cross border or international appeal. Some of these are still produced in house by broadcasters, who then own all the rights in the finished product. Some are produced by independent producers but are fully funded by the broadcaster. In either case the commissioning process will be relatively simple. The producer is contracted to deliver the programme or series for an agreed budget and by an agreed date.

Higher profile, more expensive, larger budget programmes are more likely to be produced with similar funding models to feature films, although possibly with fewer partners. In the UK, the tax credit can now be applied to so-called 'high-end' television productions with budgets of more than £1m per hour, and to animation. In practical terms this makes it pointless to produce drama in the £750,000–£1m per hour bracket, since these are not eligible for the 25 per cent tax credit. Since 2014 all children's programming has also been eligible for tax credits and is not subject to the £1m per hour threshold.

Co-production is now a regular form of television funding. Recent examples include the BBC working with Netflix, and collaborations between Sky and HBO. Creative Europe invests in television series where three or more different European countries or broadcasters are partners.

Many of the major broadcasters fund the development of television drama. They often want to be involved from the earliest possible stage, to influence the choice of writers and give notes on each stage of the script writing. Producers will normally approach a commissioning editor to discuss the project at treatment stage or even earlier, and will work closely with a development producer, executive producer or script editor. Once the scripts

are written, the broadcaster may also become involved in seeking other investors or pre-sales, and may work with the independent producer to achieve this. Contracts are drawn up to acquire the right to show the programmes for an agreed number of transmissions over an agreed number of years. It is normal to include at least two repeat showings, and often more.

One consideration when you approach a broadcaster for investment in your project may be the terms and conditions of their funding. Some broadcasters, such as the BBC and C4, may offer to invest their contribution during the production and partly cash flow it. Others, such as ITV, may only pay on delivery of the finished programmes, or even on transmission. This could be a year or more after you have paid for everything, and can involve you in expensive borrowing costs. Before committing to the deal make sure you have worked out all the hidden costs.

SHORT FILMS AND MICRO-BUDGET FEATURES

In the UK, the BFI and the different regional funds all have schemes to support emerging filmmakers and short films. These change with the organization's current priorities, and you should check their website regularly and register for updates to receive the most recent announcements and opportunities. Creative England has a low budget, first feature film programme 'iFeatures', and Film London has a number of initiatives to support new talent, including 'Microwave' and 'London Calling'. Some broadcasters support short films and have space in their schedule to show them. Channel 4 has a strand titled *Random Acts* dedicated to three- to four-minute art films, and encourages 'bold expressions of creativity' and practitioners to 'use the screen as a canvas'.

Many national and regional funds and some broadcasters have similar projects for supporting new talent. Competition for these funds is always intense, and in most cases the rules will be strict about who can apply and what projects qualify.

APPLYING FOR FUNDING

Before making an application for funding you should read the guidelines carefully and make sure you understand them fully. All funding bodies publish clear criteria, which must be met. Don't waste your time applying for a grant if you already know you don't meet their requirements.

Second, you should pull together everything you need for the application. The following list includes those items most commonly requested:

- Evidence of copyright: proof that you have an option agreement for the source material, research and the screenplay. You will be asked to provide copies of signed agreements.
- A short synopsis or creative proposal. Normally one A4 side or less. Clearly explain what the story is, and the themes it explores.
- Screenplay or treatment or detailed research for a documentary.
- Director's statement: a personal note outlining the director's vision for the film, to include some indication of style and tone. If you don't yet have a director attached, a writer's statement might be included instead.
- Biographies or CVs of key cast and crew committed or confirmed, with notes about their previous work, if appropriate. Include links to IMDb, showreels or websites.
- Audience: it is very important to provide a statement detailing who the film is aimed at, and how you plan to reach this audience. You might also note what certificate you are aiming for – for example PG, 12A, 15 or 18.
- A full project budget, including one-page summary.
- Detailed production plan, including timelines and production schedule to delivery. Include any information already known about when and where you plan to shoot.
- Details of any finance already committed or offered.
- Sales estimates (if available).
- Finance plan: how do you propose to raise the money?
- Distribution and marketing plan: will you launch through festivals, or at the opening weekend?
- Marketing plan: does your project have digital and cross-media opportunities? If so, explain how.
- How does your project meet the funder's stated objectives?

TAKING YOUR PROJECT TO MARKET

The documents and tools you need to launch your project into the marketplace may be slightly different. All the above will be necessary later, but if you are heading off to Berlin or Cannes with a great idea at an early stage, what you need first is a pitch, a logline, and a great image. Film and television markets are scary places, especially the first time you experience them. Spend a few hours inside the Palais des Festivals at Cannes during the Marché du Film or MIP TV, and you will quickly realize that this is a business, not an art form. You will see stand after stand of sales teams trying to get the best price for items in their catalogues, and it can be disheartening to discover that your beautifully made work is being offloaded to the highest bidder in this way.

In the event that you find yourself in a meeting, at a party, or in the lift with a buyer, you will need a logline, and a proposal or pitch document.

LOGLINE

Writing loglines is difficult but essential. The logline sums up your project simply and clearly. It might be one or two short sentences, but never more. It is different from the tagline, which will be used after the film is made to sell it to audiences, appearing on the poster or digital marketing. A great example of a tagline is from *Alien* – 'In space, no one can hear you scream'. This will intrigue audiences, but it won't help you sell the project in advance.

A good logline reduces your project down to its essential dramatic narrative. It should answer the question 'what is the film about?' without getting bogged down in the detail. You are 'selling' the story, not 'telling' it. Your only objective is to make whoever reads or hears it want to see the film, or at least read the script. Look up good loglines for previous films online. IMDb has lots of examples. We should know from a logline what the film is about, and who the protagonist is; for example, 'A troubled child summons the courage to help a friendly alien escape Earth and return to his home-world' (describing *E.T.*).

Think about three basic questions, and try to answer them all in your logline:

- Who is the main character (the protagonist), and what does he or she want?
- Who (the antagonist) or what (the obstacle) is standing in the way?
- What makes the story unique?

You might also want to think about the genre of your project. If it's a comedy, try to make your logline funny, or at least raise a smile. If you are selling an action project, try to get as many verbs into your logline as you can. Most successful loglines don't use the main character's name. It doesn't add anything except extra words.

And never, ever give away the ending.

PROPOSAL OR PITCH DOCUMENT

In addition to the logline you need a proposal. This should be short and eye-catching. Note that the pitch is not the same as a treatment, which is written by the writer and tells the whole story from beginning to end. The pitch is a tease, and to do it well you need to think like an advertising executive, not like a storyteller.

The proposal should include the following items, but must not be too long. At all film markets there is far too much paper, and most of it gets left behind or thrown away. Consider creating your marketing materials in a digital format. Show them on your iPad or tablet, and email a link later. Recipients will be grateful.

Include the following information in your proposal:

- A strong, professional and appealing cover image;
- Title, format, length, genre;
- A short synopsis of the story, no more than one page at the very most;
- A mood or storyboard or images to communicate the film's visual style;
- Short biographies (a paragraph or less) of the creative team – producer, director, writer, and any confirmed talent such as DoPs or composers;
- Cast or talent wish list;
- Budget top sheet;
- Financing plan, including information about any already confirmed;
- Target audience, distribution and marketing strategy;
- Production schedule – roughly when you plan to shoot and deliver.

Remember that your goal is to attract interest in your project. You will probably have less than twenty minutes to sell your idea. You don't have to answer every question now: if a buyer is interested, he or she will happily follow up later and ask for more detailed information, such as the script, research documents, full budget, and more details on the funding strategy.

THE ART OF THE PITCH

Pitching is a key skill that all producers must master. You may be frightened, or think you are no good at it, but it is essential that you teach yourself how to improve.

Remember that throughout the life of your film you are always selling it. You may already have sold your idea to a writer, director or cast; now you are selling it to potential funders. If you are successful you will soon be selling it to an audience. Try to think of all these people in the same way.

What goes into the pitch is quite different from what you include in your proposal. The pitch is verbal. Think of it as the difference between the work of a solicitor and a barrister: the solicitor prepares the case for court, and the barrister stands before the jury and argues it. Your job is to engage your 'audience' and excite them about the project. That's all.

Although you need to perform well, the pitch is not a performance. Don't overact, or you may alienate the people you are trying to win over. Try to relax. You want to work with these people, and are starting a conversation to discover whether there is common ground between you. You want to be memorable, but not so memorable that they think you are a freak. It's like a first date, but without the worry of whether you will have to kiss or be kissed at the end of it. You might keep in mind the following guidelines:

- Spend time working up your pitch before you go into any meetings. Write a series of questions about the project and answer them. Then delete the questions. You are only interested in delivering the answers.
- Keep practising your technique. Shut yourself away and rehearse your pitch out loud. You can even record it and play it back. The first time you do this you will hate it (and yourself). But the next time it will be better.
- Be brief. Don't expect to speak for more than two minutes without interruption. If you can keep it even shorter, so much the better.
- Start by identifying the genre. Say up front if it's a comedy, a horror movie, or a coming-of-age drama. Don't leave your audience wondering about this during your pitch.
- Introduce your main character and explain what makes them and their story special. You don't need to use their name, give lots of backstory, or talk about the colour of their hair.
- Don't tell the whole story. This is the most common mistake made by new producers in pitch

meetings. And don't ramble. Remain concise and focused always.
- Try not to reference too many other films or similar projects. Avoid saying things such as 'It is *Mean Girls* meets *Black Mirror*'. You need your film to appear original and unique.
- Talk about the audience, and who you are making the film for. And do say why this project is important, and why it should be made *now*.
- Try to anticipate the questions you may be asked, and have answers ready.
- Always look at the person you are speaking to. Don't look down or out of the window.
- Only pitch one idea. Offering up a number of projects makes you seem uncommitted, vague and desperate.

JUGGLING

Raising production finance, whether for a short film, a low budget feature or a television series, is frequently a long and time-consuming business. It can literally take years, and can be frustrating and exhilarating in equal measure. As the producer you have to become a cheerleader, and convince everyone else that the film is really happening, even when you privately have real doubts.

It is really important to remain committed to your project and have faith in it. You knew it was a good project ten months ago, and it is still a good project now. The closer you come to having everything in place, the more difficult it can sometimes be to hold it all together. Some of your funding may be conditional on a particular actor, but you can't offer them a contract until all the money is committed. Other funding may be tied to a location or studio, which is only available on certain dates, and these may not be compatible with your main actor's schedule. And so on. In these last stages of fundraising the producer has to hold their nerve and continually reassure everyone else.

To misquote a line from the 1989 film *Field of Dreams*: 'If you build it, they will come.'

'The filmmaker requires money, camera and film.'

6
PRE-PRODUCTION

While the poet can write poems on a napkin in prison, the filmmaker requires money, camera and film.

Robert Stam,
Author and Professor at New York University

Pre-production (also known generally in the industry as prep) is arguably the most important stage of any production. This cannot be said too often or emphasized too strongly. Meticulous planning and preparation now will save you a vast amount of time and money during the shoot. In pre-production you can anticipate many of the problems you are going to encounter and prepare strategies for how to tackle them. If the producer gets the prep right, then his or her job during the shoot will be made much easier.

In theory, pre-production cannot begin until your film or series is fully financed and all the contracts have been signed. However, in practice there are many occasions when it is necessary for some of the pre-production to start before this has happened. The start of pre-production marks the moment everyone is committed to making the drama and the shoot dates are set. It is also the time when money starts to be spent in increasingly larger sums as the weeks go on. It's a critical time for the producer as the team that will make the programmes or film is assembled, and how they work together may determine the success or otherwise of the project.

SCRIPT MATTERS

As the producer, one of the most useful things you can ensure at the start of prep is that the script(s) are 'locked' and major changes can no longer be made. This is what would happen in an ideal world – but as few of us live in that, it almost never does. Changes are likely to continue (whether large or small) throughout this time. This can make life difficult, as the script is the blueprint for the film and the document from which everyone will work.

Once individual crew members arrive and start work, each of them will begin the process of 'breaking down the script' for their own purposes. Art department will make lists of all the sets, locations and props. The first assistant director will begin work on the shooting schedule, and the script supervisor will start timing each scene and marking story days (*see* below). But if the script continues to change substantially, much of this work will be worthless and it will all have to be done again.

So your first priority should be to ask all your investors, funding institutions, commissioners and executive producers to formally commit to making *this* script and stop giving you and the writer any more notes or asking for any further revisions. Next you need the director to agree to the shooting draft, and then it can, and should, be locked.

There are examples of script pages and their standard layout in Chapter 3 'Scheduling and Budgeting'. At the start of prep it is important for someone to read through the script carefully, to check that everything is correct and to make a list of notes and queries. Writers are very talented individuals but not always the most meticulous, and they can make mistakes. You need to find these and correct them now. In television production this would normally be the job of the script editor, but on low-budget films there may not be such a person and it might be you, the producer, who does this, since you already know the script better than anyone else. Or you can delegate this task to the production assistant or associate producer if there is one.

SCRIPT CHECKLIST

Scene numbers
Scene headings – INT or EXT/DAY or NIGHT
Set description
Characters – who is in the scene?
Story days
Time of day

STORY DAYS

Story days, also known as script days, must be identified in the shooting script and given a number. A story day means a new day in the story of the film. Your film may take place over a six-year period but only contain fifteen story days. For example:

Story Day 1: Sam and Jane meet – 1 July 2010
Story Day 2: Sam and Jane go on a date – 4 July 2010
Story Day 3: Sam and Jane get engaged – 31 December 2012
Story Day 4: Sam and Jane move in together – 1 April 2013
Story Day 5: The day before their wedding – 5 June 2014
Story Day 6: Wedding day – 6 June 2014
Story Day 7: Sam starts a new job – 3 January 2016
Story Day 8: Sam meets Rachel at work – 10 January 2016
Story Day 9: Sam and Rachel go for a drink after work – 12 February 2016

Story Day 10: Sam and Rachel spend the night together – 1 April 2016
Story Day 11: Sam forgets their wedding anniversary – 6 June 2016
Story Day 12: Jane finds out Sam has been lying to her – 1 July 2016
Story Day 13: Jane accuses Sam of cheating – 2 July 2016
Story Day 14: Sam moves out – 4 July 2016
Story Day 15: Jane files for divorce – 3 September 2016

Identifying story days is important for many reasons, and vital for the art department, costume and make-up, as not only will characters' clothes change with each story day, but there may be other physical changes, too. Over a six-year storyline they may change their hairstyle, grow a beard or gain weight. If one of your characters gets into a fight on Story Day 6, is punched and has a black eye, then the make-up team will know he or she has the black eye in the following days until it heals. As most films and series do not have the luxury of shooting sequentially, marking the story days is an important way of ensuring continuity.

It is normally the job of the script supervisor to identify and mark up the story days.

SCENE TIMINGS

Another important part of the script supervisor's job is to time the script. As the producer, you may already have done a rough timing some months ago to ensure you don't have too much or too little material. The first assistant director might also do their own timing when they sit down to do the first shooting schedule. What you are looking for now is a really accurate timing for how long each scene will be in the final edited version of the film.

The script supervisor will give you a full list of scene timings and a running total length. Look at this carefully. Despite all the previous warnings about locking the script, now is still the best time to deal with one that is too long or too short. Whilst there may be some flexibility in the running time for feature films, there is very little for the running time in television or other forms of drama series. The contract you signed with the network will specify a precise length for each episode. If you are delivering to a commercial channel, then a television hour might in reality be no more than forty-two minutes to allow for commercial breaks and trailers. Even a non-commercial broadcaster such as the BBC will want something less than sixty minutes to allow time for announcements and to promote other shows.

Therefore if you are contracted to deliver fifty-five minutes, then this is what you must do. And that time also includes credits in the form of an end roller of a specified length. So if your total script timing comes in at forty-seven minutes now, you should start to worry. And you should do the same if it comes in at seventy-five minutes. Clearly you want a little bit of flexibility for the edit, but you definitely do not want to shoot twenty minutes too much material and then end up with it lying on the cutting room floor.

During the shoot your editor will compare the estimated scene timings with the actual cut he or she is assembling, and should alert you if there are major discrepancies. This information is kept by the production co-ordinator, added to the daily progress report, and shared with key individuals, including the investors. If, after two weeks of a four-week shoot, you appear to have shot more than half the film, they may want to talk about cutting material or trimming scenes.

SCRIPT REVISIONS

When the script is formally locked, certain things can no longer be changed. In particular the scene numbers must be fixed, because if this doesn't happen it can cause chaos, and everyone working on the project becomes upset, for good reason. If there are changes after the script is locked (and there certainly will be some minor ones, at least), then a system for revisions must be strictly followed.

If a scene is cut, the scene appears in the script as:

SCENE 24 – OMITTED

If a scene is added, the scene is given a letter in addition to its number and appears in the script as:

SCENE 25A – INT CAFÉ DAY

The script supervisor will make detailed timings for each scene.

The next scene will be scene 26.

If another scene is added between 25A and 26 it will be numbered 25B.

Scene 26 does not change its number, however many scenes are inserted before it; so whenever anyone on the unit talks about 'scene 26', they all understand and are referring to the same scene.

The same system should also be applied to the script pages. So there may be new pages numbered 30A, 30B, and there may also be pages that are marked as 'PAGE 31 OMITTED' to show that its contents are no longer necessary and have been replaced or cut completely. This sounds confusing, but it is essential and it does work in practice.

Once the script is locked, there is also a system of coloured pages for further revisions. Even if the pages are not actually copied on to different coloured paper, they must still be given a colour. Traditionally the first colour is pink, so the first set of revisions to be issued after the shooting script will be known as the 'pink pages'. Thereafter it is usually blue, yellow and green, but really it is up to the production office, so long as everyone knows what the system is. Most films end up with multicoloured scripts.

It is also important to make sure that the colour and date of issue (for example, 'BLUE' 20.12.2017) is typed on the top of every page, so if it is photocopied on to white paper or read in a digital format it is still clear that there is a new or revised scene.

It is useful if the production co-ordinator who issues the pages also adds a cover note detailing the changes, and marks them with an asterisk as well. This makes it quicker to identify whether the change is to the action, which may impact on what and who is needed to shoot the scene, or is merely an amendment to the dialogue, and of interest mainly to the cast.

It is very important that all script changes are formally issued by the production office to all departments, cast and crew. I once worked on a film where the writer insisted on issuing her own script changes and coloured pages, and missed out some vital people when circulating the revisions. As a result we ended up without a costume for one of the characters who was added into a scene.

Negative Checking

Negative checking is a very necessary part of pre-production and must be done at an early stage. This is usually outsourced to specialized companies or people, sometimes former script editors, who have a keen eye for detail and know what to look for. Negative checking involves going through the script (or scripts) carefully and identifying any potential legal problems or issues. A written report on everything found should be sent to the producer.

To begin with they will need to check the names of all the characters, however small the part. They will want to make sure that if the drama is a fiction, there is no real living person of the same name who can claim their reputation has been damaged by association. For example, if your writer has created a fictional doctor who prescribes medication that accidentally kills a number of people, you need to make sure there is no real doctor with the same name, especially if it is an unusual one.

But you may need to be even more precise than this. For example, if your writer has created a fictional thirty-year-old, bi-racial female general practitioner living in a small town in the Midlands, and it turns out there is only one person like this living in that town, you could be accused of basing your character on them, even if their name is different. You might then have to change where they live, or their age, or something else about them. Unfortunately some writers get quite upset about having to change their characters' names and other details, but it is important to do so to avoid any potential legal action against the film.

In the same way you must check addresses. Is there a 10 Rillington Place in Newcastle, and if so, who lives there? Is there a Chief Inspector Hound? Names, addresses, phone numbers, car number plates and so on all need to be checked against the truth, and either cleared or amended to ones that are all right to use. Some production companies have lists of phone numbers that have been cleared for use in this way and have never been issued to the public.

Using Copyright Material

At this time it is also useful to mark up and make a full list of any copyright material, which you need to clear for the production. This may include:

Music and songs
Radio jingles and idents
Mobile phone ringtones
Works of art
Audiovisual material
Photographs
Posters
Book jackets and album covers
Logos
Computer screens
Newspapers and magazines
Toys and games

All these are in copyright, and you need permission from the owner to use them in your film. In many cases there will be a fee payable, so it is worth deciding how vital it is to use the actual image or footage, or whether someone on your team can generate the material instead. Most locations don't want to be identified by your film, so even with permission to film at a particular restaurant, hotel or business, you may be asked to change its name and create new signs and nameplates. The art department can also create fake packaging to avoid using real takeaway cartons, design new logos, mock up book jackets and newspaper front pages, and create graphics for computer screens.

Music and Songs

If your drama or documentary includes any scenes where actors, musicians or any other kind of performer are playing or singing live, in vision, there is some key planning to do now during prep. This could include, for example, scenes of someone singing in a nightclub, playing a piano in a bar, children singing in a school play, or adults performing karaoke. Crucially, you must make sure that you have obtained clearance to use the song or music in question.

Music copyright is broadly divided into two different types – publishing rights and performance rights. They are often owned and controlled by different companies. If your actor is performing the material in the film, then for now you only need to worry about the publishing rights. There is more information about performance and other music copyright in Chapter 8, 'Post-Production'.

The publishing rights to any song or piece of music will normally belong jointly to the composer and the lyricist and, as with all copyright, this extends for a period after their death. There may also be an original arrangement or orchestration, which is also subject to copyright. Most musical works are managed by a music publisher or controlled by a publishing library. They will collect the fees and royalties on behalf of the composer and lyricist, and distribute these to them on an agreed percentage. You don't need to worry too much about this distribution, you just need to make sure that you have cleared the track and obtained the rights you need. In the UK the quickest way to find out who owns the publishing rights for a song is to check with the Mechanical Copyright Protection Society (MCPS). They can advise if the song can be licensed and how much you will need to pay, and will issue a licence.

It is important to make sure that you obtain all the rights you need to satisfy the investors and distributors of your programme or film. Normally this will mean obtaining worldwide rights in all media. But if you know that you have no intention of selling the programmes abroad or releasing them theatrically, you may instead obtain a more limited, and therefore cheaper, licence.

Audiovisual Material including Archive Footage

If your programmes contain scenes where your characters are watching television, are at the cinema, or are viewing moving images on any other kind of screen, you need to source this material and clear its use. There are numerous film libraries, and their charges vary greatly depending on the age and popularity of the material and how many minutes or seconds you wish to use. There are also some libraries who will allow you to use material free of charge, especially if the end product has any educational benefit or is being produced by students. This may apply to some historical material and archive film. The BBC Motion Gallery, BFI National Archive, British Pathé Film Archive and British Council Film Collection are a few places to start.

If you require some very specific footage and want to show your characters watching a football match, other sporting event, or daytime quiz show, you will need to approach the companies who produce this content and own the copyright, and ask if it is available. If it is, they will quote you a price from their rate card, which will depend on who you are, what you are making, and how long the clip you need will be on screen. In some cases it may very well be cheaper for you to create your own material, or to use something you have produced in the past and own yourself.

You should never assume that footage is available and that you can clear it later. This is a far more expensive option, especially if the scene in which it appears is critical to the story and cannot be cut out in the edit.

PHOTOGRAPHS, POSTERS, PAINTINGS, MAPS, BOOK JACKETS AND ALBUM COVERS

Images are also subject to copyright, which must be checked and permission sought. This may be another situation where it is cheaper for someone in the art department to create something new for your fictional set, maybe even in the style of something already existing but with different detail.

In documentaries the original image may be needed for authenticity, and in this case a fee will almost certainly be payable, although the amount is usually negotiable.

LOGOS

All commercial logos are copyright designs and cannot be used without permission. Accidental use might occasionally be ignored if it is in the very back of shot, but any prominent featuring of logos should be avoided whenever possible. Clothing such as football shirts, T-shirts and handbags can be quite problematic. So are pizza boxes, takeaway coffee cups, drink cans, chocolate bars, mobile phones, and so on, and so on. Again, the advice is avoid where possible, or get substitutes designed and made.

COMPUTER SCREENS

Another area of concern can be the material featured on computer screens. Search engines and social media sites such as Google, Facebook, Instagram and Twitter all have copyright logos. Look closely at some major films and you will see that when characters are using these sites they feature screens where the layout is similar enough for the audience to assume it recognizes the brand, but different enough to avoid any accusations of stealing their designs or infringement of copyright.

NEWSPAPERS AND MAGAZINES

Many national newspapers are happy to allow drama producers to mock up fake front covers featuring 'news' stories, but you need their permission before doing so. Contact will usually be made by the production designer or art director. Once granted, their team can use the newspaper's own template and cover design to insert their own headline or photographs to suit the scenes in the film.

OTHER

There are many other products that fall under copyright rules, but they cannot all be listed here. They include games such as Scrabble and Monopoly, toys such as Barbie and Lego, and many other original designs. If you are in any doubt, make sure to check with lawyers or experts in this area.

PRE-PRODUCTION WEEK BY WEEK

The length of pre-production will vary considerably according to the complexity of the programmes or film you are making. For period films, those with lots of action, special effects or large set builds it will be longer. But for a contemporary low budget feature film with a four to five week shoot, you will probably have between six and eight weeks of formal prep. It cannot be stated too often that prep is a really important time. The more problems you can resolve then, the more smoothly the shooting period will run. Cutting prep time saves money in the short term, but may prove costly in the end.

Once pre-production starts, the number of people who are suddenly working for your production, and are therefore your responsibility, starts to expand considerably. Until now there have probably only been a very few people on board. You have been working closely with the writer for months or years. The director will have been with you for a few months at least. You may have employed a casting director or a location manager on an occasional or part-time basis to get you this far. And it is likely that a line producer or production manager has been involved in drawing up a budget and schedule. If this is a television series you have probably been working with a script editor. If you work for an organization you may have had some office support, but at most there has probably been a tight team of just four or five people.

Between the start of prep and the start of the shoot your team will expand rapidly until there are around sixty or more staff. This excludes the actors and supporting artists who are another large group. As the producer you must know everyone, remember their name, their job, and hopefully recall if you have worked with them before, where and when.

In the following example we will assume that this production has six weeks prep.

Week One: Shoot Minus Six

Aside from the line producer and the director, the first two people you will need to engage will be the location manager and the production designer. You will also need a casting director, but they will almost certainly have been with you for a few months already. For the director, finding and confirming locations, set design and casting will occupy most of the first two weeks of prep. It is to be hoped that during the later stages of development (soft or 'pre'-prep) you have already identified some key locations, and made decisions about whether you will be building sets in a studio or not.

Whilst the director is out on the road with the location manager and designer, the production office is being established. If you are fortunate enough to move into a space that's already set up, that's great. But it is quite common to find yourself working from an empty 'shell' where you have to bring everything in. I have set up production offices in an old hospital (for a medical drama), a school (for a police series) and even in an abandoned convent. None of them had any furniture, or a phone line, internet connection or heating. All of this had to be brought in fast, as well as hiring a photocopier and making sure the building was secure. Even with most people working from mobile phones, you will still need a landline and broadband connection, and probably an ISDN line, too. This can often be the hardest thing to install at short notice.

As the producer, another substantial amount of your time at this stage may be spent in interviewing and engaging heads of department (HODs). Although you may already have met many of the people you aim to be working with, the nature of production means that when you finally get the 'green light', some of these people will have become unavailable and taken other jobs. The key creative roles you need to appoint are production designer, director of photography, editor, production sound mixer, first assistant director, costume designer, make-up designer and production accountant. You may also need to appoint a special effects company.

You may have to get the approval of your investors or commissioning editor before you appoint some or all of these key roles. HOD contracts will be reasonably standard, but terms, credit, and any special conditions must be agreed by both the line producer and the producer as they have financial implications. These may include whether HODs are being provided with a hire car by the production, or are expected to use their personal vehicle and claim mileage or petrol; also, whether or not any accommodation or *per diems* are offered as part of the contract, and if so, how this will be arranged: is

there an allowance they can use to make their own private arrangements, or is the production office making these bookings and picking up the bills? The arrangements may be different if the production is shooting in multiple places, but it should all be made clear at the start to avoid any misunderstandings on either side.

Once all the HODs are appointed, they become responsible for selecting the remaining members of their team. Most will have regular crew with whom they like to work. However, they should run all appointments through you and the line producer for approval before confirming them. The line producer will negotiate the deals, and the production office will issue each member of the

Building a set on location in Scotland.

Image attribution: Silent Storm Productions / Neon Films

Image attribution: Silent Storm Productions / Neon Films

The construction team includes carpenters, plasterers and painters.

crew with a contract of employment when they begin working on the production. Once the individual contract is signed, the production is normally committed to paying that person for at least two weeks, which is the standard notice period should anything go wrong and the production be forced to close down.

CASH FLOW AND ESCROW

The production accountant is one of the first people to join the production office, and their first task is to set up a cash-flow schedule. As prep and production progress, the weekly outgoings will rise exponentially, and this must be anticipated and managed. Some broadcasters and distributors will advance their contribution to the budget during this time, and pay it to the production on a monthly or weekly basis. Other investors will not pay until they receive delivery of the finished film and all its elements. This means that arrangements may have to be made to borrow the money to ensure weekly costs can be met.

It is normal practice to set up a separate bank account to fund the production; in most cases this is a legal requirement. Strict rules will be in place about who can approve payments from the account – normally the production accountant plus one of either the producer or line producer. In addition, in many circumstances there is a requirement to hold at least two weeks' wages for everyone on

Production design is one of the largest costs for any production.

Image attribution: Silent Storm Productions / Neon Films

The finished church as it appears in the film, *The Silent Storm*.

Image attribution: Silent Storm Productions / Neon Films

the payroll (including the cast) in what is known as an 'escrow account'. This is to ensure they can be paid what is due to them in the event that production stops for any reason.

Don't be surprised if your production accountant talks directly to staff in the accounts or business affairs department at the broadcaster, distributor or sales agency. It is quite normal for there to be a dialogue between them. Everyone worries about how the money is being spent, and likes to be reassured that it is being properly managed and controlled.

Week Two: Shoot Minus Five

Five weeks away from the start of principal photography the production designer will be on board and will be adding to his or her team. This will include the art director and production buyer. It may also include a construction manager if there are sets to design and build. The design team will be breaking down the script and preparing a budget for your approval. Design is one of the most expensive areas of production, and the one where it is easiest to overspend if you don't keep a constant and careful check on it. Insist on regular weekly meetings with the production designer and the line producer from now onwards, schedule them into everyone's calendar and don't let this slip.

THE CASTING PROCESS

You may already have attached some of your key cast to the project in order to confirm the commission and funding. But during prep a great deal of the director's time will be taken up with casting the other parts. These will range from cameos, to day players and children. Experienced directors may know who they want for some of these parts, but may still want to meet them to talk about the part, or see if they have changed a lot, gained or lost weight, or aged significantly since their last meeting. This means setting up auditions, meetings and casting calls. The number of actors seen can vary hugely. Actors should

always be contacted through their agents. Even if you know them personally and have worked together in the past, it is unprofessional to approach them directly.

In the UK, most actors are members of the actors' union, Equity. In the USA they belong to the Screen Actors Guild, known as SAG. Children under the age of eighteen cannot join a union. Equity has a website for actors called Spotlight, where you can search from hundreds of profiles and can also advertise paid jobs. An alternative UK site is Mandy.com, where many different film and television jobs are advertised, including both cast and crew. Professional casting directors don't generally advertise acting jobs in this way, but many student filmmakers or short filmmakers do. If this is your approach you must first write a clear 'casting brief' explaining what the part is and giving a summary of the project, who the team is, where you are filming, and the approximate dates. It is very important when advertising a role that whenever possible you make it clear the part is openly available to actors from all racial groups.

Early in pre-production the director will sit down with the casting director and discuss a 'wish' list of actors for every one of the characters who speaks or has lines in the film or series. Both will make suggestions, and as producer you may also want to have an input. The casting director will normally bring recent headshots and, following the meeting, may share links to a particular actor's recent work.

Armed with the wish list, the casting director's office checks the availability of all the actors, and crosses off any who are not free during the dates you plan to shoot. There may be some actors who have limited availability and they might stay on the list for now, but with the limitations clearly marked. At the next meeting, the director and casting director decide who should be called in for a first round of meetings and auditions. The casting director then begins to make the arrangements by calling their agents.

The actual times and appointments for the casting will be arranged by the casting director, their assistant, or someone in their office. The production office is responsible for booking a room or space where these auditions and meetings take place. It may need to be quite large if the director wants the actors to do anything more than sit and read. It has become normal practice to film the auditions and meetings for later reference and to show to others, so an unsophisticated camera on a tripod will be required as well. Ideally this is simple enough for the director or casting director to operate – it is unhelpful to have an extra person attend auditions just for this task.

It is also important to have a separate place away from the audition room for actors to wait before they are called to meet the director. It can be embarrassing for actors to run into other people who are up for the same part, although most are sanguine about this and understand it is inevitable.

Prior to the audition the actor should have received an email confirming the exact time and place for the casting, and a mobile phone number for someone in the building or attending the session in case they get lost, delayed, or can't find the entrance. Trust me, it happens. Ideally there should be someone available who is not required in the actual audition, but is there to meet and greet them, show them where to wait, and offer water or tea.

They should also have been sent in advance the script pages for the scene or scenes they will be reading on the day. Depending on the size of the part, they may ask to read the whole script before the meeting, or they may just want to know more about the character they are auditioning to play. Before sending out the audition pages, known also as the 'sides', the director may choose to remove any physical descriptions of the character first. This includes hair and eye colour, height, skin tone and so on. Some writers love to include this kind of detail in scripts, but it is far better to open the casting as widely as possible.

Whether you, the producer, decide to attend all the casting sessions or not is up to you, and how you decide to prioritize your precious time. Some producers sit through them all, while others only attend for key roles, catch up by watching

the filmed content, and leave meeting day players and decisions about the minor roles to the director.

The director may wish to see some actors again, either alone or alongside someone with whom they will be working. This is known either as a 'recall' or a 'call back'. This may be especially important if casting children, when you may wish to see how well they interact with those who might be playing their parents or siblings.

This is a good place to mention something else about the management of casting sessions. It is very important that there is always someone in the audition or casting room with the director and the actor he or she is meeting. All producers should be aware of the potential dangers associated with anyone meeting actors privately or in inappropriate or unprofessional situations.

Experienced actors are used to attending auditions, and understand that the director will be seeing a number of different people for every part. Younger and less experienced actors are likely to be more nervous and may need a little reassurance or conversation at the start of their audition. In general, for most parts, a first audition should not be any longer than twenty minutes at most. It will begin with a brief chat, hopefully to relax the actor and answer any questions they may have about the role. They will then 'read' the sides once. Usually the casting director will read in the lines for the other main person in the scene. If the producer or someone else is in the room they might read any other parts. It is preferable that the director does not read, and can focus on observing the actor.

After the first 'cold' read there may be notes from the director about an alternative reading or approach. The scene is then read again. On the third reading it may be filmed. After this the actor leaves, and there is usually a brief discussion between director, casting director and producer before the next person is called in.

A full day of auditions and casting can be an exhausting process. Sometimes the first person seen is obviously perfect and everyone following feels wrong. Sometimes you can spend a whole day and none of the actors is right.

OFFERING THE ROLE

When you and your director have selected the actor you want to engage for a particular part, you make them an 'offer'. The system of offers is well established, and an offer is considered binding even before a contract has been signed or any paperwork exchanged.

Once you have made an offer to an actor you cannot offer the same part to anyone else until the conversation with them and their agent has been concluded, whether successfully or not, and the actor contracted. Only if the negotiations are un-successful for some reason can the offer be with-drawn and the part become available again and offered to your next choice.

Sometimes you will be asked by an agent if it is an 'offer' before the actor will agree to meet you. This can be an awkward situation to manage. It normally only applies to well known actors, or if an agent thinks their client should not have to audition for the role. It is important to be very clear in this conversation, and ideally to let the casting director manage it for you. Don't agree to meet any actor in these circumstances unless you are absolutely certain that you and the director want them for the role. And double check first with anyone who has approval that they want them too.

When the actor has been confirmed, the cast-ing director issues a 'casting advice note'. This document summarizes the agreement reached, and allows time for a full contract to be prepared. Information on the casting advice note will include the name of the role and the actor who has been cast, contact details for both the artist and their agent, performance dates, the agreed fee, de-tails of billing, and any special stipulations that might apply. This may then be shared with other members of the production team, particularly the assistant directors and costume departments. The production office needs certain information about the actors, including private addresses, phone numbers, health issues and dietary restrictions. However, this information must remain strictly con-fidential and absolutely never shared with anyone outside a small and agreed group of people.

Different forms of standard cast contracts are available from Equity. These include an agreement for students making short films – and these can change, so check the website and download the most recent and most appropriate contract for your particular production. Normally contracts are issued by the production office, but they should be carefully checked by you first. Information about dates and special conditions must be shared with the first AD, as this will impact on the schedule and management of the shoot.

CASTING AND WORKING WITH CHILDREN AND MINORS

There are special rules for working with children and minors under the age of eighteen, and it is es-sential that you understand these and follow them precisely. This is not only industry practice, but is part of government legislation regarding the cir-cumstances in which children are allowed to work. The rules vary slightly in England, Northern Ireland, Scotland and Wales. Different rules will also apply when filming abroad, and in different states within the USA. You must check locally exactly what these are, and how they differ from the UK. Also remember that if you are taking UK-based children abroad to work, UK law will still apply.

Any child under the school leaving age in the UK must have a special licence to work. The pro-ducer, casting director or production co-ordinator needs to apply for this licence from the relevant local authority where the child lives or goes to school. In some areas, such as London, these are issued by the local borough, for example Camden or Westminster. In the rest of the country it will be the county council, for example Kent. It can take up to twenty-one days for a licence to be granted (some do issue them more quickly), so you must allow at least this amount of time to obtain one. The child's parent will also need to provide a medical certificate, and the written permission of their headteacher for the child to miss school if required.

All children under sixteen must be supervised and accompanied on and off set at all times by a 'chaperone'. This can be a parent, but does not have to be. There are professional chaperones who do this for a living, have been checked by the police, and are licensed. In most cases they have a better understanding of the demands of film production than the child's parents, and often take better care of them. In my experience of working extensively with children and teenagers I have generally found their parents to be more difficult and time-consuming than the young performers! If you can persuade them to agree to you hiring a chaperone instead of coming to set themselves, this can sometimes be a big advantage, even if it is more expensive. The chaperone must stay with their charges at all time, whether on or off set, in rehearsals, or whilst travelling to and from work. One chaperone is allowed to supervise more than one child, depending on their ages.

How many hours a child is allowed to work each day is determined by their age, but minors are never allowed to work more than five days in a row without a rest day. They are not permitted to start work before 7am or finish after 11pm (10pm for under five-year-olds). Travel to and from the set is considered part of the working day, and the child must also be accompanied by the chaperone during their journey. If they need to stay overnight, the chaperone must also stay with them in the same place. The table below shows the hours of work for different aged children. The younger the child, the fewer hours they are permitted to work. A child between five and eight years old is permitted to travel to and from the place of work, rest, learn, eat and be with the unit for eight hours, but they can only be 'working' for three of these. Work includes rehearsal time on set, so this is a clear restriction to the working day.

In all cases it is advisable to cast a child as old as possible, even if their playing age is younger. Casting a young-looking nine-year-old to play a seven- or eight-year-old will allow you two further hours with them on set, and they will also be more mature. With very young children and babies it is sometimes common to cast a pair of twins and therefore double the number of available hours.

Except at weekends and during statutory school holidays, children must also be tutored or schooled to make up for work they are missing. A room must be made available, and the tutor must be paid for by the production.

Additional risk assessment will normally be required if you are planning to work with children. Their safety and well-being must always be a priority. Care must be taken not to expose them to any danger or health risks. They cannot be asked to undertake 'activities beyond their physical and psychological capabilities'. They must be given regular fifteen-minute rest breaks. Local authorities in the UK are allowed to turn up unannounced on a film set and check that children are being properly cared for and supervised. If they feel the rules

Age of child	Maximum number of hours in one day at place of performance or rehearsal	Maximum total number of hours of performance or rehearsal in one day	Maximum continuous number of hours of performance or rehearsal in one day
Birth until child reaches five	5	2	30 minutes
Five until child reaches nine	8	3	2.5 hours
Nine to school leaving age	9.5	5	2.5 hours

Working with Children: Log of Hours

Production/Film: _____

Producer: _____

Date of Production: _____

Child Peformance Licence _____

Parent's Name: _____

Chaperon's Name: _____

Place of Production*: _____

*If UK, please specify England, Scotland, Wales or Northern Ireland

Child's Name: _____

Child's Date of Birth _____

Age on Date of Production: 0 Years, 0 Months _____

Legal Guardian's Name: _____

Chaperone's Licence No.: _____

Start Time (hh:mm)	End Time (hh:mm)	Total	Activity	Comments

Total Times		
Rehearsal	
Performance (On Set)	
Meal Break	
Rest Break	
Wait Time	
Education/Tutoring Time	
Other	
Total	

_____
Producer's Signature, Date

_____
Parent or Chaperone's Signature, Date

All children's working hours must be recorded.

are being ignored or broken they can close down the set.

The production office must keep a detailed record of all the hours worked by every child, and what they were doing. This includes when they were collected, when they had a costume fitting, when they rehearsed, and when they arrived on set for filming. All their rest and meal breaks must be listed, as well as the amount of time in tutoring. This must be signed by a member of the production team, either the first AD, producer or line producer, and by the chaperone or parent. This is a legal requirement and should not be overlooked. It is also a legal requirement to keep these records for at least six months after filming is complete.

One final consideration for working with children is the use of their image in publicity and other material, especially if it may appear on the internet. Again, there are strict child protection rules to preserve their privacy and safety. You must obtain written permission from the child's parent or guardian for each photograph you wish to use, and in this case the chaperone's permission is not enough. This applies to any 'behind the scenes' photographs, as well as to photographs of underage supporting artists and passers-by. Care must be taken not to film children in the street accidentally without obtaining consent. The permission form should clearly state the purpose of the photograph, and the circumstances in which it may be used.

Take special care not to use photographs of children in inappropriate clothing, such as swimming costumes, and never allow photographs of children in any state of undress. Children should not be named or identified in the photograph, and all pictures of children should be kept securely to avoid any danger of their misuse. If you film children during auditions and castings you are advised to delete the footage as soon as the casting process is complete.

Week Three: Shoot Minus Four

It is to be hoped that by now the main locations are all confirmed, and contracts are being negotiated and drawn up by the location manager and then issued by the line producer.

This week the first assistant director (known as the 'first AD') will normally start working full time on the production. This is a role that can literally make or break a successful shoot. The first AD is responsible for running the 'floor'. They manage every day of the shoot, and ensure the production remains on schedule and that each specific day's filming is completed. Their responsibilities also include giving direction to the supporting artists, child welfare and working hours, as well as health and safety on the set. But their first job when they start on the production is to begin work on the shooting schedule.

Although you, or the line producer, may have already produced a schedule in order to budget the project, the first AD will now prepare a more detailed one for the actual shoot. He or she will take into account where the locations are, when the actors are available, the best time of day to film, and how long each scene or sequence will take to film. They should have conversations with the director about how many set-ups they anticipate for each scene, and detailed discussions about any action sequences, special effects or stunts.

At the end of their first week, the first AD should be able to present their first draft of the shooting schedule for discussion at the first main production meeting. This meeting should be scheduled by the production co-ordinator, and will probably take place on the following Monday morning, allowing everyone concerned to spend the weekend going through the first schedule.

COSTUME AND WARDROBE

With most of the casting in place, the costume designer will also normally start full time on the production four weeks before filming. If this is a period or science fiction film with a lot of complex costumes to be made individually, they might have started earlier. As soon as any member of the cast is formally agreed and a casting advice note issued, production staff can approach the actor to arrange costume meetings and wardrobe fittings. Depending on his or her schedule, the director may be present at some of these, or may look at photographs, samples or footage after.

The costume department will do their own breakdown of the script and work out how many different outfits each character needs, and how many 'repeats' of each outfit might be required. 'Repeats' are necessary when one outfit might be ruined during the filming and a second, third or fourth might be needed for subsequent takes. For example, if the character has to jump into a lake or pool they will need an identical set of dry clothes to put on for take two, when they have to do it again.

The rest of the costume team will join in in subsequent weeks as production approaches. The costume department comprises the costume designer (head of department), the wardrobe supervisor (their main assistant) and one or more wardrobe assistants. During the shoot it may also be necessary to have additional staff or 'dailies' on particular days when cast and crowd numbers are high.

You will already have discussed the costume budget with the line producer. The costume designer will be given this figure, and must be asked to provide you with a budget breakdown to show how they plan to stay within it. It is important to make sure everyone understands what is included (or excluded) from the budget. For example, does the budget include all payments to daily staff, all transport and travel expenses when out buying or attending fittings, and so on. The costume designer and team must keep receipts for everything they buy, and account for how the money has been spent, including petty cash as well as major purchases and hires. Regular reports and updates on this are essential to avoid any unpleasant surprises later.

PLANNING PUBLICITY

One of the key responsibilities of the producer is to oversee publicity and marketing. You may hire a professional publicist, appoint an agency, or work with the marketing department of your broadcaster or distributor, but there are still some important things you will need to take care of yourself.

The first of these, in pre-production, will be when to issue press releases, and when to make announcements on social media. It is customary to issue a statement announcing the commencement of filming, and to put a notice in one or more trade publications. Investors like this, and feel comforted that something tangible is finally happening with all their money.

Insist that all press releases must be approved by you. You know the production best, and understand the personalities involved. You need to strike the right balance between giving information and not releasing too much. Keep details of the plot to a minimum, and never give away any spoilers. You must make sure every detail is correct. Are the cast listed in the correct order? Actors' agents check these things rigorously, and if their client is meant to have second billing and appears third in the list they will be on the phone to you in an instant.

Local film offices can be a fantastic support to productions but in return often expect publicity. I've worked on films where they have made their own announcements with genuine excitement at having a famous actor filming in their town. However, if this means that your sleepy village exterior is suddenly full of sightseers and movie tourists, it can only make your shooting days harder. So try to encourage them to wait until after you have filmed, and offer them photos of the star on location in return for this.

As soon as you have a draft shooting schedule from the first AD you can also start to plan which days you wish to have a stills photographer on set, and to check their availability. Stills photographers are freelancers, and the good ones are often busy on a number of different productions. You should aim to have a photographer for at least ten days if possible, so that you get a variety of shots. Think about which scenes and locations are likely to be visually strong. But also remember to get photographs of all your main cast in costume and working.

Week Four: Shoot Minus Three

You should expect all casting and locations to be confirmed by now. The director needs to focus their energy on making the film, and this week should be in meetings with the production designer and director of photography, and starting work on his or her shot list. It is not helpful if he or she is still out on the road for days, or in long casting sessions.

This week the second AD will probably start to assist the first AD, and will begin breaking down the script for crowd numbers in each scene.

PRODUCTION MEETINGS

From now until the shoot starts there must be weekly production meetings. Different departments will need other meetings between themselves, but a formal weekly meeting of all the key personnel including each of the heads of department is vital. The production co-ordinator should manage these meetings and add them to everyone's calendar. At the first meeting the main subject for discussion will be the first draft shooting schedule, which was hopefully circulated to everyone at the end of the previous week.

CAMERA TEAM

Most directors have a strong view about who they want to work with as their director of photography

(DoP) or cinematographer. The appointment of this key individual will usually be their choice, in consultation with the producer. Conversations with the DoP should start early and must include the production designer, who needs to be part of any discussion about the tone and colour palette chosen.

But there is very little real preparation the DoP can do until most of the sets are built and the locations are finalized, and they do not normally begin working full time until three weeks before the shoot. They are one of the most highly paid members of the team, and it is costly to have them on board too early. You may agree to pay a daily or half-daily fee to attend some of the early meetings.

The camera department provides lists of all the equipment they will need.

For production, a crucial decision will be the choice of camera and whether you are shooting on film or on a digital format. This has financial implications, and you must be involved in the discussion. The DoP is asked to provide a full equipment list, detailing everything they want for the whole shoot. This can be eye-watering. The line producer will then have to obtain quotes for the list, and sit down with you and the DoP to decide what the production can afford and what it can't. This is never easy, but in my experience, DoPs frequently ask for more than they really need, and it is essential to make sure you are not hiring expensive equipment that never gets taken off the truck. There may also be a discussion about additional camera crew if you decide to use a steadicam, or other specialist equipment.

Another decision to be taken is whether the DoP will operate the camera or bring someone on to take this role. I have worked with both systems. Provided communication between them is good, it is usually quicker to have an operator as well as a DoP. You may also want to discuss whether any scenes or sequences will be shot using more than one camera. For action scenes or large crowds it can be useful to get as much additional footage or 'coverage' as possible, and having a second camera with you on these days will save time. Possibly the DoP may elect to operate the second camera for some sequences, or you will need to budget for an additional member of the team on these days.

When shooting with two cameras in this way, it is essential that both point in the same direction and shoot down the same line. There is another kind of multi-camera shooting used in studios, mainly for continuing dramas and comedy, where cross shooting is employed, and this is a very different technique.

Next you will need to decide on the aspect ratio. The aspect ratio refers to the shape of the image, and describes the relationship between the width and the height. There are some common formats used in film and television. In the early days of television a standard 4:3 ratio was used, which suited the square shape of the television screen well. More recently the 16:9 ratio has become the standard for high definition television production. For features the 1.85:1 widescreen ratio is popular. The choice of aspect ratio is an aesthetic decision, but you should also check your contracts with distributors or broadcasters to see if they have made any stipulations about this.

If you are shooting on film, a decision about which laboratory to use for processing is necessary. If you are shooting with a digital camera there are further decisions to take on precisely which camera to choose, and then on frame rate, resolution, and the optimum shooting ratio. You will also need to decide on what lenses to order, and how many. Most camera packages come with a standard set of four or five different lenses, but your DoP may want to add others for certain shots. Producers must remain up to date with developing technology, and understand the implications of all these choices. There are regular trade events where you can meet and talk to the major camera and lighting rental houses, suppliers and manufacturers.

The DoP will select the other members of their team, including the first AC, the second AC, the grip and gaffer, and will give their details to the line producer. But once again, these all need your approval.

Once the choice of camera and lenses is decided, the camera department will arrange a series of camera tests. There will also be a meeting with production and the first AD to discuss any special equipment requested for certain scenes – for example cranes, cherry pickers, drones, tracking vehicles and so on.

STORYBOARDS

A storyboard is a visual or graphic tool used to illustrate how certain sequences will appear in the finished film. They can be extremely useful when explaining to others how the shots will be constructed and framed. The storyboard looks something like a comic strip and consists of a series of squares, with pictures to represent each shot in the sequence. The picture may be an actual photograph, an elaborate drawing, or just a very rough sketch. The point is not to make a great work of art, but to convey information clearly. The dialogue from the script may be included in the picture or immediately underneath. The pictures are annotated with notes about what is happening in the shot, and may include decisions about lens size, camera moves, angles, framing and so on.

Previsualization software (normally shortened to Previz) is now a very useful tool for filmmakers, directors, DoPs and VFX supervisors, to illustrate how they believe a sequence or series of shots should look, and to provide information in prep, which can avoid long delays on set. Previz allows them to try out different versions of the shot before the expense of shooting it for real is incurred. It also allows directors to explain to others exactly what they are planning, and for the other HODs to question them about their ideas. It is mostly used for scenes involving complicated actions, stunts and special effects.

Week Five: Shoot Minus Two

Two weeks before the shoot you will walk into the production office and suddenly realize how many people are now involved in the production and are your responsibility. It can be a scary or exhilarating moment when the project feels real for the first time: it is no longer just an idea you discussed with a writer months or years ago, it is actually happening. Enjoy the moment now, because from here on you will not have a second for personal reflection again until after the wrap party.

The level of activity in a production office two weeks before the shoot is very intense. The production team has now confirmed equipment deals for camera, lighting, grip and sound as well as catering, location facilities, transport, accommodation, studios and edit suites. Meetings will be taking place to agree any special requirements

Storyboards for an action sequence.

such as visual and special effects, animals, drones, cranes and so on. Things are arriving, and the office is filling up with people and stuff. If you don't already have one, you definitely need an office runner from now.

In the production design department the props master will have set up the props store and started to log everything for easy access. Make sure your director finds time to visit the store and test any complicated props to see how they work. Many hours have been wasted on shooting days when a particular prop fails to perform as it is meant to. Check now, when there is still time to change or amend it.

The costume department will now be arranging fittings with all members of the cast. This is a good time to meet and introduce yourself to any you have not already met at auditions, or to say hello and welcome them on board if you have. It will be appreciated. During the shoot, one of the producer's key jobs is keeping the cast happy so they can do their best work. Dropping in for a brief chat now is a good start to your ongoing relationship. They may also mention anything that is worrying them, from accommodation to a particular scene. It is good to find this out now, and offer reassurance that their worries are being taken seriously.

Depending on the scale and complexity of the production, the make-up designer may begin this week. On some films there is less for them to do during prep, but they may be arranging hair dying, contact lenses or wig fittings, or 'on camera' make-up tests.

Another important person who joins this week is the script supervisor. They will time the script and produce a list of scene times, assign the story days and discuss the exact time of day each scene is meant to take place. You should arrange a meeting early in the week with the script supervisor, as they may have questions about the script that only you can answer.

A second draft of the shooting schedule should appear this week, and further meetings arranged to discuss it in detail with relevant HODs.

The end of week five is the time for the technical recce, also known sometimes as the 'tech scout', or more often simply as the 'recce'.

RECCE

The recce is a very important part of the pre-production, and should be carefully planned by the location manager so that it runs efficiently and smoothly. Essentially this is a chance for all the key individuals to visit each location or set in advance of filming there. As a general rule the recce will take two full days or longer. I recommend taking as many of your team as possible, but as a minimum the following must all go on the recce:

Producer and line producer
Director
First AD
Location manager and assistant
Production designer
Art director
DoP
Camera operator
Gaffer
Grip
Production sound mixer

Normally the production office books a minibus and driver to take everyone around. This may be the first time some of these people have spent time together, and the discussions on the bus between locations can be a valuable exchange of information. On arrival at the location, the director should explain briefly which scenes are to be shot here, and how much of the area will be seen. The location manager should inform everyone of any specific restrictions associated with the location, any areas out of bounds, and where the unit base will be located. I have been on recces where it has only become apparent at that time that the unit base is actually in the middle of one of the shots the director has in mind.

There will also be a discussion with the DoP and gaffer about power. Is a generator required, and if so, where will it be parked? The grip will want to examine the condition of the ground, and comment on the practicality of laying track or boards. The production sound mixer will be listening out for any problems such as distant traffic noise, flight paths and so on.

I recommend that when possible, a location should be recced at the same time of day as you are planning to shoot there. You might recce a street at 11am and find it quiet and peaceful, and then turn up for filming at 3pm and discover a school is coming out and the previously quiet street is full of children and their parents.

After the end of the recce a production meeting takes place with everyone attending. This meeting is chaired by the first AD, and the agenda will be a discussion of each of the breakdown sheets. Every scene should be talked through, and special

requirements agreed. You should allow at least four hours for this meeting. At the end, many decisions will have been taken and agreement reached. But there will also be a list of questions still to be resolved, and these will be everyone's priority for the final week of prep.

RISK ASSESSMENT

Risk assessment is an important part of all productions, however small. It is a legal requirement, and your insurance company may wish to see a risk assessment for each location and for any dangerous sequences. The purpose of risk assessment is to do the following:

- Identify all potential hazards and all those who may be affected by them;

Any Production - Risk Assessment Form

Production Title: Date(s) of Shoot: Assessor: Date of Assessment:

HAZARD	PERSONS WHO MIGHT BE HARMED	RISK CONTROLS IN PLACE	ACTIONS TO MINIMIZE SEVERITY OF ANY INCIDENT	LEVEL OF RISK
Working at heights (up to 27m) on Ferris wheel - risk of camera, equipment and/or objects falling.	Cast/Crew and Members of Public	Camera will be attached securely to fixed part of cabin. Any equipment inside cabin to be secured so it cannot cause injury in the case of wind or the Ferris wheel stopping abruptly. Camera will not be leant / placed outside the area of the cabin at any time.	First aid kit on set. Details of local A&E department on file on set. Check phone reception at location.	LOW to MEDIUM
Filming interior with boiling pot on the stove - risk of accident /injuries	Cast and crew	Film wide shots with boiling pot and for medium shots remove it from set or turn it off. Minimum distance of 1m from boiling pot for crew and equipment. Do not fill pot with liquids to top. Ensure that pot is stable on the stove before bringing water to boil.	First aid kit on set. Fire extinguisher on set Have the contact details of the local medical facilities and emergency services on location. Check phone reception at location.	LOW
Filming exterior locations - risk of hot / inclement weather /exposure	Crew/cast	Have a garden umbrella or a large umbrella for camera. Check weather forecast. Accordingly advise crew and cast to wear appropriate clothing and footwear for location. Have refreshing drinks available on location.	First aid kit on set. Have the contact details of the local medical facilities and emergency services on location. Check phone reception at location.	LOW
Filming cattle - risk of accidents	Cast and crew	An animal wrangler will be on set and supervise cattle movements. Crew and equipment are located in minimum 2-metre distance from the cattle. When filming cattle still, tie his legs to strong beams with rope.	First aid kit on set. Have the contact details of the local medical facilities and emergency services on location. Check phone reception at location.	LOW

Sign and Date: Assessor..   Checked by ....

An example of a risk assessment.

- Evaluate the risk of each of these hazards;
- Identify and prioritize appropriate measures to control or eliminate the risk;
- Review and update these measures as necessary if the situation changes.

In your risk assessment you must anticipate all potential hazards, and provide an explanation for how the risk will be mitigated. Examples of this may include the following:

- Carrying a first aid kit with you to treat minor injuries;
- Ensuring loose cables are secured and covered, and are not a trip hazard;
- Having an extinguisher close to any action involving flames or fire;
- Providing warm clothing when filming in extreme conditions or on water;
- Clearly marking emergency exits and escape routes;
- Making sure that all equipment has been professionally tested and fitted.

For some filming situations the independent contractor you have hired may need to provide their own additional risk assessment, for example if you are using an animal handler, action vehicle or special effects company.

INSURANCE

All film productions, including shorts and student films, must have adequate insurance cover in place before shooting begins. If you don't, you could become personally liable for any claims against the production. For larger productions you may need to have some types of insurance in place earlier in pre-production, as soon as you begin employing cast and crew. The main kinds of insurance required for films are described below, but you should also take legal advice to ensure you have covered all possible risks.

Public Liability (PL) insurance protects you from any claims brought against the production for injury to third parties, or damage to third party property – for example, if a member of the public injures themselves by tripping over a cable, or if a lighting stand damages the polished wooden floor of a location. Public liability is not a legal requirement, but you will not be able to get a permit to film without it. All locations, including local authorities, public and private landlords, will ask you to produce proof of PL cover before giving you permission to film or work on their premises. Normally they request a copy of your Certificate of Public Liability Insurance, also known as the 'Verification of Insurance'. Cover is usually in bands of £1m, £2m, £3m, £5m and £10m, although most local authorities ask for a minimum of £5m or £10m.

Employers' Liability insurance protects you from claims brought against the production for injury to people who are working for you. This is mainly your cast and crew, who are your employees. But the definition of 'employee' can include volunteers, freelancers and supporting artists – even your friends who come along to be part of a crowd in the pub scene. Legally someone does not need to be paid to be an employee. If you ask them to turn up at a particular time and a particular place, they are your responsibility whether you pay them or not. If you engage the services of someone who is working under your control, then by law you have what is known as a 'duty of care' towards them. So it is your legal responsibility to have employers' liability cover, and you are also required to display the certificate of cover in a prominent place on the wall of the office to prove this.

Equipment Insurance covers all 'hired-in' equipment used on the shoot. This includes camera, grip equipment, lights, sound equipment, editing equipment as well as any office equipment such as photocopiers and printers. When you discuss their hire, the rental company will give you a valuation figure, known also as the 'sum insured', which is the cost of replacing each item new at today's price. This figure may be used to calculate the premium you will need to pay.

The hire company may also give you a figure for 'loss of hire' or 'continuing hire'. This is the usual amount they charge for hiring out the equipment you are renting. This may be a different figure from the price you have negotiated with them, and will normally be the price on their standard 'rate card'. If a piece of equipment is damaged while on hire to you, the rental house can change you 'loss of hire' for the time it takes to be repaired and when it is not available to be hired to another production.

If a member of the crew is providing their own equipment, you should check that it is already covered and they have their own insurance policy. It should not be included under the production policy.

Producers' Indemnity insurance (also sometimes referred to as an 'all risks' policy) is an optional insurance that covers the additional costs of completing the production in certain circumstances – for example, if a member of the cast became ill or broke their leg, and filming could not be completed on schedule. It may also cover rescheduling if a location were damaged by fire just before you were due to film there. Not everything is covered, and some circumstances will not be included, so check the small print very carefully.

Errors and Omissions insurance covers legal liability and your defence costs against lawsuits brought against you or the film. This covers the production against infringement of intellectual property, breaches of confidentiality, failure to give credit for authorship, trademark infringement and so on. It can be quite an expensive policy, but some investors and funders will insist that you obtain E&O insurance.

Filming Abroad and in the USA. If you intend to film abroad for all or part of your production you may need other types of insurance as well as all the above. Employers' liability won't cover your foreign crew, although it will extend to anyone from the UK whilst they are working abroad. In the USA you need to obtain 'workers compensation' insurance for your employees there. In Europe there are other local regulations, which must be complied with.

If you take UK cast and crew to film abroad you should check what medical insurance may be required. In Europe there is a reciprocal arrangement between the EU member states and Switzerland to provide emergency health care if you are in possession of a European health insurance card (EHIC). But not everyone carries one of these, so it is worth checking if all your cast and crew has one. If you plan to film outside Europe you will certainly have to purchase medical cover to ensure your cast and crew can be treated if they become sick or are injured abroad.

It is normally assumed that individuals will have their own insurance to cover travel, in the same way that they might if they were going on holiday. But make it clear from the outset that you are not expecting to pay out if their luggage is lost in transit.

Vehicle insurance. Normal car insurance will not cover a vehicle if it is used for filming. You may need to purchase additional cover if you plan to use a car as a prop or action vehicle during your shoot. All other vehicles such as unit cars and trucks need to be insured by law in the same way as private cars.

Other Specialist Insurance. Individual contractors should be asked to produce proof of cover for activities they are supplying to the production. Examples include stunt co-ordinators, animal wranglers, drone operators, boats, helicopters and planes.

Duty of Disclosure. Since the Insurance Act became law in the UK in August 2016, it has become the duty of anyone purchasing an insurance policy to make a fair representation of the risk. If you don't do this, your insurance may be invalid. In other words – don't lie. You may be asked to declare any previous claims or convictions, and give details of any particularly unusual circumstances that the insurer needs to know.

Insurance Checklist. There are a number of insurance brokers who are specialists in the area of film. They are mainly very helpful and usually happy to provide cover for short films. Many are keen to establish good relationships with new producers, who may go on to provide them with more business in the future. I recommend that you obtain at least two quotes for comparison, though check carefully that both are offering the same level of cover. Also check what the 'excess' on each section of the policy will be. This is the amount you have to pay towards every claim. Some companies put this as £250, others at £500, and some are more.

Here is a list of information you should gather before approaching an insurance broker for a quote:

- What is your 'sum insured' and the cost of hiring all your equipment?
- Is the rental house asking you to cover 'continuing hire'?
- What is your total production budget?
- What is the hire period for the equipment? Remember to include pick up and return dates, not just the shoot;
- You may be asked for risk assessments for any dangerous sequences, so have these prepared in advance;
- Collect details of any previous claims, including dates;
- Check what the public liability limit requested is for your most expensive location;
- Where will the equipment be kept overnight? Is this a secure location?

Advice on what to do if you have to make a claim is included in Chapter 7, 'Production'.

Week Six: Shoot Minus One

In the final week of prep, the whole team will be working long hours to get everything ready for the shoot.

READ-THROUGH AND REHEARSALS

A read-through, or table read, may be arranged for the start of this week. Read-throughs are popular with executives and screenwriters, who may insist that one takes place. I have often found the read-through can get in the way of other important work in the final week of prep, since it takes up half a day, but they do serve a useful purpose as well. During the read-through the whole script is read from start to finish. All the main actors are invited to attend, and as many of the other members of the cast as possible. Some will be unavailable and their parts will be read by others. The writer usually reads the stage directions. The producer, director, first AD and second AD will normally attend, along with other HODs as required.

After the read-through refreshments may be served, allowing everyone to meet each other in an informal way before the start of filming the following week. This is a good opportunity for the ADs, costume or make-up to see anyone they haven't already met. I also usually invite the unit publicist to the read-through so they can meet the cast and chat about any interviews or other publicity matters with them.

The danger of a read-through is that sometimes the writer will go away afterwards and start changing the script. Hopefully this will only be certain lines of dialogue, and will not have a major impact on production planning.

The director will try to spend at least some of this last week of prep with the main actors in rehearsals and meetings to prepare with them for the shoot. The production office may be asked to book a room or rooms for this purpose. Ideally this will be somewhere away from the production base to allow the director uninterrupted time with the cast.

Preparing for production.

FINAL DAYS OF PREP

The first AD will gather any new information from the recce and production meeting, and will produce the final shooting schedule to be issued to all cast and crew in this week. The full schedule, including all the breakdown sheets, should be given or sent to everyone, not just the stripboard pages.

The production co-ordinator will be confirming arrangements for the first week's filming, and re-checking equipment lists to make sure everything has been ordered, is arriving, and works correctly.

The art department will be checking their props lists and dressing studio sets or locations to be used in the first days and weeks of the shoot.

Any rented vehicles will be fitted out and may begin loading this week. This includes the camera truck, lighting truck, props truck, wardrobe and make-up buses. These vehicles are generally rented from specialist suppliers, and may already have racks and shelving, make-up mirrors and lights, hanging space for costumes, changing rooms and so on.

During the last week of prep, the lighting crew may be pre-rigging or pre-lighting sets, especially if you are working in a studio.

At the end of the final week the editor may start on the production and begin setting up his or her cutting room. From the first day of principal photography, the editor will be receiving the daily footage, known as 'rushes', and assembling it into a loose cut of the finished film.

On the final day of pre-production, the production co-ordinator will issue the first call sheet, which has been prepared and authorized by the first AD. This is accompanied by the first movement order, which is prepared by the locations department. There may also be a specific risk assessment for the day, or a more general one to cover the whole shoot. A sample call sheet is included in the following chapter. It is customary also to issue the day's script pages, which are known as 'sides', to certain departments, including cast, ADs, sound and camera. This is to ensure that everyone is working from the very latest version of the script.

At the end of pre-production the co-ordinator also issues a full unit list with everyone's names and contact details. They may also issue a full cast list to certain departments, although some of this information should remain confidential. There is also sometimes a facilities list and a locations list. The more information that is shared, the more smoothly the following weeks will run.

PRE-PRODUCTION CHECKLIST

The following pre-production checklist is intended primarily as a prompt and a reminder for producers making short films, micro or very low budget films.

Set up a calendar of events with deadlines to cross off. Break down complex tasks into manageable units.

Script:
Is it locked? If not, when will it be?
Have you checked that scene numbers and scene headings are accurate, as well as who and what is in each scene?
Have you timed the script?

Shooting dates:
Are these fixed? If not, when will they be?
Remember that 'check-ins' and 'check-outs' also need to be planned and logged on the calendar.

Studio dates:
Are these booked and confirmed? Has the contract been agreed and signed?

Location dates:
Are these all confirmed? Do you have a signed contract with the location owner or owners?
Do you have permission forms/council agreements for filming in public places?
Have you worked out/booked space for unit parking?

Casting:
Is the cast confirmed? If not, when will it be?
Who is issuing the contracts?
Do you need to apply for any child licences? (This can take up to twenty-one days.)

Recce:
Who is organizing the recce? When is it? Who is going? Has the transport been arranged?

Risk assessments:
Have these been completed and signed off?
Have you checked health and safety guidelines?
Do working hours comply with regulations? Especially if working with children.
Have you planned for all potential hazards?

Insurance:
Have you confirmed insurance, including public liability, equipment hire and employers' liability?

Catering:
Who is doing the catering?
Have you checked cast and crew dietary requirements and any allergies?

Transport:
How will you get equipment/lights/props and so on to the location or studio?
Who is organizing this?
How will the cast get to the set? Who is paying for this, and how?

Green room:
Have arrangements been made for the cast to have a space to rest between set-ups?
Where is it? Who has booked it?
Where are the nearest toilets to your set/location? Who has access? Do you need a key? From whom?

Budget:
Have you accounted for all the above in your budget?
Do you have a contingency for any unexpected costs?

Shooting schedule:
When will the schedule be available? Has a meeting been arranged with heads of department to discuss it? When? Where? Has the room been booked?

Production meetings:
Have meetings been arranged and put into the calendar?
Who is communicating this information?

Test shoots:
Where and when will these take place? Who needs to attend?
What arrangements have been made to view footage/rushes from test shoots?
Who needs to attend?

Rehearsals:
Will rehearsals be held? Where? When?
Have actors been informed and space booked?

Contracts:
Do you have copies of all the necessary contracts?
Do you have blank permission forms for passers-by and/or volunteers to sign?
Who is responsible for getting these signatures on the day?

Equipment lists required:
Camera, sound, lighting, grip, additional equipment, walkie talkies

Crew and cast contact lists:
Who is compiling this information? Who is sending it out?

Daily call sheets:
Who will create these? Do you have a template? What information needs to be gathered? Where is the nearest hospital or medical facility?
Have you checked mobile phone reception where you are filming?

Special requirements:
What special requirements are there for the following:
Art department, design, props
Camera department: lenses, lighting, gels, stock, memory cards
Sound department: playback, additional crew, microphones, batteries
Costume and make-up

Stills photographer:
Have you booked a stills photographer or assigned a member of crew to take photos?

First aid and emergency numbers:
Do you have a first aid kit?
Whose number will you call in an emergency? (There may be more than one for different types of emergency.)

Post-production:
Have bookings been made for the following:
Editing
Grade
Sound editing/sound effects/final mix
Titles and end roller
Archive material, inserts
Music
FX

Paperwork:
Do you have the following:
Scripts, script pages, sides – for actors and additional crew
Marked-up scripts
Storyboards
Floor plans
Call sheets
Movement orders
Shot lists
Crew lists and phone numbers

What have you forgotten?
Go through again and double check!

Production is like a military operation: it requires careful planning and preparation.

7
PRODUCTION

The way I approach producing is like part book editor, part cheerleader. There are times where you have to hold it all together, so they know they can get through it. Like when you're working in the snow or on a mountain and all of these things. Our job is to create a safe place for people to do their best work.

Stacey Sher, Producer
(*Erin Brockovich, Pulp Fiction, The Hateful Eight*)

Production is a very intense time for everyone in the cast and crew. They will be working long days with barely a break, and on a long shoot tiredness can set in. It requires stamina and good humour from everyone, especially the producer. The irony is that if you have done your job well until now, you have less to do during the shoot. If you have picked the right team, managed the development and the prep correctly, and brought everyone together, then in theory they should all get on with doing their various jobs, leaving you to sit back, view the rushes and prepare for the next stage.

If only….

Every producer manages a shoot in a different way. Some arrive on set for breakfast and stay there all day until the unit wraps eleven or twelve hours later, normally placing themselves right next to the monitor. Others prefer to stay in the production office for part of the day, and only visit the set at certain key times and for particular scenes. To some extent this depends on the nature of the project. On television series the producer might be in script meetings with writers of future episodes, or viewing cuts of episodes already shot. On a film there may still be some elements of post-production to organize, and there are likely to be publicity visits and marketing meetings to arrange, too.

On my first ever shoot as producer I was firmly told off by my very experienced director when both the line producer and I arrived on set together early one morning. I was told it looked 'heavy', and would be taken as a signal to the crew that something was wrong and we were worried. In actual fact I'd only gone to set that morning because the location was round the corner from where I was living, and I thought I'd drop in on my way to the office. I don't know why the line producer was there, but it was an unfortunate coincidence and one I have tried to avoid repeating.

During the shoot one of the producer's main jobs is to make sure the cast are happy and stay happy. Unhappy actors can have a very bad effect on shooting, not least by slowing down the pace and causing delays. As producer you should talk to them most days, especially in the first week, to find out if they have any concerns or worries, which can be swiftly addressed before they escalate. Actors are the most important part of the filmmaker's tool kit. They need to be valued, cherished and looked after – even when their requests seem demanding, and you are filming miles from the nearest outlet for a no calorie soya latte. They are the ones who have to appear on screen, often looking deliberately terrible, sometimes forced to deliver awful lines and perform unspeakable acts.

One of my personal irritations with students and 'no budget' filmmakers is when they complain about having to pay their actors the minimum wage, whilst at the same time are prepared to spend £4,500 or more hiring a camera for a week. In my experience actors are only awkward when they are taken for granted or ignored. As the producer I don't want to receive calls from any actor's agent during the shoot. If they can't come and talk to me about what's wrong, there's a problem. In most cases it is something that can be quite simply resolved.

Running the floor and the daily management of the shoot is the job of the first assistant director, and they should be left to do it their own way. They are the key to a happy and productive crew. A good crew should work together like a well oiled machine, and a good first AD will ensure this happens. It all starts with communication, and the first way this happens is through the daily call sheet.

The Daily Call Sheet

The call sheet is issued at the end of every day and is an essential list of information to prepare everyone for the following day's filming. The detail is drawn from the full shooting schedule, but includes additional vital information as well. Every first AD has a slightly different way of arranging the information, but the key elements will be the same. The most important is the 'call time', or 'unit call': this is what everyone looks for first. Other useful details include the time of sunrise and sunset, what the weather prediction is for the day, when breakfast will be available from, and when lunch is expected to be served.

The next key information is the name and address of the location, and the address of the unit base.

Next come the phone numbers and contact details for key personnel, particularly locations, assistant directors and the production office. Although most of the shooting crew and cast should already have these, they are always included for the benefit of new cast or daily labour.

The front page will include the scenes planned for shooting that day. This information is taken directly from the shooting schedule, although the order may be amended to take account of local conditions, weather, and any last-minute changes.

Another key element is health and safety information. This includes the address and phone number of the nearest hospital or medical centre and the location of the first aid kits. The call sheet also gives special instructions for that day. For example, it might state that high visibility jackets must be worn if you are shooting on or near roads, that shoes must be removed when entering the location, or it may make recommendations about warm and waterproof clothing.

The call sheet also lists the pick-up times and transport arrangements for all actors. These times have been worked out in advance by the second AD to allow each to get to the base through the local traffic and then have enough time in wardrobe, hair and make-up before they are needed on set. It should list which unit car and driver is collecting each actor, at what time, and where they are being picked up. And it should say when they are expected to arrive at the unit base.

The call sheet does not need to reveal private information about where the actors are living or staying. There is always a concern that this kind of information will be leaked to journalists and paparazzi. The call sheet should say something like, 'Pick up Joe Bloggs from Hotel' or 'Pick up Mary Brown from Flat'. Only the driver concerned needs the actual address.

Any additional crew or equipment may also be noted on the call sheet, for example action vehicles, cranes, animals and their handlers, and special effects.

The call sheet should also note any visitors to the set, such as executive producers, publicists and journalists. It is polite to warn everyone that there will be extra people around, and to inform them who the visitors are.

The call sheet usually gives the advance schedule for the day after, and may also be used for

UNDER THE SUN
UNIT CALL : 08.00

Call Sheet No. 6 (of 28)	**Wednesday 23 May 2018**
Ready to rehearse : 08.00	**Breakfast available from: 07.15**
Sunrise at : 04.48	**Weather Forecast : 15°C - 19°C**
Sunset at : 20.57	**Mainly Dry, Light Winds**
Lunch at : 13.00	**Approx Wrap : 19.00**

Producer – Sue (phone)	Production Office	Unit Base for today
Director – Tracy (phone)	No. 1 The Road	Address
1st AD - Gemma (phone)	London	Postcode
Locations – Tony (phone)	Phone	2nd AD – Greg (phone)

Location 1 – Smith's Warehouse, Smith Street, NW10
Location 2 – Land behind Smith's Warehouse

Sc.	I/E	Set/Synopsis	D/N	Pages	Cast	Notes
12	INT	**ABANDONED WAREHOUSE** Sandy warns the rebel leaders	D	1 1/8	1, 2, 4, 6,	
23	INT	**ABANDONED WAREHOUSE** The rebels plan their next move	D	7/8	2, 4, 6	10 SAs
14	INT	**WASTEGROUND** Sandy talks them into joining him	D	1 5/8	1, 2, 4, 6	10 SAs
5	INT	**WASTEGROUND** Sandy runs off	D	1/8	1, 2	

Total Pages   3 6/8

No	Artist	Character	Pick-up	Arrive	M-Up & Hair	Costume	Ready / On Set
1	Bill Smith	Sandy	06.15	07.00	07.45	07.15	08.00
2	Sarah Jones	Jules	06.00	07.00	07.10	07.45	08.00
4	Tom Jacks	Rebel Leader 1	06.00	07.00	07.30	07.10	08.00
6	Sally Brown	Rebel Leader 2	06.15	07.00	07.30	07.10	08.00
	Lucy Green	Stand-In	N/A	0830	N/A	N/A	08.00

Supporting Artists call time at Unit Base 08.00. To have breakfast and then report to M-Up/Costume as per Greg's instructions but to be ready / on set at 10.00.
Peter Pan (armourer) on set from 13.00

Notes:
Visitors to Set : Unit Publicist – Toby will be bringing Helen Blah from the Gazette to interview Bill at lunchtime.

Transport

Car 1 Tommy (phone)	Collect Bill from flat at 06.15.
Car 2 David (phone)	Collect Sarah from hotel at 06.00
Car 3 Annie (phone)	Collect Tom from flat at 06.00 and then collect Sally from flat at 06.15.
Car 4 Harry (phone)	Collect Tracy (director) from flat at 06.45
Car 2 David (phone)	Collect Toby and Helen from station at 12.00

Police Station	Hospital	First Aid Kit 1
15 Kilburn High Road	North London General A&E	Unit Base – 2nd AD office
Kilburn	Great North Road	First Aid Kit 2
London NW10 5AA	London NW19	c/o Trevor, 3rd AD on set

REQUIREMENTS

CAMERA:	As per:	To include: (any special requirements)
ELECTRICAL:	As per:	To include:
GRIP:	As per:	To include:
SOUND:	As per:	To include:
DESIGN:	As per:	To include:
CONSTRUCTION:	As per:	To include:
MAKE-UP:	As per:	To include:
COSTUME:	As per:	To include:
SFX:	As per:	To include:
LOCATIONS:	As per:	To include:
HEALTH & SAFETY:	As per:	Copies of all Risk Assessments with Producer, 1st AD and in Production Office
RUSHES:	As per:	To include:
ANIMALS:	As per:	
CATERING:	As per:	To include lunch for: 65

Advance Schedule – Thursday 24 May 2018. Unit Call 09.00

Sc.	I/E	Set/Synopsis	D/N	Pages	Cast	Notes
8	EXT	**OLD HOTEL** Sandy and Jules meet	D	4/8	1, 2,	
87	INT	**OLD HOTEL** Sandy and Jules make a plan	D	2 6/8	1, 2	15 SAs
88	EXT	**OLD HOTEL** Sandy and Jules say goodbye	EVE	1	1, 2	5 SAs
89	INT	**OLD HOTEL** Sandy is left alone	N	1/8	1	

Total Pages   4 3/8

Gemma James
1st Assistant Director

PREVIOUS PAGE AND ABOVE: A sample daily call sheet.

other messages and information, such as lunch-time meetings.

With the daily call sheet comes a movement order and a map. This is prepared by the locations department, and contains full instructions for how to get to the unit base and set. There may also be a risk assessment related to the particular day's filming.

If you are arriving for the first day's filming and are driving yourself, you will be directed to park at the unit base, along with most of the other vehicles. Normally the locations team will have put up signs along the route to help you navigate. Unfortunately,

in many places the unit base will be some distance from the filming location. At the unit base you will find a small mobile village including the catering facilities – kitchen and dining bus – mobile toilets (known as 'honey-wagons'), mobile dressing rooms for cast (sometimes called 'three ways'), wardrobe bus, make-up bus, and security. A shuttle service is usually provided to take cast and shooting crew from the base to the set and back.

Some vehicles need to be closer to the set and must be on hand for equipment. These will normally include the camera, lighting, grip and props trucks, sound car and mobile generator.

A TYPICAL DAY ON SET

Anyone who has been on a film set for more than one day will know that there is no such thing as a typical filming day. But let's imagine there could be.

Breakfast is normally served from about forty-five minutes before the unit call time. It is good for the producer to be there, especially in the first days, to observe how the unit is working together and to be aware of any potential difficulties. Unit call is the time everyone is expected to be ready to start work. Whatever job you have on a shoot, especially if you are starting out, always make sure you plan to arrive at least thirty minutes before the call time to allow for traffic problems and to be calmly ready to start the day's work.

EARLY ARRIVALS

By now the cast may already have been at the base for an hour or more. After the locations team, the hair, make-up and wardrobe departments are always the first to arrive each morning, and they will have been preparing some of the cast for the day ahead. If you don't already know them, spend time chatting with these departments. They are the ones who know everything about your cast and all their insecurities. They know who arrives late and with a hangover, who is worried about childcare, who struggles remembering their lines and likes to run them through, and much more. These are the people who send the actors out on set more confident than when they arrived at 6am. Nobody looks great that early in the morning, and these teams have normally worked miracles before you and the rest of the crew arrive.

Make-up, hair and wardrobe personnel have a lot of unfair nicknames on film sets (the 'fluffies' being one of the kindest!). In part this is because so much of their work takes place off set rather than on it, and it may not be understood. But don't underestimate or undervalue their contribution. In my experience they provide an invaluable amount of emotional support to the cast, and handle a lot of dramas and tantrums that the rest of us only learn about after the wrap party.

If you are working in a studio, if you were at this location the day before, or if there is a particularly complicated lighting set-up, then it is possible that part of the set may already be 'pre-lit'. But in most cases you will be lighting it from scratch on arrival. At unit call I would hope to see some electricians – in the UK always known as 'sparks' – to at least be unloading equipment from the van and setting up some lighting stands.

I would also hope that the camera assistant has started to set up the monitors and construct what is known as the 'video village'. The size of this seems to get larger and larger with every technological advance. When we shot on film there were no monitors and only the operator really saw what the shot was. Now there are cables running everywhere, multiple monitors, and a host of tents under which various people huddle to watch the action.

BLOCKING

At unit call the director should be on set alone with the actors involved in the first scene to conduct a walk-through. This is known as 'blocking'. Experienced directors will let the actors play the scene the way they want, before offering them suggestions or adjustments. Inexperienced directors often tell the actors what they want them to do. Normally this takes place with just the director and the main cast, but I have known directors who invite in the DoP and the first AD to observe. The rest of the crew are kept away from the set. When they are happy with the action, the first AD will call in other members of the crew to 'show' them what has been agreed.

LIGHTING THE SET

Once this has taken place the actors normally return to make-up and wardrobe to be 'finished off', while the DoP and the gaffer begin to light the set, and the camera operator works out the moves with the rest of his or her team. This can take a long time, especially at the start of the day. Other members of the crew should stay out of the way to allow the electricians to work as quickly as possible.

However, some may need to observe what's going on: for example, the production sound mixer and boom operator need to see where the lights are pointing, and work out a plan to avoid boom shadows; the third AD should be planning where to place any extras in the scene and what actions they may have; the stand-by art director and stand-by props may have to adjust or move furniture in or out of the shot. During the lighting period, it may be useful to have one or more junior members of the crew, probably one of the floor runners, available to 'stand in' for the actors.

REHEARSING THE SCENE

Once the lighting is complete, the actors are called back to the set, and this time they need to be ready for filming, in full costume and make-up. The scene is rehearsed for the camera. The operator, grip and focus puller all need to check and re-check their movements, and may need to place marks on the floor to show actors where to end their action. This is known as 'hitting the mark'. During this process other checks are made, including eye lines. The script supervisor will usually let the director and camera operator know if either the actors or the camera are 'crossing the line': this is an indication that the scene can't be edited correctly later.

I spent a long time at the start of my career listening to people talking about 'crossing the line' without fully understanding what this meant. So here is a simple explanation – it really isn't too complicated. Try to imagine that a 180-degree line has been drawn across the set. The camera needs to stay on one side of this line and not 'cross' it. Imagine there are two characters in the scene, a man on the left and a woman on the right of the frame. If the camera stays the right side of the line he will always be on the left and she will always be on the right, even if you change the angle of the shot and adjust the size and the lens. But if you cross over the line and set up a shot from the other side, the man will now be on the right of the frame and the woman will be on the left. So it won't cut together with the other shots.

If they haven't already done so, it is at this point that the director should let everyone know how many shots or 'set-ups' there are going to be for this particular scene. It is normal to start with the widest shot or 'master' first, before moving on to mid-shots and then close-ups. The camera operator will let everyone know which size lens will be used for each shot. All this information must be recorded on the camera sheets and continuity reports.

After the blocking, lighting and rehearsal are complete, it is time to shoot the scene. There is a well rehearsed script and set of announcements for this, which is adopted on film sets throughout the world, and it is an important part of set discipline to follow this procedure.

SHOOTING THE SCENE: ON-SET ANNOUNCEMENTS

Once everyone is happy, the first AD will announce something like 'Shooting next time'. In a studio, this is the time the floor runner or third AD presses the red light and bell. This is pressed once for shooting and twice for cut. This shows everyone outside the set that shooting is underway and they must remain quiet.

The first AD will then ask for 'Final checks'. This is an opportunity for hair, make-up and wardrobe to confirm they are 'happy' or to make any adjustments.

The first AD then says something along the lines of 'Quiet please', 'Shooting this time', 'Stand by' or 'Going for a take'.

The first AD then asks 'Camera ready?'.

The camera operator replies 'Ready'.

The first AD then says 'Roll Sound'.

The sound mixer replies, 'Rolling'.

The sound mixer then says 'Speed'.

The camera operator may also say 'Speed'.

The term 'speed' comes from the early days of film. Once you started rolling actual film through a camera, it took a few seconds for the film literally to get up to speed. The cameraman would only call out 'speed' when it was filming at the correct frame rate.

The first AC says 'Mark it'.

The second AC stands in front of the camera with the clapperboard on which is written the scene number and take number, and announces, 'Scene 1, take 1' and claps the board.

Although most productions now shoot digitally, the clapperboard is still always used at the front of every take. The original purpose was as a marker used by the editor or assistant editor to synchronize the sound with the picture.

The camera operator says 'Set'.

The first AD may then say 'Background action' if the scene contains any extras.

The first AD then says 'Action'.

And at the end of the scene (or before) the director calls 'Cut'.

Sometimes the first AD might call for an 'end board'. This time the clapperboard is held upside down and clapped as before. This is normally only when there has been a false start, or more than one take has been recorded without cutting.

After the take, the entire unit prepares to 'go again'. Even if it turns out that the director is happy and wants to move on, it is still usual for everyone to be ready for a new take, just in case it is called.

The first AD will say 'Reset' or 'First positions', and everything should then be moved back to where it was at the start of the shot in preparation for another take. This can involve props or art department refilling glasses and replacing props, and may involve make-up, hair and wardrobe in further checks.

Whilst this is happening, the director should talk quietly to the actors about what changes he or she wants for the next take. At this point the director is normally inside a small tent or huddled over the monitor in the video village. He or she will have headphones or 'cans' on, to listen to the dialogue. It is very rude if the director simply shouts at the actors from this position and doesn't go over and talk to them directly. However, I have seen this happen. It may be that the actors have done everything perfectly and the reason for going again is something technical. But it is still good if the director can tell them this, be encouraging, and ask for a repeat

Film clapperboard.

performance. If the director is a really long way from the actors, it is sometimes the first AD who has to pass on a note to them, but this is far from ideal.

There may be a number of different 'takes' of the shot to get it exactly right. When everyone is happy, including the director, actors, DoP, camera operator and sound mixer, the first AD will announce they are 'Moving on'. The script supervisor should make a note of the director and DoP's preferred takes. This may not always be the same. Sometimes the director prefers the performance in one take, but the DoP or camera operator believes the quality of the shot, lighting or camera movement is better in another. If shooting on film, only the preferred takes are 'printed'.

In the days of shooting on film it was customary to 'check the gate' after a successful take. The 'gate' is the window on the camera body through which light from the lens passes. Occasionally something became stuck in the gate and would be visible on the exposed film. This was known as a 'hair', although in fact it could have been anything and was normally a sliver of film that had dislodged as it passed through. The gate was checked by looking at the front of the lens with a flashlight, and if the operator declared there was a 'hair in the gate' it was necessary to go again. With digital filming this is no longer necessary, but sometimes the take is played back to check quality.

With luck, adjustments to lighting for the next set-up won't take too long. If this is the case, it is preferable if the actors can remain around the set, rather than travelling back to the unit base. Chairs should be made available, or another room at the location might be offered where they can relax for a few minutes. It is best if the actors are not kept on set whilst lighting adjustments are made. Very young or very elderly cast members must definitely be found a private space between takes.

Filming continues until all the set-ups for the scene have been shot. Depending on the complexity and number of shots, this could be anything from two hours to a whole day. After a scene has been completed, the production sound mixer may ask for quiet on the set to record some room noise, atmosphere or 'wild tracks'. Sometimes the stills photographer will ask the actors to hold their positions for a photograph, or will position them for a production still on this particular set. When all this is finished, the first AD declares the scene is 'complete'.

An efficient first AD will try to complete a scene before lunch is called. If there is only one more set-up to shoot, they may ask the crew to break fifteen minutes later to complete the scene. It is generally considered bad practice to ask the crew to work more than fifteen minutes over in these circumstances unless this has been advertised in advance for special reasons. If part of a scene is held over lunch, it is essential that someone is left behind to literally 'guard' the set and make sure that nothing is moved or changed before everyone returns.

LUNCH BREAK

On most film sets lunch is a fixed hour. However, the hour begins from the time everyone is back at unit base, not from the time you wrap on set. If the base is a long way away, or a short journey but the traffic is heavy, then the lunch break can easily take an hour and a half or more. This is why some productions now work a 'running lunch' or 'French hours', as described in Chapter 3, 'Scheduling'.

I normally try to go to the unit base for lunch. This is really the only time I can talk to the director or first AD. Often the line producer also comes to set at lunchtime, and occasionally there may be a meeting arranged to discuss something specific coming up in the following days. During the lunch break the first AD will be discussing the next day's call sheet with the second AD, who will already have produced a draft to show him or her. After everyone else has gone back to continue filming, the second AD will make any requested amendments to the call sheet, and then send it over to the production co-ordinator in the production office.

Feeding everyone within an hour can be a challenge, and good film caterers are worth their weight in gold. The shooting crew and cast must take priority in the lunch queue. Anyone who is normally working at unit base can go later. Unfortunately, the supporting artists are always sent to the back of the queue, and they only get to eat when everyone else has been fed.

THE SECOND HALF OF THE DAY

The second half of the day follows the same pattern as the first. Things often slow down after lunch, but a good first AD will keep pushing everyone to keep on schedule. The last hour of the day is almost always the most fraught, especially if you have to finish work in that day's location. In this case I am always back on set an hour or more before wrap to see how things are going. I have seen directors perform miracles with an hour to go and achieve the impossible. And I've also been in the cutting room weeks later with an executive producer who is complaining about the lack of close-ups in a scene which I know we filmed in twenty minutes with the light going and nowhere to hide.

If it really is impossible to finish the day's filming in a location, there are limited options, none of which are easy decisions. You can try to negotiate a return date – highly unlikely and generally too expensive. You can drop a scene entirely – if so, you may be called on to decide which scene you can afford to lose, and still make the story work. Or you can consider whether it is possible to relocate any of the remaining shots or scenes to another set later. Sometimes this can be done with extreme close-ups – assuming you can find a space for these in the already packed schedule. Or, the director can simply go for it and try to shoot the whole scene 'in one'.

CALLING A WRAP

After the final set-up has been completed, the first AD announces the end of the shooting day by calling a 'wrap'. The first thing that should now happen is that the actors still on set are 'released' and taken back to the unit base to change and be taken home. All props, costumes and wigs must be left with the unit, and actors should never be allowed to take home any part of their costume. The wardrobe department may need to wash, iron or repair costumes for the following day.

Everyone else will be trying to complete their remaining tasks as speedily as possible in order to get home. At this point all the crew should pitch in and help, especially if you are working with a reduced or smaller unit. Unless you are returning to the location the following day, all the lighting equipment, including all cables and stands, will need to be packed up and loaded on to the lighting truck. The camera also needs to be packed up and loaded. The second AC will complete the camera sheets to accompany the film cans or digital storage drives. If shooting on film, the footage needs to be prepared for the laboratory. The production sound mixer completes the sound sheets, and these will be sent to the cutting room with the sound files.

Normally copies of all daily sheets are sent to the production office, along with the continuity sheets and marked-up script pages provided by the script supervisor. The production co-ordinator will extract information from these sheets for the daily progress report, before passing them all on to the editing department.

When productions were shot on film, it was necessary to get clearance on all the rushes before a set could be taken down or 'struck'. Now that most productions shoot on digital formats, this process may be somewhat faster. But it is important to check that you have all the shots you need before striking. Normally the art department will send in a team the following day to remove props and furniture and restore the location to its original state. This can involve repainting or even re-wallpapering in some cases.

When all the trucks are loaded and have moved, the locations department will make a final check to ensure nothing has been left behind and that all rubbish has been cleared. It is always advisable to leave the location in a better state than you found it. Members of the location team are not only the first to arrive each morning, but are normally also the last to leave at night.

DAILY PROGRESS REPORTS

The daily progress report is an important document that is shared with executive producers, commissioning editors, investors, the Bond company and other key individuals. They all want to know how the shoot is progressing, and should study the document carefully to keep informed. It is normally produced by the production co-ordinator, and signed by the line producer or production manager. Whilst the call sheet tells everyone what you are planning to shoot each day, the progress report documents what actually happened. On some occasions this may be quite different.

If you haven't been on set all day, you will want to look closely at this report and see how well the team is working. Did they complete all the scheduled scenes? How long did it take for the unit to turn over and complete the first shot of the morning? How many slates were completed? How many total minutes have now been shot? And so on. If the report shows the unit is dropping scenes

DAILY PROGRESS REPORT SHEET

Date	Production Title	Page of
Director	Production Company	1st AD

		Scene Nos:
Started:	Finishing Date:	Scenes scheduled:
Days to date:	Location:	Scenes shot today:
		Scenes part shot:
Remaining Days:	Weather:	Scenes not shot:

TIME

SCRIPT:

	total scenes:			pages:				
Call time:	scenes deleted:			pages:				
1st set up completed:	scenes shot to date:			pages:				
Lunch break: to	scenes remaining:			pages:				
Supper break: to		No of		no of		no of		
Breakfast break: to		setups	mins	pickups	mins	retakes	mins
Unit wrap:	Prev:							
Total hours:	Today:							
	Total:							

ACTORS (s-start day, w-days worked, sb-standby, c-call, s-set, f-finish)   CROWDS

Name	s	w	sb	c	s	f	rate

PICTURE NEGATIVE   SOUND

	exposed	N.G.	Print	waste
Prev.				
Today:				
Total:				

STILLS - COLOUR/B&W:

ARRIVALS:	
TRANSPORT:	
CATERING:	
PROPS:	
EFFECTS:	
XTRA CREW:	
ABSENTEES:	
REMARKS:	

Sample daily progress report.

and failing to complete each day, you need to act quickly. The report also records the number of hours worked by each member of the cast, which you should check to ensure they are not going to start claiming overtime. You also need to make sure children's hours are not being extended beyond the legal limit.

RUSHES

The producer should always receive a copy of the day's rushes (or 'dailies'). In the days of shooting on film it was standard practice for the rushes to be screened for all the heads of department at the end of the day, but this no longer happens. Sometimes rushes only become available for viewing the next day, after they have been synced with the sound by the assistant editor. Nowadays they are normally loaded on to a private channel for viewing by those who are allowed access. This will include the director, DoP, production designer and some commissioning editors and executive producers. Normally the director has already seen everything on the monitor, and the DoP is only looking at the lighting anyway.

Personally I like to watch all the rushes, especially if I haven't been on set all day, and I always make sure I watch them during the first few days. Early in the shoot you can still ask for changes to costume and make-up if you feel something is really not working, and you can get a good sense of how the unit is working by the number of takes. It is also an important way of assessing the cast performances, and of checking to see that all the scenes are being adequately covered and that nothing is missing.

SPECIAL DAYS AND UNUSUAL CIRCUMSTANCES

All shoots have difficult days, complicated scenes, and special circumstances. As we said earlier, there is no such thing as a typical day on set. Outlined below are some of the most common circumstances where additional elements are required. In all cases the main rule is to plan these scenes properly, discuss them fully with everyone involved, and carry out numerous rehearsals. Although the first AD is responsible for the health and safety of the cast and crew on set, as the producer you are ultimately going to be held accountable if something goes badly wrong.

Always make sure there is an adequate and full risk assessment of every potentially dangerous activity. Always check with your insurance company that they are aware of what is being planned, and that it is covered within your policy. Always hire in additional expert and specialist help when it is needed. Never cut corners or do things on the cheap, as this is how accidents happen.

SAFETY BRIEF AND SEPARATE RISK ASSESSMENT

For all dangerous activities a safety brief and separate risk assessment will be needed. If you plan to smash any glasses, plates or windows you need to discuss with the art department that these props are supplied in a substance known as 'sugar glass', which can break safely. If you want any kind of fires, barbeques, bonfires or other flame effects you need a special effects supervisor to assist the filming, and must have fire extinguishers and fire blankets on standby. Snow is usually safe, but messy, and involves a lot of clearing up afterwards. Anything involving pyrotechnics is potentially very dangerous and requires expert control and supervision. In these cases a specialist company will be hired in for the day to make the effect work.

STUNTS

As we have already discussed in Chapter 3, 'Scheduling and Budgeting', there will always have been a long discussion when planning to film any stunts. The first thing to establish is how dangerous the action is. For really dangerous sequences – jumping off buildings, into water, skydiving – you will have to hire a stunt performer to undertake the action on behalf of the actor. For less dangerous activities it may be safe for the actor to perform the action him or herself, but only under strictly supervised conditions. Examples include fighting, falling, running or riding a bicycle. Depending on the age and fitness of the actor, the surface on which they are falling, the speed they are running, or the terrain over which they are riding, this could be very dangerous or reasonably safe.

If it is agreed the actor can undertake the action, you will need to have a stunt co-ordinator or stunt arranger on set with you for the filming of these scenes. They will carefully choreograph the action and show the actors how to perform it safely. This can include providing 'crash mats' for them to fall on to, or showing them how to 'throw a punch', which cleverly misses the person at whom it is aimed. Any time a stunt is performed you must have a stunt arranger there, and this person cannot perform the action as well. So, stunts are expensive and dangerous, and should be approached with caution at all times.

With any dangerous or potentially dangerous activity, a safety briefing should be held, either at unit call or before the start of rehearsals for the scene. Everyone should be clear how far away they need to stand from the action, exactly what will happen, and what to do if anything goes wrong. It is also usually necessary to have a nurse or paramedic standing by on set, and sometimes an ambulance.

All the action must be carefully rehearsed as many times as it takes to ensure it can be carried out safely. The golden rule of filming stunts is never to change the action after rehearsals. I was on a set once where this happened, and the result was that an actor was hurt. Fortunately it wasn't a serious injury, but it could have been, and I learned a very valuable lesson as a result. This is that almost all serious accidents on set are caused by someone (usually the director) asking for changes to an action that has been prepared and rehearsed. Don't let it happen on your set under any circumstances.

WEAPONS

Any scene involving a weapon requires an 'armourer' to be on set. This includes scenes with

Shooting an action sequence.

guns, even if they are replicas and don't actually fire. The armourer is the only person who is allowed to handle the weapon, apart from the actor or stunt performer. They are entirely responsible for the weapons at all times, and all guns must be kept in locked boxes during transportation to and from set. The armourer should hand the weapon directly to the actor for the rehearsal or the start of the shot, and take it from them immediately the director calls 'cut'. They must obviously ensure the actor fully understands how to use the weapon, and brief everyone else on where to stand and what to do.

Even if the gun is firing blanks there can be dangerous accidents, and guns must never, ever be pointed at anyone who is in close range. If shots are to be fired, members of the crew should be issued with ear defenders. Swords, knives and even scissors are dangerous weapons. It is normal practice to use a plastic replica, hired from a specialist prop house.

If you are filming in a public place with replica guns or any kind of imitation weapons, the local police must be consulted in advance, and the production must obtain a 'Film Weapon Cad Number'. The point of replica guns and weapons is that they should look realistic, but members of the public who see them on the streets may be frightened and call the authorities. In the current state of alert to terrorist activities, armed police can arrive, take action and ask questions later. They must know you are filming, and that it is not a real incident. For this reason you should also ensure that all crew are wearing high visibility vests when filming in public places.

VEHICLES

As with everything else, there are many variations and different ways to achieve a shot involving a car or other moving vehicle. One safe and easy way is to have the car stationary inside a studio or large shed and use back projection, green screen and lighting effects to make it appear to move. This can be very effective, especially if the scene takes place at night. There is a technique known as the 'poor man's process', which really does work. Look it up and watch the videos showing how to do this on YouTube.

If you want to see the car moving for real, the easiest shot to achieve is a 'drive-by'. This involves a stationary camera position, normally on the side of the road or on a bridge, to capture the car passing. In most cases the car will be sufficiently far away from the camera for the driver to be someone other than an actor. The driver should be fully insured and licensed and know the vehicle. It may be an 'action vehicle driver' who works for the company from whom you have hired the car. Action vehicles come under the art department and are normally sourced by them. Production may be consulted to check insurance details.

If you want to see the actors in the car, there are ways of safely mounting a camera on to the front or side of the car to shoot the scene. This must always be done by a qualified grip using the correct equipment. If this method is selected the actor should not be driving the car as they cannot focus on performance and drive at the same time. If you want a shot from inside the car, this can be achieved with a smaller camera, usually hand held, and the operator lying or crouching on the back seat. Such scenes can be achieved most safely if a road closure has already been agreed with the local police and council. Or they can sometimes be filmed on private land, where you can be sure there are no other vehicles. Examples may include farms, old army bases, country house hotels, sports grounds or large parks. Always double check with your insurance company that what you are planning is covered by the policy.

If the scene is longer, and there is a lot of dialogue between the actors, you will need a low loader or an A-frame and a towing vehicle. The camera operator, director, first AC and script supervisor will be in the camera car in front, and the actors will be in the car behind, which is being towed. The sound recordist may also be in the car with the actors if there is enough space for them and they can be hidden out of shot. The actors are not actually driving and can focus on their performance. This works wonderfully, but is expensive and it takes a long time to shoot.

The route must be worked out carefully, as everyone must turn around and drive back to the starting place each time you want another take. Normally you will want to control who is driving behind your main car to make sure of continuity in the edit, so you may need a second vehicle following. In some cases you will need to apply for a road closure, or will need a police escort. Where possible you should try to film on a road that you can control completely.

WATER

Filming on, near, or in water is another hazard requiring extra precautions. If you plan to put any member of the cast into the water, make sure they are a competent swimmer and comfortable with the scene. Remember that clothes become very heavy in the water, and even a strong swimmer can struggle with this. In the UK the sea is cold most of the year, so a wetsuit under the costume will be necessary. Always have safety equipment, including lifebuoy rings, available. In many cases you will need a trained lifeguard on hand as well. Warm clothing, including emergency foil blankets, should also be carried to warm up actors when they come out of the water. During planning you should also check water quality and find out whether there are any known diseases in the particular river or lake.

Filming on boats, especially small ones, is another dangerous activity. You must agree the distance from shore – ideally not too far. And you will probably have to have a second 'safety' boat within range of the first in case anything goes wrong. Everyone in the crew must wear lifejackets, and the camera will need to be in a waterproof protective cover.

Underwater shots are normally filmed in a special tank located at a film studio. Lower budget films often achieve excellent substitutes in swimming pools. If the camera is going into the water it needs to be waterproof.

Whenever you are filming near or in water, be aware of the need to protect all your equipment,

When shooting in public places always wear high visibility vests.

most of which is sensitive to water damage. Also remember that electricity and water is never a good combination, and keep lights, cables and plugs well away.

SPECIAL EFFECTS

Special effects vary enormously, but nearly always take time to achieve. Preparation, discussion and testing is important to save time during the shoot.

I've been on sets where the director was disappointed or surprised by the effect, and this might have been corrected if more discussion had taken place earlier. So it is always advisable to test the effect in advance to ensure it provides exactly what is required. Even something relatively simple, such as creating rain or wind, will involve special equipment, resources and possibly extra personnel as well.

Using a low loader to shoot scenes with moving vehicles.

The camera is mounted on the towing vehicle.

For rain effects you will normally require a bowser full of water and may need arrangements to refill it from a safe water supply, or have a second one in case the first runs out. All this costs money and takes time. When hiring any special effects company, always get more than one quote for the job, and check with other producers that they can deliver what they say they can.

Aerial Filming and Drones

Drones are increasingly used on film shoots, even comparatively low budget ones. They can achieve fantastic shots, similar to those previously created using much more expensive methods, such as helicopters, gliders and cranes. There are strict rules about using drones in the UK, and you are advised to check the guidelines published by the Civil Aviation Authority (CAA) for the area where you wish to film. In most cases you need their permission to use a drone for filming legally, and this will never be granted within a certain distance of an airport. The CAA also prohibits the use of drones within 150 metres of any built-up area, which rules out most cities and towns, and generally restricts their use to rural areas.

Drones must be operated by someone who is qualified and licensed. There are also rules about how high they can fly, and who is in the area over which they are operating. You may have to clear quite a wide area of all personnel for the filming to be approved. It is also important to have permission from the landowner, and to check that you are not breaching any privacy rules. A full risk assessment is required, and additional insurance may be needed. In most cases it is advisable to use a registered drone company to make sure you comply with all the current regulations.

Animals

All animals must be brought to the set by a qualified animal handler or wrangler. They should have their own insurance, and may also provide a separate risk assessment. Once again check the production insurance policy to see what animals are covered and which are not. Most policies

Even well trained dogs don't always behave as promised when confronted by cameras and a crowd of strangers.

include 'domestic' animals, but double check if this includes cows and sheep, or only dogs and cats. Remember there are also strict rules in some countries about the movement of animals.

Like children, animals need rest times, and cannot work all day long without adequate breaks. The handler must remain with them at all times. In the UK the RSPCA has the right to inspect a film set to check on the conditions in which animals are being kept. The main problem with any animal on set is that they may not do what you are expecting them to do, or what you were told they would. Even well trained dogs don't always behave as promised when they are confronted by unusual situations, cameras and a crowd of strangers. The hardest domestic animals to control are cats. Asking them to do anything other than sit still is a challenge, and even that doesn't always work.

Children

The rules for working with children and young people are outlined in the previous chapter. Their hours must be strictly supervised and recorded, and because of these time restrictions it is always advisable to rehearse and light scenes with a stand-in, and only bring the child to set when everyone is absolutely ready to shoot. Sometimes the director will decide to shoot the rehearsals because the child may give a more natural performance. Children have to be chaperoned at all times, and must never be left alone or unsupervised. They should be provided with a space to relax, as close to the set as possible, and must never be asked to do anything that makes them feel uncomfortable or scared.

ELDERLY ACTORS

There are no special regulations covering the employment of older actors, but you should check any restrictions on your insurance policy before casting. Sometimes it is necessary to notify insurers if you have actors over a particular age (normally eighty), and you may also have to declare any pre-existing medical conditions. Although it is not a legal requirement, you should still take care to provide older actors with additional comforts where possible. They will appreciate a chair for their use between takes, someone to bring them water or tea, and they may need extra breaks to use the bathroom.

NUDITY AND CLOSED SETS

Any scenes involving nudity or sex should always be declared as a 'closed set'. This means that only the essential crew can be there for the filming of these scenes. Absolutely no visitors or press are allowed. Anyone who doesn't have a specific job to do should be asked to wait outside. Actors should be allowed time to become comfortable with the scene, which should be rehearsed privately with the director first. If the crew is predominantly male, and the scene involves an actress, it is advisable to have at least one female member of the crew on set. Bathrobes and towels should be available for a quick cover-up after each setup and between takes.

SUSTAINABLE PRODUCTION

In recent years the film production industry has made great efforts to become more sustainable, and to support initiatives that consider its impact on the environment. It is now very important for producers to be aware of these guidelines, and ensure they are implemented on all film shoots. The BFI has adopted BS 8909, the new British Standard for sustainability, and is working closely with BAFTA and their ALBERT initiative to promote better working practices throughout the industry.

STAYING WITHIN BUDGET AND COST REPORTING

Throughout the pre-production, production and post-production period, you need accurate financial information about how well each department is managing its budget, and whether any area is likely to be going over. The production accountant and line producer gather this information from each department and prepare weekly 'cost reports' to show the current situation. It is quite likely that some lines in the budget may be showing an overage at certain points during filming. There may also be some that show an underage, and the two can balance each other out. For example, you may have estimated an amount for hiring in the camera package, but then done a deal that is better than the estimate. But you might not have budgeted for a particular lens that the DoP wants, and have to add this in.

Even when filming has started there are ways to cut back on future expenditure, such as reducing the number of supporting artists in a scene (saving not only their fee but also their catering and travel), or turning down some additional equipment requests. Don't be tempted to start cutting items from the post-production budget during the shoot. This will only cause you problems later. A weekly meeting is usually held to discuss the current situation and any steps that may need to be taken to address problems. The cost reports will be sent to the main investors and to the bond company. If there are major red flags they will swiftly send someone from their organization to discuss how you plan to get everything back on track.

INSURANCE CLAIMS

The point of having insurance in place is to be able to recover costs if something goes wrong. This can involve replacing damaged equipment, paying for the cost of repairs or, in some cases, mounting a full re-shoot of certain scenes. But before any of this can happen you will first need to make an insurance claim. Below are some ground rules issued by a specialist film insurance provider. They apply equally to larger productions and to low budget films and shorts.

- Make sure everyone is safe. Call the emergency services if needed.
- Report the incident to the appropriate authorities immediately.
- Advise the production office or person designated on the call sheet.
- Collect evidence while the incident is fresh in everyone's minds.
- Take photographs of everything relevant as evidence.
- Gather witness details, including phone numbers and email addresses.
- Contact your insurance broker and report the incident as soon as possible.
- Get together all receipts and invoices relevant to the claim.
- Advise all interested parties, for example hire companies or location owners.
- Put together an estimate of the total claim.

And the following is a list of 'don'ts':

- Panic or get angry;
- Admit liability;
- Sign anything;
- Offer to pay for the damage or say your insurance will;
- Destroy any evidence that will be useful as part of the claim;
- Hide any facts from your insurer, or lie about the claim;
- Delay reporting it or sending in evidence to support the claim;
- Stop filming, unless it is unsafe to continue;
- Assume that a claim is an opportunity to upgrade to better equipment;
- Answer any correspondence without first checking with your insurer.

WRAP

The end of filming is usually a great relief for everyone, and most will be totally exhausted. It is customary to hold a wrap party to reward everyone for their efforts. Whether you want to go or not, it is part of your job, as the producer, to attend. It is also best if you don't relax too much or get drunk. You will still be working with some of these people in the following weeks, or on another job.

Depending on their particular role, members of the crew will have different amounts of wrap time. Some will finish on the last day of the shoot. Some will have one or two days to check and return equipment. Others, such as costume and props, will have longer to return or dispose of everything purchased and hired in. Any props or costumes that have been bought for the production must be sold and the money raised returned to the production accountant. Investors have the right to audit this.

Sometimes actors ask if they can have a certain item from their costume, such as a dress or a pair of shoes, and I would normally allow this. But I've also known executive producers who request expensive props and assume they can have them for nothing. It is a delicate situation, but the sale of props and costumes can raise many hundreds of pounds, which you will surely need for something later.

Before everyone leaves, the production accountant and line producer will also need to reconcile individual petty cash accounts and purchase orders, and go through each department's actual budget with them, and compare it to the original

Weekly Cost Report

Category Title	Budget	Costs to Date	Commitments	Estimate to Complete	Final Costs	Variance
Story/Scripts/Development	179,769	169,734	0	0	169,734	10,035
Producer/Directors	161,280	150,281	6,996	0	157,278	4,002
Artists/Performers	246,060	238,393	(6,978)	0	231,618	14,442
Production Unit Salaries	131,888	124,442	6,962	0	131,404	484
Assistant Directors	55,222	58,948	(3,258)	0	55,690	(468)
Crew Camera	95,892	105,285	(5,083)	0	100,202	(4,310)
Crew Sound	34,461	35,005	(2,542)	0	32,463	1,998
Crew Lighting	72,851	77,884	(4,435)	0	73,449	(598)
Crew Art Department	140,544	151,989	(9,349)	0	142,640	(2,096)
Crew Make-Up/Costume	118,360	113,141	(4,832)	0	108,309	10,051
Crew Post Production Picture	43,793	34,540	9,530	0	44,070	(277)
Materials Art Dept	183,460	133,757	18,792	0	152,549	30,912
Materials Wardrobe/Make-up	24,000	22,449	(837)	0	21,612	2,388
Production Equipment	149,605	151,403	3,593	0	154,996	(5,391)
Studios	100,250	91,348	1,155	0	92,503	7,747
Other Production Facilities	131,328	112,856	109	0	112,966	18,362
Film Tape Stock	3,543	3,513	0	0	3,513	30
Post Production	161,810	87,645	24,760	31,238	143,642	18,168
Graphics	101,000	67,330	19,060	0	86,390	14,610
Music	17,550	11,050	5,250	0	16,300	1,250
Travel and Transport	69,102	69,257	(973)	0	68,284	818
Hotel and Living	122,715	121,481	1,176	0	122,657	58
Other Production costs	18,525	18,057	2,257	0	20,314	(1,789)
Production Overheads	1,500	3,000	0	0	3,000	(1,500)
Production Fee	75,000	75,000	0	0	75,000	0
Contingency	0	0	0	0	0	0
Total	2,439,507	2,227,787	61,352	31,238	2,320,580	118,927

An example of a weekly cost report prepared by the production accountant.

estimates. The cost report produced at the end of the shoot will be closely scrutinized by investors, and if it is showing an overage at this point there will be discussions about how to recover this from post-production.

The line producer and production co-ordinator normally have two weeks' wrap. They need to supervise the returns, deal with claims for anything that has been lost or damaged, approve final invoices and clear the office. Normally the producer, post-production supervisor and production accountant move to a smaller office space for the post-production period. The main production office must be returned to the state it was in before everyone arrived.

The production co-ordinator should also collate all the paperwork from the shoot and make sure it is all in order for the final delivery. He or she will normally hand this over to the post-production supervisor. The file should include all of the following:

cast contracts
crew contracts
location agreements
release forms
supporting artist time sheets
daily call sheets
daily progress reports
camera sheets
continuity sheets
sound sheets
log of children's hours
risk assessments
accident report forms
insurance paperwork
music licences
permission for the use of artworks, photographs
   and so on

After completion of the shoot and wrap, the producer moves on to the next stage of the process: post-production.

Delivering the finished film is a complex process.

8
POST-PRODUCTION

A film editor often has to coax the director's vision of the film out of the director. Often, it is like a hidden dream that the director has yet to articulate. The editor must challenge the hidden dream with alternative scenarios until the desired vision is revealed.

Walter Murch, Editor
(*The Godfather I, II and III,*
Apocalypse Now, The English Patient)

The period between the end of the shoot and final delivery of the film or series is known as post-production, commonly shortened to 'post'. It includes the time spent editing the picture from the rushes, track laying, recording the music, sound design, grading the picture, and adding any CGI or visual effects. There is also a lot of paperwork to be prepared as part of the delivery materials. In this chapter we will explain the different elements, and provide details and examples of some of the 'deliverables'. Throughout post-production the producer must make sure that each stage is completed on schedule and on budget. It is often assumed that once the shoot is finished, there won't be any further problems or cost overages – but this part of production can be as demanding and complex as everything that has gone before.

PLANNING

A lot of planning should already have taken place in pre-production and production to ensure a smooth post-production and delivery. The line producer may be involved in some of this planning with you, but you should also have an experienced post-production supervisor on board early, and consult with them on all the arrangements before bookings are confirmed. The post supervisor creates and updates the post-production schedule, and liaises regularly with the production accountant to inform them of any additional budget costs. They may also hire other key post-production personnel in consultation with the producer. They should also set up meetings for you with all the selected post-production facilities houses, including the colourist, sound mixer and any visual effects or graphics companies.

EDITING

The editor usually starts work on the first day of principal photography, and spends the shoot assembling all the footage. Working from information in the daily camera sheets, continuity reports and sound sheets, the editor uses the preferred takes to produce a version of the complete film, which is known as an 'assembly'. This is normally available for the director to view in the cutting room one or two days after production has wrapped. Almost all editors now work with non-linear editing software, the most commonly used being 'Avid' and 'Final Cut Pro'. Once the rushes have been digitized, this software enables editors to move shots and change sequences rapidly. Throughout this process the editor will create 'back-up' versions of everything, and store these on an external hard drive as a safety measure.

It is important to remember that the assembly is not a 'cut'. There has been no creative input from the director: the purpose is to check that all the required shots are there, and there is a coherent narrative. The assembly follows the structure of the script. During the creative editing process that follows, scenes may be moved or dropped entirely from the film. For this reason it is important not to share the assembly with anyone else, especially investors and distributors. They may ask to see it, but producers are strongly advised to resist these requests. The assembly is always overlong and loose, and it can be disappointing viewing, especially to an inexperienced eye.

Experienced producers normally stay away from the cutting room for the first few weeks, and leave the editor and director to work alone together until they have a version they are reasonably happy with and want to share. A fresh set of eyes is always useful and it is preferable to wait and offer this when asked. For a feature-length film the first cut – known as the 'director's cut' – should take three to four weeks. The producer then views this cut with the director and editor, and offers suggestions.

Taking any notes into account, the next cut should be completed within a week, and a viewing is then arranged for anyone else who has an interest or right to comment. Ideally the viewing should take place in a screening room or cinema, where the film can be projected. It is not good to hold viewings in the cutting room on a small screen.

Receiving notes on the cut is very similar to the process of receiving script notes, and can be a delicate matter. This time it is the director who may be reluctant to implement suggestions. There may also be different opinions and contradicting views from executive producers and others. As the producer you have to stay closely involved in this process and manage the notes carefully.

When everyone is happy, the final cut is agreed and the picture is locked.

A locked picture, unlike a locked script, cannot be changed – although like every film rule, I have known this one to be broken. Once the picture is finished you can start working on the sound. If the film changes after picture lock, the time codes will be different and much of the following work will have to be done again.

SOUND EDITING

Sound editing is a crucial part of post-production, and you must allow enough time for this to be done well. A strong soundtrack enhances the film's atmosphere, and this can make a huge difference, especially for shorts and very low budget films.

The first stage is to clean up the dialogue tracks and remove any 'noise' or distortion. The sound editor will also try to even out the recording levels, which are often different within the same scene. If a line of dialogue is particularly bad the sound editor may be able to lift the sound from a different take and lay it over the shot, adjusting it to match the movement of the actors' lips.

Once the dialogue tracks have been cleaned, the sound editor will then begin to create a more complex sound track for each scene, adding atmospheres and creating new backgrounds. These may have been recorded on set as 'wild tracks' or 'room noise' by the production sound mixer, or maybe from a sound library. Most sound editors use Pro Tools software produced by Avid to create these multiple tracks. The backgrounds must be laid down on separate tracks so that the film can later be dubbed into foreign languages if required. One of the deliverables listed in all contracts is an 'M&E Track'. This is short for 'Music and Effects Track', and consists of all the backgrounds and music without any dialogue, which can then be replaced in the chosen language.

FOLEY

Foley is the creation of everyday sounds to match the specific sounds in a film. It is named after Jack Foley who invented the process when he worked at Universal Studios in the 1920s. Foley is recorded in a sound studio, and is used to enhance the soundtrack and sometimes to mask or cover up something on the original production tracks, such as a plane. Foley artists are sometimes known as 'footsteps artists', because one of their key jobs is to create footstep sounds in the studio to match the way the actors walk in the film. They may also be asked to produce noises such as doors slamming, glass breaking, punches, sighs, screams, cloth tearing, clothes rustling, and so on.

Frequently Foley artists use something entirely different to create a sound. Bacon frying is a common trick for recreating rain, and coconut shells have been used for horses' hooves. The 2012 film *Berberian Sound Studio* features some wonderful examples used in early Italian horror films. Watching experienced Foley artists at work is a great treat.

AUTOMATED DIALOGUE REPLACEMENT (ADR)

Sometimes it will be necessary to call back one or more of the actors to re-record a line that is unusable from the original production tracks. It may also sometimes be necessary to record additional dialogue and new lines to add to a particular scene. This is normally to make it easier for the audience to understand what's happening, or to explain something that may have been missed or lost in the edit. This process is known as 'ADR', or 'automated dialogue replacement', and it is always done at a specialist sound studio. It may also be referred to as 'post-sync' sound or 'looping'.

Arranging the ADR bookings is done by the producer and the post-production supervisor together. The post supervisor will probably arrange the studio and book the sound editor, but the producer may be better placed to contact the actors' agents and find time in their schedule. Arranging ADR can be complicated, as it normally takes place many weeks after the end of the shoot, and actors are often engaged on another production, sometimes even filming abroad. It is customary to pay actors to attend the ADR session, unless this was previously included and specified as part of their original fee. Most actor contracts have a clause that makes it very difficult for producers to revoice their work without first obtaining their permission.

The director must attend the ADR sessions to explain to the actor what they need from their performance, and what is wrong with the original. Normally they will be asked to give more than one version to provide options for the sound editor. At the sound studio the actor is shown a video playback of the scene in question, and asked to reproduce the line from inside a sound recording booth, ensuring it is lip synced to the original. The clip is played back with a white line or visual mark to cue them in.

SOUND MIXING OR DUBBING

When all the separate tracks have been laid down, the sound editor hands over the project to the sound mixer. The sound mixer ensures that the different tracks are mixed in the right relationship to each other – for example, making sure dialogue is always audible in relation to background sounds and music, or bringing up music levels during silent or montage scenes. The director, editor, sound editor and producer should all attend the final mix. Prior to this the sound mixer will already have done some preparation, but most directors have strong feelings about the final soundtrack of the film. During the final mix each section is played, notes given, adjustments made, and then played again. The whole process can take two or three days, depending on the length of the production.

Dubbing theatres have some of the most advanced sound systems available, and the quality of sound you will hear in them is wonderful.

However, you should always ask to listen to the finished product through the ordinary television speakers as well. This is how most audiences will experience the film. It is important to check that the dialogue is still audible through these speakers, and not drowned out by the music or other elements.

After the mix is completed and signed off by the director and by you as producer, the next process is known as the 'layback'. This is when the finished soundtrack is put in sync with the picture and is literally 'laid back' on to the film to match it frame by frame.

PICTURE POST-PRODUCTION

At the same time as the sound editor is track laying and preparing for the final mix, there are still some steps to be taken to complete the picture post-production. These will be different, depending on whether you originally shot on film or on a digital camera.

If your original format was digital (as is increasingly the case now) and you want to achieve the optimum picture quality for delivery, you will first need to do an online edit, also known as a 'conform'. During the edit so far, the editor has been working with low resolution images to increase speed and reduce the amount of storage needed. Now you need to return to the original high resolution images created in the camera. The editor should produce an EDL or 'edit decision list'. This provides digital information, which is used to replace all the low resolution materials with exactly the same frames from the high resolution original masters. At the same time any visual effects shots and graphics will also be added to the conform, producing a finished high resolution digital master.

If your original format was film, you may need to go back to this for your finished master. In this case the EDL can be used to provide information for the 'neg cut'. Negative cutting is highly specialized work, and means literally cutting the original negative and producing a finished film by splicing together the required frames. But in recent years it has become more common to create a 'digital intermediate', or 'DI', instead. In this case the full selected takes are digitally scanned and spliced together to create a new selected roll of negative, which is then used to produce the final master.

For television productions shot on film you may decide to telecine your negative to produce your finished master.

VISUAL EFFECTS

Visual effects is another area of filmmaking that is changing rapidly. A visual effect shot (or VFX) is one that is created or manipulated digitally in post-production. It can range from a simple 'composite', where one static frame is laid on top of another, to a highly complicated sequence combining live-action footage shot on location with computer-generated imagery (or CGI). Some elements, including actors performing a scene, may be shot against a 'green screen', and the background may be added to the scene in post. This is often done on period films or science fiction where no appropriate location can be found. The simplest kind of CGI or VFX shot involves nothing more complicated than 'painting' out something you don't want to see in the shot, such as a satellite dish or parking meter. The most complex include creating whole new worlds.

Producers should try to stay up to date with changing technologies, and should regularly attend trade fairs and exhibitions where the latest software is being demonstrated.

For post-production planning it is preferable if all VFX shots can be completed and inserted into the film before final grading.

GRAPHICS, TITLES, CREDITS AND END ROLLERS

Some films and television series commission complex animated title sequences. Others may be much simpler, involving nothing more than the actual title of the film superimposed over one of the early shots. There are specialist companies who can design your titles and graphics, or you may decide to use someone already working on the production to provide you with exactly what you want. The post-production supervisor will be able to make suggestions.

One of the most awkward jobs for the producer is agreeing the credits for the front and end titles. It is amazing how upset some people get about this. For all main cast, the stipulations are agreed from the start – who comes first, second, third, fourth and so on. There may also be conditions about the size of the font, the height of the lettering, and how large their name appears in relation to other members of the cast. It is really important not to make any mistakes. For the end roller the cast are also normally listed again in the order they appear in the film.

Crew credits can be equally difficult and contentious. For television programmes there are strict rules about the length of the roller, which cannot be exceeded. This means that you may have to leave out some members of the production simply because they won't all fit. I've also had television executives refuse credits, or who want to change the name of the job, which also upsets people.

You may also need some on-screen captions, for example 'one year earlier', or the name of a place. There may also be sub-titles if some of the dialogue is in a foreign language. When preparing these, be very careful about the background against which they are placed. Using a 'drop shadow' around the text can help with readability. And make sure to double check how long the words are on the screen. Can they be read comfortably, or are you only half way through before they disappear?

COLOUR CORRECTION AND COLOUR GRADING
Colour correction is the process by which the finished master is adjusted to create the cinematic look that the director and director of photography want. It is standard practice to invite the DoP to attend the sessions with the director, and to pay him or her for their time. Being a 'colourist' is a skilled job, and the best are highly paid and highly sought after by post-production houses. During the first colour correction sessions they will perform a number of small miracles, including matching scenes shot in different locations on different days and in very different weather conditions, fixing crushed blacks or bad exposures, and much more.

The final stage of colour correction may add highlights and shadows (luminance) or adjust the colour balance (chromiance), and this can profoundly affect the final look of the film. There are numerous colour correction and grading softwares available, but the one most commonly used by professional filmmakers is DaVinci Resolve.

MUSIC

You will almost certainly want to use music in the soundtrack of your film. There are two different types of music to consider, and we will deal with these separately.

Originally Composed Music

'Originally composed music' means music that is composed and recorded specially for your production, and which does not already exist in any form. There are many highly talented composers who work mainly in the field of film and television production. All are represented by agents, or have websites where you can look at their credits and hear samples of their work. Normally the director will suggest who they want to do the music, but producers are also involved in the choice of composer. This is a major creative role and must usually be approved by the main commissioning editor or financiers of the production.

Once the choice of composer is approved, the producer must negotiate their deal. Again, there are different models. In some cases the composer is offered a 'package fee' in return for delivering the full music soundtrack. In this case the composer pays any musicians, singers, arrangers, transcribers, fixers, recording studios and other staff from the package fee. The advantage to the producer is that the music budget is fixed and you know from the outset how much you will be spending on it. There will be no hidden costs.

If you decide on a package fee you must ensure the composer understands that any payments to musicians or singers are made on a 'buy out' basis, and no future royalties will fall due for which you may become liable later. Musicians are members of the Musicians Union, and there are agreements in place to regulate minimum fees and future royalty payments. You can find details of these on their website.

The second option is to commission the music but agree to pay the costs of recording directly from the production budget. This will be a more time-consuming process but could possibly save money.

The process for deciding where to place music in the film is known as 'spotting', and is done with the director sitting together with the composer and the editor discussing points in the film where music will enhance the action or the emotional content of the scene. During the spotting session the director should indicate what kind of music he or she has in mind, the 'in' and 'out' points for the cue, and the mood he or she wants to create with the soundtrack at this point. Although the composer may be selected before picture lock, spotting can really only take place after. Make sure you are aware how many cues are being discussed. Composers may wish to renegotiate their deal if there is substantially more music to write and arrange than they had originally expected.

When all the various cues have been recorded and mixed, they are played back against the picture in the cutting room. Producers should attend these sessions, and should ask for changes if they think the music is not doing what was

requested. When everyone is in agreement the final music will be delivered to the sound editor on digital format.

Existing or Copyright Music

Music that already exists and has been previously recorded is subject to copyright in the same way as literary works, artistic works and other existing material. In this section we will only discuss copyright as it applies to music recordings and performance. Please refer also to the section on copyright in Chapter 2, 'Development', for more details about the general rules.

There are two types of licence or rights you need to secure if you decide to use existing music in your film. These are known as 'performing rights' and 'publishing rights'.

MUSIC PUBLISHING OR SYNCHRONIZATION RIGHTS

These rights are also sometimes referred to as the 'sync' rights, and relate to the person or people who wrote the music or song. In some cases this may be more than one individual, for example a composer and lyricist or a composer and arranger. Publishing rights are subject to the usual length of copyright, which is seventy years after the death of the last author, although this may differ in some countries so it is always worth checking if your chosen music is still in copyright or not. Even if the composer is dead, there will still be fees to be paid to their estate.

To check who controls the publishing rights there are a number of useful websites to help. In the UK the MCPS – Mechanical Copyright Protection Society – is a good source of information. In the USA there are four main performing rights organizations who between them represent a huge number of composers and musicians. BMI, ASCAP, SOCAN and SESAC all collect licence fees on behalf of their members when their music is publicly performed. But this also means they hold information about who controls the publishing rights. Another good source of information about recordings and record labels is Discogs.com.

Once you have found out who the publisher is, you need to contact them to request permission to use the music or song in your production. You should clearly state the rights you are seeking, which will probably be 'all media worldwide in perpetuity' if your budget can afford this. But you could ask for less than this for low budget films or television projects where you don't expect to make many international sales. You should try to get as many rights as you can afford. Clearing only two years can limit your festival run for a short film, and rule out any further sales or distribution. Clearing only some territories means you would either have to turn down a sale to any others, or go back and pay an additional fee later.

You may be asked whether you want the licence on an 'exclusive' or 'non-exclusive' basis. For most productions 'non-exclusive' is fine. If you ask for an 'exclusive' licence and want to be the only film ever to use this particular track, you will have to pay a lot more money for it.

Performing or Master Recording Rights

The other rights you may need to acquire are the performing rights. These rights belong to the musicians, singer or the band who are performing the track you wish to use. If you are trying to clear a performance from a very well known or popular group this can be very expensive, and you may decide instead to re-record the song with a different performer.

If you wish to use the original recording you need to contact the record label who released it. This information is fairly easy to find online using a site such as Discogs, or on the CD case if you have a physical copy of the album. Once you know the label you should contact their rights department and ask whether the song is available. They will want to know more about how you plan to use it. It is common for the record company to ask for details of the particular scene in which the song will be played or used. This is

because they may not want their performers to be associated with particular acts of violence, illegality or sex.

They will also want to know how the song will be used – for example, over the final credits, in vision, or purely as soundtrack, such as over a montage, or coming through a radio. You will be asked exactly how many minutes and seconds of the track you will use, and what rights you are seeking. Once again you will normally want to start by trying to acquire all media worldwide in perpetuity.

If there are multiple recordings or versions of the song you want to use, think carefully about which artist and label to approach. The bigger the artist, the less likely it is that you will get a good deal. You might also consider approaching the band or their management directly. I once cleared some tracks for a film this way. I was assured that the particular artist never granted permission to use his work, but by talking directly to his manager, and not the record company, we were able to interest him in our film and get permission. Sometimes a direct and very passionate appeal from you or your director can make all the difference.

If there is a strong reason why you must have a particular song, and have cleared the publishing rights already, then re-recording it may be your best option. This is common practice, and there are many artists and companies who can provide you with versions that sound uncannily and deliberately like those of other people. I used a company to provide me with a version of *Que Sera Sera*, which was essential to the narrative of our film. The new recording was very close to the Doris Day original, but cost vastly less. If you listen carefully you will notice that many commercials appear to be using songs by Frank Sinatra, when in fact it is actually someone singing in the same style. This is how they avoid paying a huge sum of money, and how you can use the song you want if you are turned down by the original recording artist.

If you have a lot of copyright and recorded music in your film you might find it useful to hire a music supervisor to help you with the clearances. They have personal connections and a lot of experience, and can often clear tracks and negotiate preferential deals. A music supervisor will advise on alternative tracks if the director's first choice is unavailable or too expensive. They are normally paid a fee and given a budget within which to work.

Almost all master recording labels and music publishing companies operate on a basis known as MFN or 'most favoured nations'. This means that whatever price you agree to pay for the sync licence will also apply to the recording licence, and vice versa. If you believe one side is likely to give you a better deal you should negotiate these rights first. Then the other side will usually agree to the same terms. MFN can also apply to all the songs in your film, in which case you need to treat all recording artists and music publishers in the same way, and agree the same terms with each.

Finally, it is important to remember that even if the music you have chosen is out of copyright, the recording may well not be. Mozart and Beethoven may have been dead for centuries, but their works are not necessarily free to use if the orchestrations, arrangements or recordings are still in copyright. If you don't want to pay to use classical music recordings, then you need to find a version that is affordable or available free of charge. One place to look for these is Creative Commons, but there are many other similar websites.

Library Music

For some projects you may decide to use music that is royalty free. This is known as library music. There are numerous websites where you can listen, and decide whether the work is appropriate for your project. When you have chosen the track you pay a fee to the library and obtain a licence for the required duration and length of time. The advantage is that it can be very quick and cost effective compared to other sources of music. The disadvantage is that the music is not original to your film, or composed and recorded

specially for it. You may find it appearing in other film soundtracks as well.

Television

Some broadcasters, including the BBC and PBS stations in the USA, have negotiated blanket agreements that allow programme makers to use some music without having to clear the recording or publishing rights first. Not all recordings are included, and it is therefore very important to check with the company's music department first before assuming it will be OK. You should also remember that the agreement may only apply to transmission by that broadcaster in that country. If you are making a series intended for wider international distribution you will still need to go through the clearance process for the rest of the world.

Music Cue Sheets

After your film or programme has been mixed, you will need to complete a music cue sheet as part of the delivery paperwork. This is normally done by the post-production supervisor. The cue sheet details exactly how the music is used – whether 'in vision' or 'background', the precise duration in minutes and seconds, and provides information about publishing and recording rights. This information is necessary for distributors and particularly broadcasters, as it helps them to collect and make PRS (Performing Rights Society) payments to artists on an annual basis.

DELIVERABLES

When you signed contracts with the distributors, broadcasters or sales agents who helped to fund your film you were given a list of 'deliverables'. This is literally a list of all the items you are expected to deliver to them when the film is completed. Some of these will be physical materials and others will be paperwork. Different distributors will have different requirements, and it is essential that you check their list carefully and make sure

MUSIC CUE SHEET

Programme Title
Episode No.
Episode Title
Production Company and Contact Information
Programme No.
First TX date

Completed By: _____ Phone: _____ Producer's Signature: _____ Date: _____

Please list all music used in the production.

TIME CODE	MUSIC TITLE OR NUMBER (CUE)	COMPOSER (C) AUTHOR (A) COMPOSER/AUTHOR (CA) ARRANGER (AR)	PUBLISHER	PERFORMER(S)	RECORD or VIDEO LABEL AND NO.	DURATION Mins / Secs	TYPE OF USE	
							Record Code*	Music Use Code*
00.00-02.26	THE GREAT PRETENDER	B.RAM	SOUTHERN MUSIC	THE PLATTERS	MERCURY/ UNIVERSAL	2m 26s	C	VB
03.06-04.15	ORGINAL CUE 1	NAME OF COMPOSER	ABC Music	N/A	N/A	1m 10s		X
04.16-04.41	RADIO LONDON JINGLE	NAME OF COMPOSER(S)	JINGLE INC	N/A	N/A	25s		VB

*Music Use Codes: B = Background, F = Featured S = Signature X = Commissioned P = Live Performance V = Vocal
*Music Record Codes: L = Library recording C = Commercial recording PPL = PPL member

Page _____ of _____

An example of a music cue sheet.

your post-production supervisor and others know what is expected. Adding items you have omitted later can be costly. Moreover the final cash flow payments are often held back until the full delivery has been made.

STANDARD DELIVERABLES

DCP (digital cinema package): Most contracts now require producers to deliver a DCP, which is the standard way in which films are now screened in cinemas and at most film festivals. This is generally delivered unencrypted.

A digital cinema digital master (DCDM): This consists of all industry standard elements including textless sections, subtitles and delivery trailer. This is normally encrypted.

HDcamSR: You will also be asked to deliver HDcamSR digital master files in either 16 × 9 full frame or 4 × 3 full frame format, or both. Some contracts ask for both 'texted' and 'textless' master files.

Apple ProRes files: 2K and 444 file type. Sometimes 422 is acceptable too.

Both the above items should include either 5.1 or Stereo sound mix.

DVD or Blu-Ray copies for screening, press and backup.

Trailer: Sometimes two of different lengths are required.

Electronic press kit: *See* Chapter 9 for more details.

Sound elements: Master sound stems for all dialogue tracks, music tracks and sound effects tracks.

Channel 1: 5.1 track: left
Channel 2: 5.1 track: right
Channel 3: 5.1 track: centre
Channel 4: 5.1 track: LFE
Channel 5: 5.1 track: left surround
Channel 6: 5.1 track: right surround
Channels 7+8: full mix stereo L&R

Separate music and effects tracks
Two-track master
Original source music

PAPERWORK

You will be expected to deliver the following paperwork when the film is completed:

- Post-production script: this is a transcript of the final edited film and it may be very different from the shooting script. Some dialogue may have been changed or omitted, and it will include new lines from ADR. It is usually required in English, and with a time code to match the finished film;
- List of all subtitles;
- Closed captioning files;
- All licences for archive footage, music or copyright works;
- Full credit list for all cast and crew;
- All cast and crew contracts and release forms
- Copies of contracts with writer, director, producer, composer and other talent;
- Laboratory access letter;
- Contractual credit block – *see* Chapter 9 for more details;
- Press pack – *see* Chapter 9 for more details;
- Advertising key artwork – *see* Chapter 9 for more details;
- A minimum of 100 hi-resolution (300dpi or higher) digital still publicity photographs, approved by producer and cast, with accompanying captions;
- E&O insurance cover – *see* Chapter 6 for more details;
- Certificate of Origin – this is normally only required in the USA;
- Chain of title documents – to show that you have obtained all the necessary script rights to legally exploit the film. This may include the original source material for an adaptation;
- List of any residual payments that may become due, if you have not 'bought out' all the cast, writers and musicians;
- Music cue sheets;
- Music contracts;
- Dolby or DTS licence.

Collecting and preparing all the above can be very time-consuming, which is why it is helpful to gather as much as possible as you go along. Despite all the other pressures it is very frustrating to get to this point and find a key contract or release form is missing. Avoid this by checking that a smooth handover takes place between the production co-ordinator and the post-production supervisor.

When you have delivered your film it is time to move on to the final stage of production and put your film or series in front of an audience.

Metrocolor

The British Broadcasting Corporation
Broadcasting House
London
W1A 1AA

Dear Sirs,

Re: *'Donovan Quick'*

In consideration of your agreeing that all or part of the laboratory work for the production of the television programme with the above provisional title ("the Programme") shall be carried out by us with the consent of Making Waves Film and Television Ltd ("the Producer"), we hereby undertake:

1.   To hold to your order the picture and sound negatives of the Programme ("the Negatives") from such time as they shall come into our possession.

2.   Not to part with possession of the Negatives except on your written instructions or for the purposes of telecining the rushes at Metrocolor London Ltd and for negative logging and cutting by the approved negative cutters in accordance with the production schedule for the Programme.

3.   Not (except in the case of material ordered by the Producer and needed for the production of the Programme and the answer print) to accept orders from the Producer or any other person for any material derived from the Negatives or created in connection with the Programme unless such orders have been confirmed in writing by you.

4.   Not to assert any right of lien or other claim against the Negatives or any other material derived from the Negatives or created in connection with the Programme except in respect of sums due to us for work carried out by us in respect of the Programme.

Yours faithfully,

Director for and on behalf of
Metrocolor London Limited

We hereby consent to the terms contained in the foregoing letter

Director for and on behalf of
Making Waves Film and Television Limited

An example of a standard laboratory access letter.

9

MARKETING, FESTIVALS AND DISTRIBUTION

When I'm making a film, I'm the audience.

Martin Scorsese, Director and Producer
(*Taxi Driver*, *Goodfellas*, *Boardwalk Empire*)

It is no longer enough simply to produce and deliver a short film, feature, documentary or drama series. If you want anyone to watch it, it is a vital part of the producer's job to be involved in its marketing and distribution as well. A successful release or festival run will make funding your next project much easier. In the UK, more than two-thirds of all the feature-length films produced do not get a theatrical release. Identifying your audience and finding ways to put your film or series in front of them is at the heart of the producer's job. You should already have been thinking about your marketing strategy since the development stage.

All producers must research and understand how audience habits are changing. You should familiarize yourself with market trends by reading the many reports produced and published by *Variety*, *Screen International*, *Ofcom*, *The Guardian* and others. The BFI publishes an annual *Statistical Yearbook* (available to download from the BFI website), in which it gives up-to-date information and data on film releases, television and video games. The yearbook includes details of box office takings, which films performed best, how many films were produced, and much more. As we all know, the demographics of cinema and television audiences are changing, and there is a growing shift away from terrestrial broadcasters towards online

subscription channels, including Netflix, Amazon and YouTube.

In previous chapters we have already referenced some of the key marketing tools and materials. In this chapter we will include more detail about what a successful marketing campaign requires. We will also look at some strategies for getting your short film or low budget feature into film festivals, and how distributors and broadcasters promote their content to audiences.

MARKETING YOUR FILM

STILL IMAGES

One of the keys to successful marketing is having good images. This is especially true of shorts and very low budget films. Do not underestimate the immense importance of strong, high resolution photographs. Unfortunately screen grabs are not good enough quality for most festival brochures and printed material, although they may be satisfactory for online content. Whatever else, make it a priority to get good stills. At least thirty decent images is better than hundreds of poor quality ones. Make sure you include some 'behind the scenes' photographs of the director and cast at work as well.

Also, despite all the other pressures, try to think about your poster image early. In many cases this

Film festivals offer great opportunities for emerging filmmakers.

shot will not actually be in the film, and you may have to set it up to make it happen. This could include arranging a photo shoot for your leading actors, in full costume and make-up. This takes some planning during a busy schedule, but is definitely best done during the shoot before everyone vanishes to work on another project.

In many cases your leading actors will have 'approval' over the release of all photographs in which they appear. This can also be a time-consuming process, but it will be written into their contracts and must be undertaken. Normally the producer and unit publicist make a first selection, and then send these to the actor's agent. Most actors are very sensitive about how they look, so don't be surprised if they reject more than they accept. Remember that it is a legal requirement that any

photographs featuring children must be approved by their parents. Also, most actors' contracts will have a clause that prohibits the use of photographs showing them naked or semi-naked without consent.

PRESS PACK

The unit publicist will either write the press pack themselves or commission a writer or journalist to do it. The purpose of the press pack is to give lots of background information and notes to journalists, from which they can create editorial content and stories for magazines and newspapers. You might remember the scene from *Notting Hill* in which Hugh Grant pretends to be working for *Horse and Hound* magazine in order to meet Julia Roberts at her hotel. Individual press interviews such as this are reserved for the most important magazines, and all the smaller publications prepare their stories from the press pack instead. This is why you might notice some papers using the same quotes from key individuals involved in making a particular film. The pack is normally sent out as a digital PDF file.

The press pack will normally contain the following information:

- Title page – with a key image from the film, contact details for the publicity and marketing team, website address and social media contacts, length, genre and format.
- Logline – *see* Chapter 5 for more details.
- Short synopsis – maximum one A4 page – less for a short film.
- Biographies of the director, writer, producer, executive producer, main cast and other talent if appropriate. For example, you would include the composer if the film is a musical, or the original author if it is based on a novel.
- Director's statement about his or her vision for the film.
- Full screen credit list, including all cast and crew. Check spellings and titles are correct and as they appear on the end roller.
- Interviews with principal cast, director, writer and producer(s).
- Longer synopsis, or episode breakdowns if a series.
- Background information. Anything journalists and magazines will pick up on and want to write about. This might include historical research or information about a particular location.
- Press clippings or links to previews or good reviews.
- Details of any awards or festival selections.

ELECTRONIC PRESS KITS

Larger productions may also produce an electronic version of the press pack, which is commonly known as an EPK. The contents are similar to those included in the press pack, except that they are produced as filmed interviews and behind-the-scenes footage rather than written content and still images.

SCREENERS

Screeners are digital copies of the film, or first episodes of a series, which are sent out to key press and critics for review, and to members of the Academy or BAFTA for awards voting. They may be sent via a secure web link with a protected password, or delivered on DVD. They are normally watermarked or identified in some way to protect against piracy, which is still a major problem for film producers and distributors in many regions.

KEY ARTWORK AND POSTERS

Most producers and distributors will engage a professional agency to create their poster, and a number of meetings should take place during production and post-production to discuss this. The purpose of the poster is to sell the film to the audience. It requires a strong image, normally one that features your main actor and introduces their character in an appealing way. Think about the genre of your film, and how your poster conveys this with its use of photography, graphics, colour, and even the font you choose for the lettering. Horror film posters will be quite different from those promoting a period romance. Spend time looking at posters on the underground or in magazines, and make notes about those that leap out from the crowd and grab your attention.

There may be a 'tag line' or 'strap line' and you will probably want to include some key phrases from reviews. Posters often include laurels from film festivals or stars from critics. You will almost certainly need more than one poster in different formats – landscape, portrait and thumbnail – but the core image needs to stay the same for audience recognition. The poster must prominently feature names likely to attract your audience. This will always include the cast, and usually the director, especially if he or she has a loyal following. If the film is based on a well known or best-selling novel, this will be there, too. There is also an obligation to include the 'contractual credit block' on all publicity material. Make sure you check these details against all the contracts.

SOCIAL MEDIA AND ONLINE MARKETING

Whatever the size or scale of your production, you must have a website, Facebook page, Twitter and Instagram accounts and YouTube presence. When you read this, there will probably be others to consider. These should be set up before production and fed regularly with new content. Building these platforms is a key part of creating audience interest and a desire to see the finished film. Many producers will hire someone to undertake this work on their behalf. It can be extremely time consuming, and may require particular skills.

TRAILERS

Trailers are essential marketing tools. Audience research shows that most people decide whether to visit the cinema and watch a film based on having seen the trailer. This is another area where you may decide to get professional help. If you have a distributor already, they will probably want to produce the trailer for you, at least for their own territories. Short films need trailers just as much as features. The trailer can be posted online and sent to festivals as part of your advance promotion.

Trailers need to be short – definitely no more than ninety seconds, and in some cases shorter. They must not tell the whole story, and should never reveal the ending. Watch out for spoilers. We have all seen trailers that give so much away it makes you wonder why you would now want to pay money to see the film. Once again, double check the end card information. Also think about the best music to use. Some of the most successful trailers use different tracks from those featured in the film.

You may be required to deliver different versions of your trailer for different audiences. If your film is rated '12' or over you will need to create a second trailer, which can be played to younger audiences.

CERTIFICATES AND 'THE WATERSHED'

From the start of development you should always know who your audience will be. For film releases this means understanding what the different certificates mean, and what is permitted and not permitted within each band. Which rating you receive will have a major impact on the available audience for your film. For television productions, you must understand what rules apply to programmes made for transmission before 9pm. This is the hour known as the 'watershed', after which broadcasters assume children are no longer watching and their rules may be somewhat relaxed.

The British Board of Film Classification (BBFC) gives each film released in the cinema in the UK a certificate to indicate its suitability for audiences of different ages. It is important to note that the certification also relates to DVD release of the film. The current certificates are as follows:

U: 'Universal' and suitable for viewers of all ages.

PG: 'Parental guidance' – suitable for most audiences, but some scenes may be unsuitable for very young children. The BBFC says: 'Unaccompanied children of any age may watch, but parents are advised to consider whether the content may upset younger, or more sensitive, children.'

12 and 12A: Containing material that is not generally suitable for children aged under twelve. No one younger than twelve may see a 12A film in a cinema unless accompanied by an adult. No one younger than twelve may rent or buy a 12-rated video or DVD.

15: No one younger than fifteen may see the film in a cinema or rent a DVD. Cinema owners may ask for proof of age before selling tickets.

18: Films rated 18 contain adult content, and children are not allowed to see them in the cinema or rent DVDs.

R18: Films rated R18 can only be shown in specially licensed cinemas, or rented through licensed sex shops. They normally contain explicit sexual content.

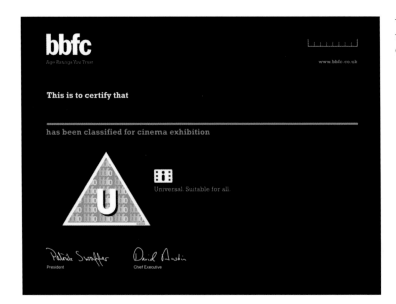

The BBFC gives each film a certificate to indicate its suitability for audiences of different ages.

You can read more about the regulations relating to each of the age categories on the BBFC website. The rules generally cover nudity, sexual content, violence, use of drugs, language and imitable behaviour. Similar rules apply to television programmes. The BBC publishes guidelines about the use of offensive language and content on its website.

FILM FESTIVALS

Attending film festivals is very valuable experience for emerging filmmakers. There is nothing more exciting (or depressing) than watching your film with a room full of strangers. Until now most of your audiences have probably been friends and members of the crew. Now you have an opportunity to test it in public for the first time.

Getting your film seen by audiences and potential distributors is the most important reason for entering a festival, and they are often the only places where short films are now screened before a live audience. But there are other benefits. Festivals are great places to network and meet other filmmakers, as well as people who can help you with your next project. Many have workshops and seminars attached where you can acquire useful knowledge and information.

Festivals can also be a place to test your ideas and potentially build towards a first feature film. Damien Chazelle made a short film version of *Whiplash*, which directly led to him raising the funding to make the full length version. Festival success, awards, prizes and reviews help you to build a reputation, and assist with funding applications. If you already have a distributor for the film, you must first check with them before entering it into any festivals.

There are now so many international film festivals throughout the year that detailed research must be undertaken to decide which ones are best for your particular film. It is very easy to spend a lot of money on festival entries without success. Talk to other filmmakers about their experience. Many festivals have a particular niche into which your film can fit. There are festivals such as Underwire, celebrating female filmmakers, horror film festivals such as ScreamFest, and LGBTQ festivals such as BFI Flare. In fact there are so many different kinds of festival it can appear to be quite overwhelming. So, like everything else, you need to plan your strategy before you start, and decide how much money you are prepared to spend.

To begin, try to be honest about your chances of getting into an 'A'-list festival, and decide if you might have more success if you target 'B'- or 'C'-list festivals, or niche ones instead. Next, think about festivals where you or your director may have local connections. Look at the films your preferred festival screened the previous year, and ask yourself if your film is going to fit into their programme and appeal to their taste. You must also think about the typical audiences who attend. There's no point sending a film with blood, gore and sex to a festival which promotes itself as 'family friendly'.

'A'-List Festivals

'A'-list festivals are generally those festivals that can offer major prizes and attract high profile international features and their directors. They may also have sections for first features, shorts and documentaries. 'A'-list festivals include Cannes, Berlin, Venice, TIFF (Toronto), Sundance, London and Tribeca (New York). Some, such as Cannes, Berlin and TIFF, have markets attached where films are bought and sold and film business is done. Some 'A'-list festivals allow applications, and others, including TIFF, only invite those films they want.

'B'- and 'C'-List Festivals

The next group of festivals (the 'B' list) are those with a strong reputation within the industry where your film can be noticed and admired. Examples include Locarno, Rotterdam, San Sebastian, Palm Springs, South by South West, Dubai, Austin and Karlovy Vary. Some of these may count as either Oscar or BAFTA qualifying festivals.

'C'-list festivals may be smaller and more regional, but they can be useful if you or your director come from the area, or your film is in the language. Examples include Dublin, Galway and Edinburgh.

Premieres

After deciding on your choice of festivals, next you have to decide where ideally you want to premiere. Your film can have only one world premiere, so it is important to plan where you hope this will be. Film festivals prefer to be the first to screen a film, as it adds audience appeal and helps their promotion. The way premiere status works is slightly complicated, so carry out your own research into this. In some circumstances you may be allowed to screen your film first in the country of origin without harming your world premiere status. But some of the bigger and more important festivals do not accept this.

You can have a world premiere, a North American premiere, a European premiere or a premiere in another geographical area. And you can also have a country premiere. So if you are a UK filmmaker and your film is accepted by the London Film Festival, your first screening there would be your world premiere, your European premiere *and* your UK premiere all in one. But you can then still have a North American premiere at TIFF or Tribeca, and a Middle Eastern premiere at Dubai.

Festival Entry and Preparation

You can enter your film into most film festivals through an online submission platform. The two most popular are FilmFreeway.com and With outabox.com. Both provide information and offer secure sites, but they have different terms and conditions, so research which is the most suitable for your particular project. Their advantage is that you only have to upload all your materials to their site once, rather than doing it endlessly for each individual festival. For some of the 'A'-list festivals you may have to make a direct submission through their own site.

Most festivals make a charge for submission. These vary considerably, but entering a lot of festivals soon becomes expensive. Work out your budget in advance, and decide exactly how much you can afford to spend. Festivals offer different entry fees at different times. Most have 'early bird' discounted rates if you submit as soon as entries open, and this is strongly advised. Festival organizers start to build their programmes from these early submissions, and your film is statistically more likely to be chosen. Avoid making a late entry as this is the most expensive option and the least likely to succeed.

Some festivals offer 'waivers', which means they waive the entry fee entirely. Normally this is if you have previously screened at their festival, or if you have a special connection, but it is always worth asking if they will do this for you. Some festivals offer travel expenses, accommodation, accreditations and festival passes if your film is selected.

Before you pay the entry fee, check to see if the festival accepts work in progress, or only considers finished films. Some will look at a film that is unmixed or ungraded, but you should make sure it is picture locked. The festival will not thank you if you send them a ten-minute film and then deliver one later that is substantially longer or shorter. Also check whether the festival has a maximum length requirement. If they say they won't consider any films longer than twenty minutes, they mean it. There is absolutely no point in paying the entry fee and uploading your twenty-four minute film.

Most festivals ask for the same list of submission materials, which normally include the following:

title
production country
production date
duration
technical specifications
camera
budget
location
synopsis and logline

nationality of director and date of birth
biographies – no more than 300 words
headshots
dialogue list with 'in' and 'out' times
stills – good quality, at least six from the film (not behind the scenes) and make sure they don't give away the plot.

If your film is accepted you will be asked to supply a DCP and a Blu-ray as backup. But you don't need to do this when you first submit it, so you can upload or supply an mp4 or Pro Res file first.

DISTRIBUTION AND EXHIBITION

Producers must understand the difference between distribution and exhibition. The distributor is the company who places your film in cinemas in one or more territories around the world. Examples of international film distribution companies include all the major studios, as well as independents such as Altitude, Vertigo, Pathé, Studio Canal and Artificial Eye. The exhibitor is the cinema or cinema chain who actually show it. There are a number of international cinema exhibitors including multiplex chains such as Vue, Cineworld and Odeon, and some smaller 'art house' chains such as Curzon. In addition there are independent cinemas in many cities. Each cinema or cinema group decides which films they will show or 'exhibit' in each of their screens. They make decisions about whether to screen in a large theatre or a smaller auditorium, and when to take the film off if it is not performing well.

The distribution company is responsible for promoting the film and persuading cinemas to show it. They acquire films either through pre-purchasing them in development (*see* Chapter 5, 'Raising Production Finance'), or buying them from producers or sales agents at film markets, after they have been completed. A distributor may acquire multiple territories or just one. It is much more common now for rights to be split amongst a number of different distributors, and worldwide distribution deals are becoming a rarity. Some distributors have particular niche interests and look for certain kinds of film. For example, Dogwoof Films specializes in documentaries, Peccadillo Pictures in LGBTQ titles, and Trafalgar Releasing in event cinema and showing live theatre shows. Others have a more general approach and will acquire any titles they think they can sell.

In most cases a distributor will acquire not only the theatrical (cinema) rights, but also DVD, VOD ('video on demand') and broadcast rights as well. This helps them to recover their investment from different places, and capitalize on the promotion they have already done.

Film distributors are responsible for marketing your film as well as placing it in the cinema. Before entering into a contract you should find out how the distributor plans to do this, and what they intend to spend on the campaign. This used to be known as the 'P&A', or 'prints and advertising'. You want them to spend as much as possible, whilst they will try to spend as little as they can get away with. Renting space on large hoardings on tube platforms and at mainline stations, paid advertising in magazines and newspapers, and paying for online advertising is an expensive business, but it is all necessary if you are going to make potential audiences aware of your film. These costs are all met by the distributor.

The film distributor reaches an agreement with the exhibitor about how the box office receipts are split. This can be a closely guarded secret, and there is no standard agreement. Cinemas make a considerable amount of their income from selling sweets, popcorn and fizzy drinks, but they pay staff costs, cleaning and cinema maintenance. On average they retain around 50 per cent of the ticket sale price after VAT has been deducted. In some cases the distributor can negotiate a better deal for themselves if they have a hot title such as the new *Star Wars*. In other cases the distributor has to take a worse deal to persuade the exhibitor to take the film at all – and this can be reduced the longer the film stays in the cinema. So the distributor might accept 45 per cent of the split (after VAT) for the first week, 40 per cent in week two, 35 per cent in week three, and so on. Most films take 90 per cent of their box office revenue in the first four weeks, so the cinemas are keen to bring in new titles as soon as takings start to decline.

Producers should be aware that very little of the money taken at the box office will eventually make it back to them. If the average cinema ticket costs £10, the likely split from this would be as follows:

£2.00 – 20 per cent VAT to the government in tax
£4.40 – 55 per cent of the balance to cinema/exhibitor
£3.60 – 35 per cent of the balance to the distributor

However, the distributor is able to recover all their expenditure from their share. This means that until they have paid for all the advertising costs, marketing, DCPs, trips to Cannes and Berlin and everything else, you won't see any money back for a long time. So don't hold your breath. Even films that win awards and seem to be doing really well, don't necessarily return a profit for many years. In 2016, the top 100 films released in the UK took 93 per cent of the box office – and this was from a total of 900 releases, meaning that the remaining 800 films took just 7 per cent between them. (For more information about box office figures, refer to the BFI *Statistical Yearbook*.)

AUDIENCES ARE CHANGING

We have noted before that Netflix has been seriously upsetting the traditional distribution models, and this is likely to continue. Unlike conventional distributors and exhibitors, Netflix has very low overheads and does almost no advertising. It does not have to pay for any physical materials to release a film, nor does it currently undertake major promotion or advertising. All it does is put the film or series on its site, and relies on word of mouth for you to find it. This gives the company an unprecedented advantage.

In the USA, but currently not yet in the UK, Moviepass has been upsetting the exhibitors. Moviepass offers a monthly subscription, allowing the purchaser to see one movie a day in almost any cinema. For serious fans this is a massive discount, since the average price of one ticket is roughly the same as the monthly subscription. Cinema owners are not happy.

Nor are they particularly happy that the window between theatrical release, DVD, VOD and television broadcast has significantly shortened in recent years. I remember when television viewers had to wait three years before they could see a film, and six months before it was released on video or DVD. Now it is more likely to be on television within six months, and could be out on DVD within less than two. In some cases films are released simultaneously in the cinema and online, known as a 'day and date' release. And it does not appear to significantly affect the box office receipts. For example, *45 Years* and *Beasts of No Nation* appeal to different audiences, but both proved that this model can work.

Audience demographics have also changed, and there is an increase in the number of over-sixties who regularly go to the cinema. Producers have noticed this, and are making films targeted at the so-called 'silver-haired' baby boomers who have more free time and more disposable income. Examples include almost any film starring Judy Dench, Bill Nighy or Maggie Smith.

Another development is the number of cinema days now being handed over to events. This includes 'live' transmissions from the National Theatre, opera performances, sporting events and even art exhibitions. Screenings that encourage audience participation, such as Secret Cinema, are also growing in popularity.

As the way audiences consume entertainment changes, producers must also change how they reach them. This is yet another example of the need for all producers to research, plan, adapt and deliver. Keep reminding yourself of this, and continue to update your skills and knowledge, and you will be a good producer.

USEFUL WEBSITES

COPYRIGHT INFORMATION

Intellectual Property Office:
www.gov.uk/government/organisations/
  intellectual-property-office
Copyright Licensing Agency: www.cla.co.uk
US Patent and Trademark Office: www.uspto.gov

TO DOWNLOAD AND READ SCREENPLAYS AND SCRIPTS

www.bbc.co.uk/writersroom/scripts
www.imsdb.com
www.simplyscripts.com
www.screenplay.com/resources/research/scripts/
  index.htm

TO PURCHASE MOVIE MAGIC SCHEDULING AND BUDGETING SOFTWARE

Entertainment Partners: www.ep.com

FOR DETAILED FILM INFORMATION, CAST AND CREW CREDITS

www.IMDb.com
www.IMDbPro.com

TO FIND CAST AND CREW

www.mandy.com

UK FILM AND TELEVISION INDUSTRY

Albert (Sustainable Production): www.
  wearealbert.org
Assistant Directors Association (ADA): www.
  adauk.org
BAFTA – British Academy of Film & Television Art:
  www.bafta.org.uk
BECTU, the film and television industry trades
  union: www.bectu.org.uk
British Board of Film Classification: www.bbfc.
  co.uk
British Film Institute (BFI): www.bfi.org.uk
Creative England: www.creativeengland.co.uk
Creative Scotland: www.creativescotland.com
Creative Skillset: www.creativeskillset.org.uk
Directors Guild of Great Britain: www.dggb.org
Equity – the actors trade union: www.equity.org.uk
Ffilm Cymru Wales: www.ffilmcymruwales.com
Musicians Union UK: www.musiciansunion.org.uk
Northern Ireland Screen: www.
  northernirelandscreen.co.uk
Producers Alliance for Film & Television (PACT):
  www.pact.co.uk
The Production Guild of Great Britain: www.
  productionguild.com
UK Cinema Association: www.cinemauk.org.uk
Women in Film & Television: www.wftv.org.uk
Writers Guild of Great Britain (WGGB): www.
  writersguild.org.uk

US FILM AND TELEVISION INDUSTRY

Directors Guild of America: www.dga.org

Filmmakers Alliance (USA): www. filmmakersalliance.org
Producers Guild of America: www. producersguild.org
The Academy of Motion Picture Arts and Sciences: www.oscars.org
The Screen Actors Guild (SAG): www.sagaftra.org
Writers Guild of America (WGA): www.wga.org

FILM FUNDING

Creative Europe: www.ec.europa.eu/programmes/creative-europe
For information about public film funds and incentives around the world: www.olffi.com
Indiegogo: www.indiegogo.com
Kickstarter: www.kickstarter.com

FOR MUSIC RIGHTS AND LICENSING

ASCAP: www.ascap.com
BMI: www.bmi.com
Creative Commons: www.creativecommons.org
DISCOGS: www.discogs.com
Performing Rights Society and MCPS: www.prsformusic.com
SESAC: www.sesac.com
SOCAN: www.socan.com

FOR ARCHIVE FILM MATERIAL

BBC Motion Gallery: www.motiongallery.com
BFI National Archive: www.bfi.org.uk/archive-collections
British Council Film Collection: www.film.britishcouncil.org
British Pathé Film Archive: www.britishpathe.com

GLOSSARY

Some common terms used in film and television:

above the line The cost of the talent, including writer, director, producer and main cast.

ASCAP The American Society of Composers, Authors and Publishers.

aspect ratio The ratio of the width to the height of an image or screen.

assignment of rights The contract or legal agreement where one party to an existing contract (the assignor) hands on the contractual obligations and benefits to another party (the assignee).

below the line The real costs of technically making the film.

blocking Planning the movement of the actors and the camera positions before shooting a scene.

BMI: Broadcast Music Inc.

commissioner The organization, person or broadcaster who asks you to make the programmes and pays for all or part of the cost of production.

crossing the line Also known as the 180-degree rule, which states that if two people are filmed in a sequence there is an invisible line between them. The camera must always stay on one side of this line. If the camera crosses it, the people appear to change position and the eye lines are ruined.

cut What a director calls to stop the camera rolling. Also used in editing to mean the change point between one shot and the next.

cutaway A shot used to break up a matching action sequence. Used in editing to avoid a jump cut.

dissolve A transition between two shots, where one shot fades away whilst another shot fades in.

errors and omissions: Insurance to cover financial losses to your production if legal action is brought against you for any accidental failures.

force majeure An unexpected or uncontrollable event, also known as an *act of God*.

green light The point of decision when a production is given the go-ahead to film.

gross receipts The amount actually received before fees and expenses are deducted.

logline A single sentence that describes the story.

M and E track Music and effects audio track, part of the standard deliverables for all films. The track contains no dialogue and is used when the film is dubbed into a foreign language.

minimum guarantee A sum of money offered as an advance on sales to a particular territory, however well the film performs there.

most favoured nation (MFN) Meaning everyone receives the same deal as everyone else in that category – for example, actors or music rights.

music cue sheet A list of all the music used in the production with exact timings and details of any royalty payments.

net profits The amount left after all the fees and expenses have been deducted from the gross receipts.

option The exclusive rights to develop a project for the screen based on that work for a limited period of time.

pari passu Meaning 'at the same time and at the same rate'. This is often used in contracts to explain how investors will recoup. It means everyone gets their share back equally. It often appears alongside *pro rata*, meaning literally without preference.

principal photography The first day of the shoot.

prime lens A lens with a single focal length, which can be wide, normal or telephoto. Considered faster and sharper than a zoom lens, which has a variable focal length.

public liability Insurance cover to protect you from claims brought against the production for injury to Third Parties, or damage to Third Party property such as members of the public and locations.

recce Short for 'reconnaissance', meaning a visit to a set or location before filming to plan logistics for the shoot there.

recoupment Literally meaning recovery of money. In film finance refers to the returns on an investment in the production.

rights Referring to copyright, or the right to copy. As a producer you need to acquire the rights to any material you plan to make into a film.

room tone A recording of the silent room at a location or on set. Used in the sound track to create atmosphere.

rushes or dailies The day's uncut footage.

SESAC: Originally the Society of European Stage Authors and Composers, but since 1940 known exclusively as SESAC.

SOCAN: The Society of Composers, Authors and Music Publishers of Canada

turnaround The term used to describe the arrangements when an option lapses and the rights revert to the original copyright holder.

wrap The end of the day's filming or the end of the shoot. From the expression 'to wrap it up'.

FURTHER READING

Aronson, Linda *The 21st Century Screenplay* (Allen & Unwin)

Boorman, John *Money Into Light: The Emerald Forest Diary* (Faber and Faber)

Eberts, Jake and Ilott, Terry *My Indecision is Final: The Rise and Fall of Goldcrest Films* (Faber and Faber)

Field, Syd *Screenplay: The Foundations of Screenwriting* (Delta)

Figgis, Mike *Digital Film-Making* (Faber and Faber)

Finney, Angus *The International Film Business* (Routledge)

Gill, Liz *Running The Show: The Essential Guide to Being a First Assistant Director* (Focal Press)

Goldman, William *Adventures in the Screen Trade: A Personal View of Hollywood* (Abacus/Time Warner)

Mackendrick, Alexander *On Film-making: An Introduction to the Craft of the Director* (Faber and Faber)

Martin, Brett *Difficult Men: Behind the Scenes of a Creative Revolution* (Faber and Faber)

McKee, Robert *Story: Substance, Structure, Style and the Principles of Screenwriting* (Methuen)

Murch, Walter *In the Blink of an Eye: A Perspective on Film Editing* (Silman-James Press)

Ondaatje, Michael *The Conversations: Walter Murch and the Art of Editing Film* (Bloomsbury)

Raskin, Richard *The Art of the Short Fiction Film* (McFarland & Co.)

Vogler, Christopher *The Writer's Journey, Mythic Structure for Writers* (Michael Wiese Productions)

INDEX